ARCHER & ARMSTRONG

FAR FARAWAY

FRED VAN LENTE | PERE PÉREZ | CLAYTON HENRY | DAVID BARON

D1265427

CONTENTS

Collection Cover Art: Clayton Henry

VALIANT.

Peter Cuneo
Chairman

Dinesh Shamdasani
CEO and Chief Creative Officer

Gavin Cuneo
CFO and Head of Strategic Development

Fred Pierce
Publisher

Warren Simons
VP Executive Editor

Walter Black
VP Operations

Hunter Gorinson
Director of Marketing, Communications & Digital Media

Atom! Freeman
Sales Manager

Travis Escarfullery
Production and Design Manager

Alejandro Arbona
Associate Editor

Josh Johns
Assistant Editor

Peter Stern
Operations Manager

Robert Meyers
Operations Coordinator

Ivan Cohen
Collection Editor

Steve Blackwell
Collection Designer

Rian Hughes/Device
Trade Dress and Book Design

Russell Brown
President, Consumer Products, Promotions and Ad Sales

Jason Kothari
Vice Chairman

Archer & Armstrong®: Far Faraway. Published by Valiant Entertainment, LLC. Office of Publication: 424 West 33rd Street, New York, NY 10001. Printed in the U.S.A. First Printing.
ISBN: 9781939346148.

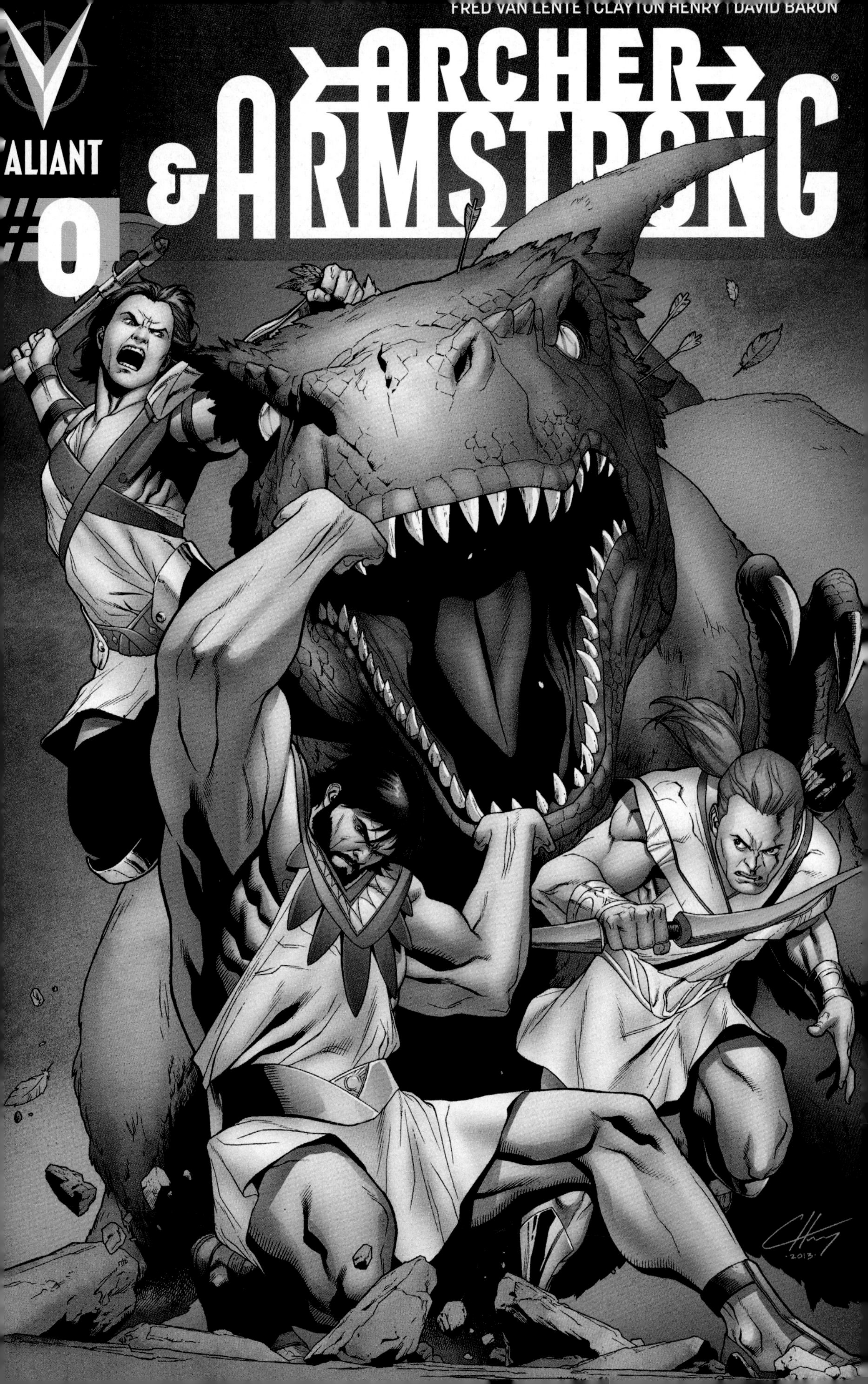
FRED VAN LENTE | CLAYTON HENRY | DAVID BARON
ARCHER & ARMSTRONG
#0

ARCHER → & ARMSTRONG

OUR STORY SO FAR...

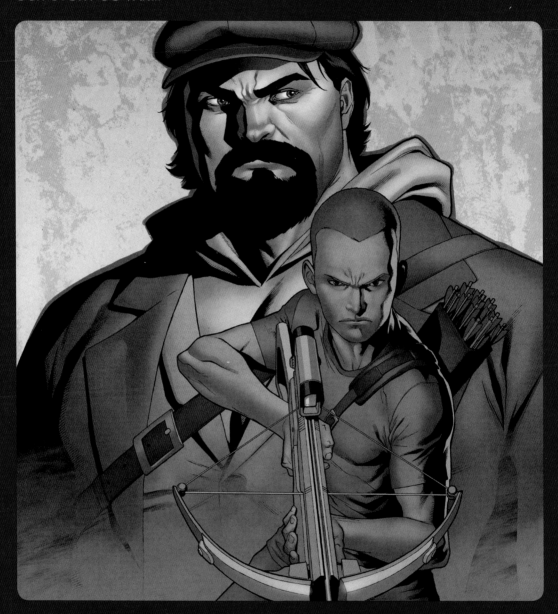

The immortal affectionately known around all the finest watering holes as Armstrong has had a busy year. Along with his naïve partner Archer, they have rescued the world by stopping the nefarious organization known as the Sect from acquiring a mystical "Boon" which grants immortality and doubles as a nasty WMD.

Soon after, they teamed up with the Geomancer and the Eternal Warrior to stop a cult from erasing existence altogether.

Good thing they went two for two.

Now our dysfunctional duo find themselves with some downtime on the Las Vegas strip...

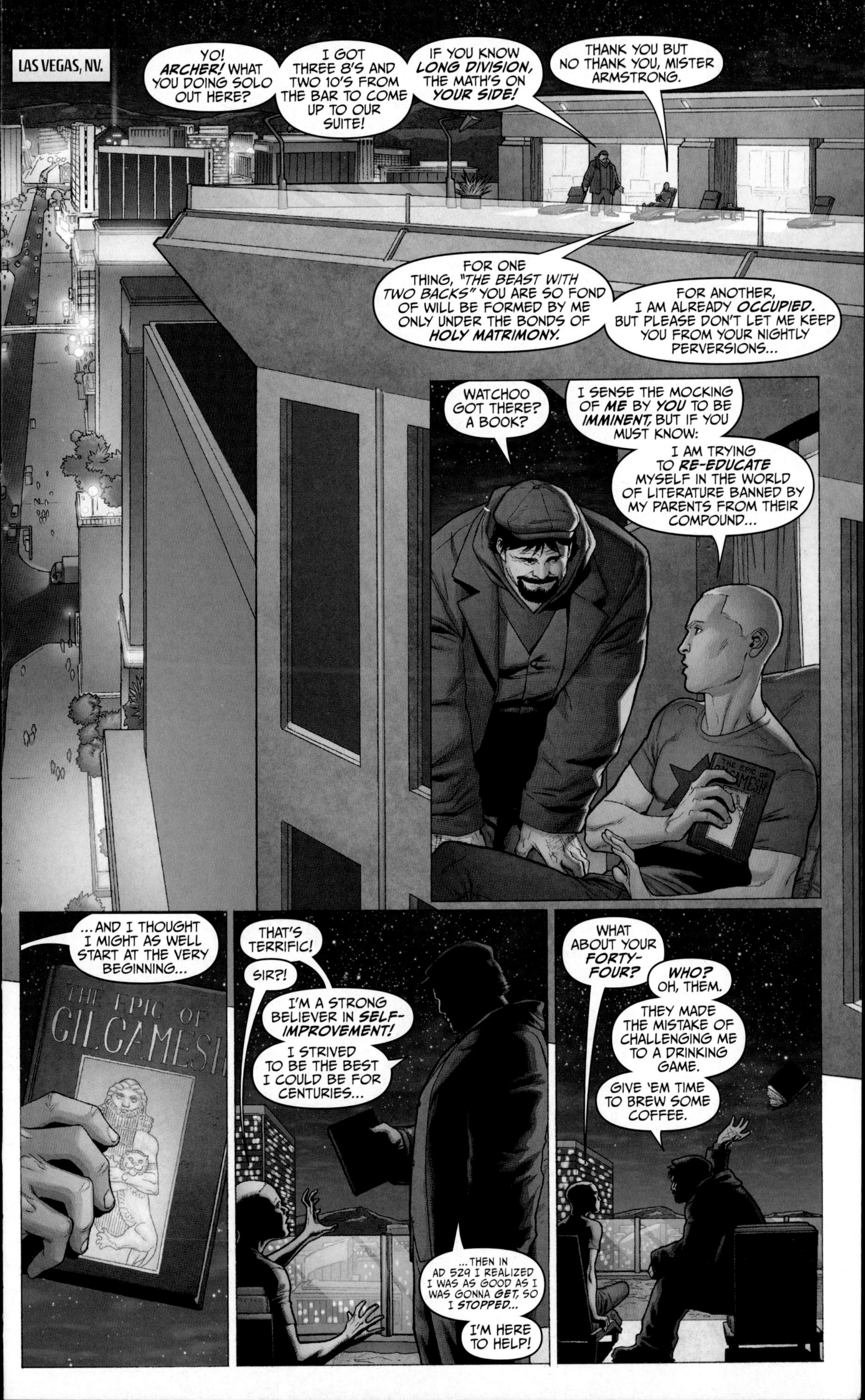
LAS VEGAS, NV.
YO! ARCHER! WHAT YOU DOING SOLO OUT HERE?
I GOT THREE 8'S AND TWO 10'S FROM THE BAR TO COME UP TO OUR SUITE!
IF YOU KNOW LONG DIVISION, THE MATH'S ON YOUR SIDE!
THANK YOU BUT NO THANK YOU, MISTER ARMSTRONG.
FOR ONE THING, "THE BEAST WITH TWO BACKS" YOU ARE SO FOND OF WILL BE FORMED BY ME ONLY UNDER THE BONDS OF HOLY MATRIMONY.
FOR ANOTHER, I AM ALREADY OCCUPIED. BUT PLEASE DON'T LET ME KEEP YOU FROM YOUR NIGHTLY PERVERSIONS...
WATCHOO GOT THERE? A BOOK?
I SENSE THE MOCKING OF ME BY YOU TO BE IMMINENT, BUT IF YOU MUST KNOW:
I AM TRYING TO RE-EDUCATE MYSELF IN THE WORLD OF LITERATURE BANNED BY MY PARENTS FROM THEIR COMPOUND...
THE EPIC OF GILGAMESH
...AND I THOUGHT I MIGHT AS WELL START AT THE VERY BEGINNING...
THE EPIC OF GILGAMESH
THAT'S TERRIFIC!
SIR?!
I'M A STRONG BELIEVER IN SELF-IMPROVEMENT!
I STRIVED TO BE THE BEST I COULD BE FOR CENTURIES...
...THEN IN AD 529 I REALIZED I WAS AS GOOD AS I WAS GONNA GET, SO I STOPPED...
I'M HERE TO HELP!
WHAT ABOUT YOUR FORTY-FOUR?
WHO? OH, THEM.
THEY MADE THE MISTAKE OF CHALLENGING ME TO A DRINKING GAME.
GIVE 'EM TIME TO BREW SOME COFFEE.

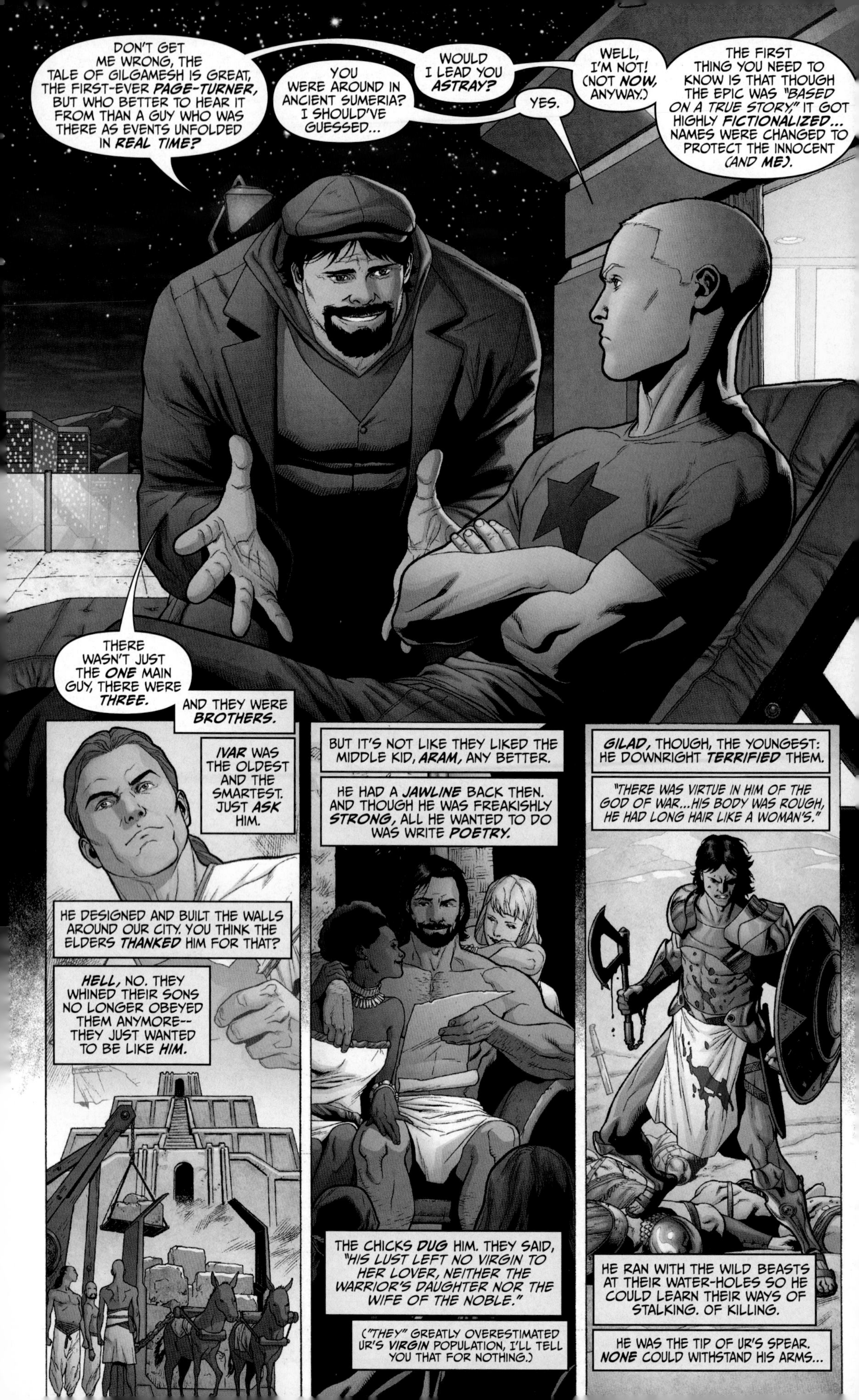
DON'T GET ME WRONG, THE TALE OF GILGAMESH IS GREAT, THE FIRST-EVER PAGE-TURNER, BUT WHO BETTER TO HEAR IT FROM THAN A GUY WHO WAS THERE AS EVENTS UNFOLDED IN REAL TIME?
YOU WERE AROUND IN ANCIENT SUMERIA? I SHOULD'VE GUESSED...
WOULD I LEAD YOU ASTRAY?
YES.
WELL, I'M NOT! (NOT NOW, ANYWAY.)
THE FIRST THING YOU NEED TO KNOW IS THAT THOUGH THE EPIC WAS "BASED ON A TRUE STORY," IT GOT HIGHLY FICTIONALIZED... NAMES WERE CHANGED TO PROTECT THE INNOCENT (AND ME).
THERE WASN'T JUST THE ONE MAIN GUY, THERE WERE THREE.
AND THEY WERE BROTHERS.
IVAR WAS THE OLDEST AND THE SMARTEST. JUST ASK HIM.
HE DESIGNED AND BUILT THE WALLS AROUND OUR CITY. YOU THINK THE ELDERS THANKED HIM FOR THAT?
HELL, NO. THEY WHINED THEIR SONS NO LONGER OBEYED THEM ANYMORE-- THEY JUST WANTED TO BE LIKE HIM.
BUT IT'S NOT LIKE THEY LIKED THE MIDDLE KID, ARAM, ANY BETTER.
HE HAD A JAWLINE BACK THEN. AND THOUGH HE WAS FREAKISHLY STRONG, ALL HE WANTED TO DO WAS WRITE POETRY.
THE CHICKS DUG HIM. THEY SAID, "HIS LUST LEFT NO VIRGIN TO HER LOVER, NEITHER THE WARRIOR'S DAUGHTER NOR THE WIFE OF THE NOBLE."
("THEY" GREATLY OVERESTIMATED UR'S VIRGIN POPULATION, I'LL TELL YOU THAT FOR NOTHING.)
GILAD, THOUGH, THE YOUNGEST: HE DOWNRIGHT TERRIFIED THEM.
"THERE WAS VIRTUE IN HIM OF THE GOD OF WAR...HIS BODY WAS ROUGH, HE HAD LONG HAIR LIKE A WOMAN'S."
HE RAN WITH THE WILD BEASTS AT THEIR WATER-HOLES SO HE COULD LEARN THEIR WAYS OF STALKING. OF KILLING.
HE WAS THE TIP OF UR'S SPEAR. NONE COULD WITHSTAND HIS ARMS...

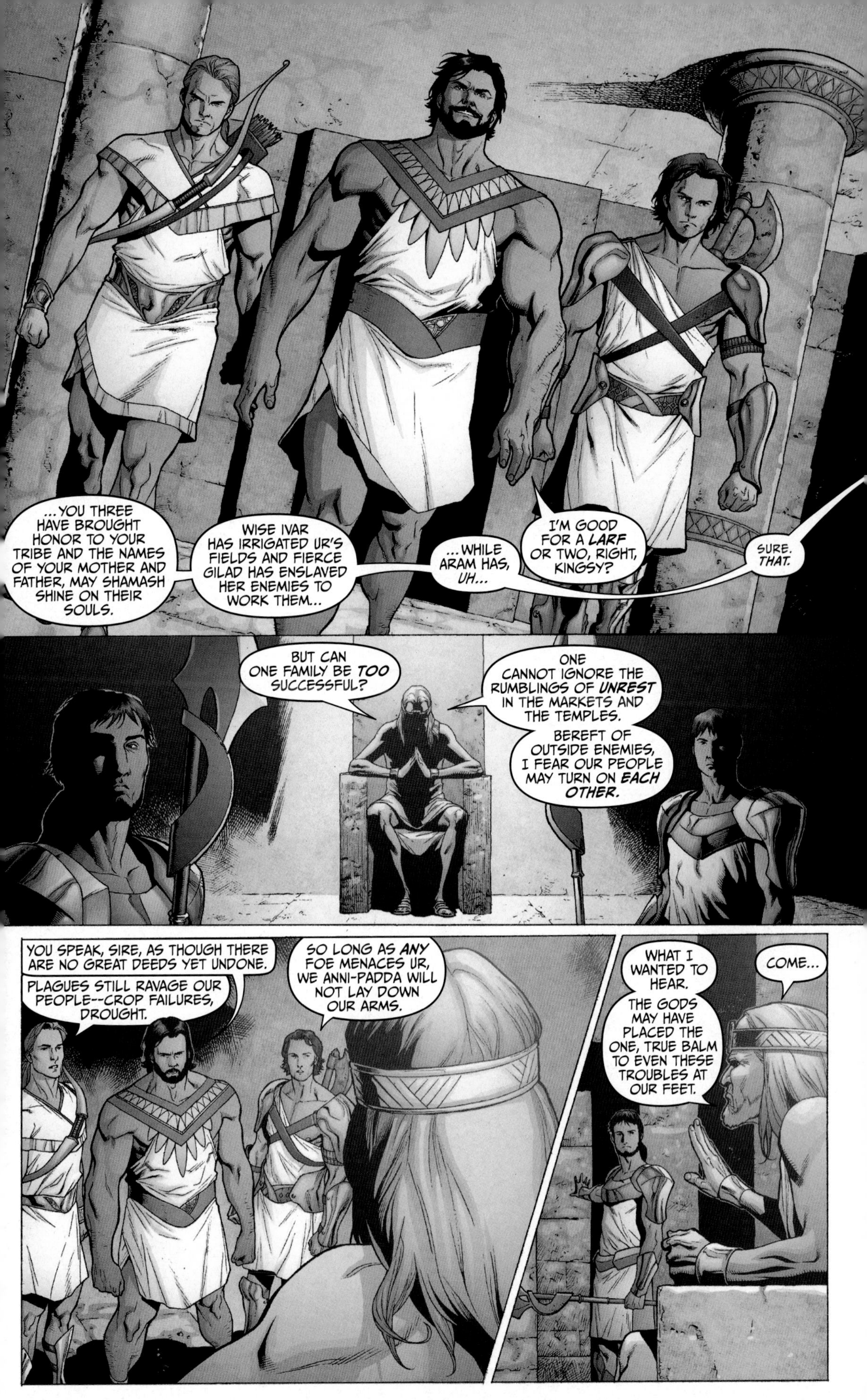
...YOU THREE HAVE BROUGHT HONOR TO YOUR TRIBE AND THE NAMES OF YOUR MOTHER AND FATHER, MAY SHAMASH SHINE ON THEIR SOULS.
WISE IVAR HAS IRRIGATED UR'S FIELDS AND FIERCE GILAD HAS ENSLAVED HER ENEMIES TO WORK THEM...
...WHILE ARAM HAS, UH...
I'M GOOD FOR A LARF OR TWO, RIGHT, KINGSY?
SURE. THAT.
BUT CAN ONE FAMILY BE TOO SUCCESSFUL?
ONE CANNOT IGNORE THE RUMBLINGS OF UNREST IN THE MARKETS AND THE TEMPLES.
BEREFT OF OUTSIDE ENEMIES, I FEAR OUR PEOPLE MAY TURN ON EACH OTHER.
YOU SPEAK, SIRE, AS THOUGH THERE ARE NO GREAT DEEDS YET UNDONE.
PLAGUES STILL RAVAGE OUR PEOPLE--CROP FAILURES, DROUGHT.
SO LONG AS ANY FOE MENACES UR, WE ANNI-PADDA WILL NOT LAY DOWN OUR ARMS.
WHAT I WANTED TO HEAR.
THE GODS MAY HAVE PLACED THE ONE, TRUE BALM TO EVEN THESE TROUBLES AT OUR FEET.
COME...

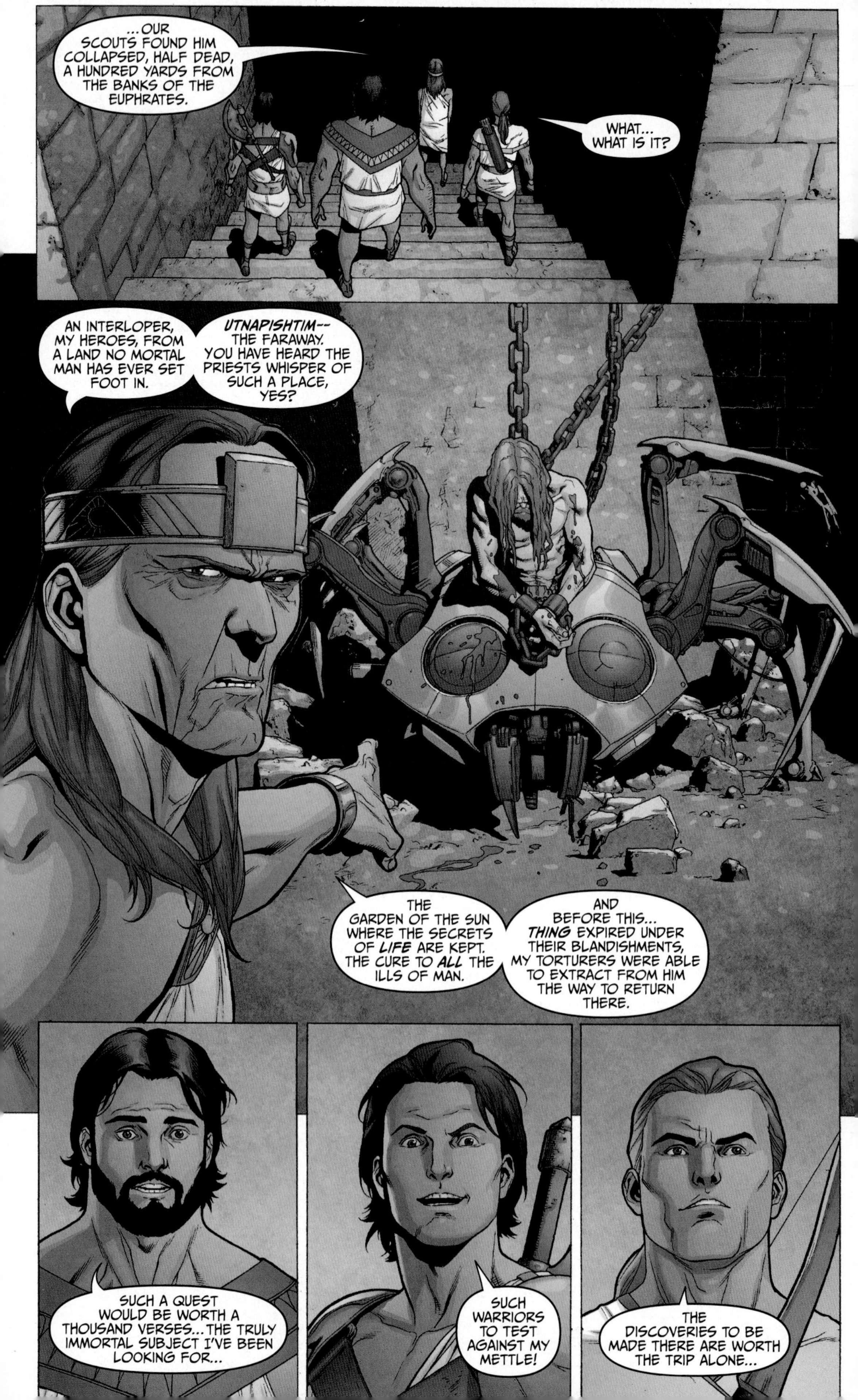
...OUR SCOUTS FOUND HIM COLLAPSED, HALF DEAD, A HUNDRED YARDS FROM THE BANKS OF THE EUPHRATES.
WHAT... WHAT IS IT?
AN INTERLOPER, MY HEROES, FROM A LAND NO MORTAL MAN HAS EVER SET FOOT IN.
UTNAPISHTIM-- THE FARAWAY. YOU HAVE HEARD THE PRIESTS WHISPER OF SUCH A PLACE, YES?
THE GARDEN OF THE SUN WHERE THE SECRETS OF LIFE ARE KEPT. THE CURE TO ALL THE ILLS OF MAN.
AND BEFORE THIS... THING EXPIRED UNDER THEIR BLANDISHMENTS, MY TORTURERS WERE ABLE TO EXTRACT FROM HIM THE WAY TO RETURN THERE.
SUCH A QUEST WOULD BE WORTH A THOUSAND VERSES... THE TRULY IMMORTAL SUBJECT I'VE BEEN LOOKING FOR...
SUCH WARRIORS TO TEST AGAINST MY METTLE!
THE DISCOVERIES TO BE MADE THERE ARE WORTH THE TRIP ALONE...

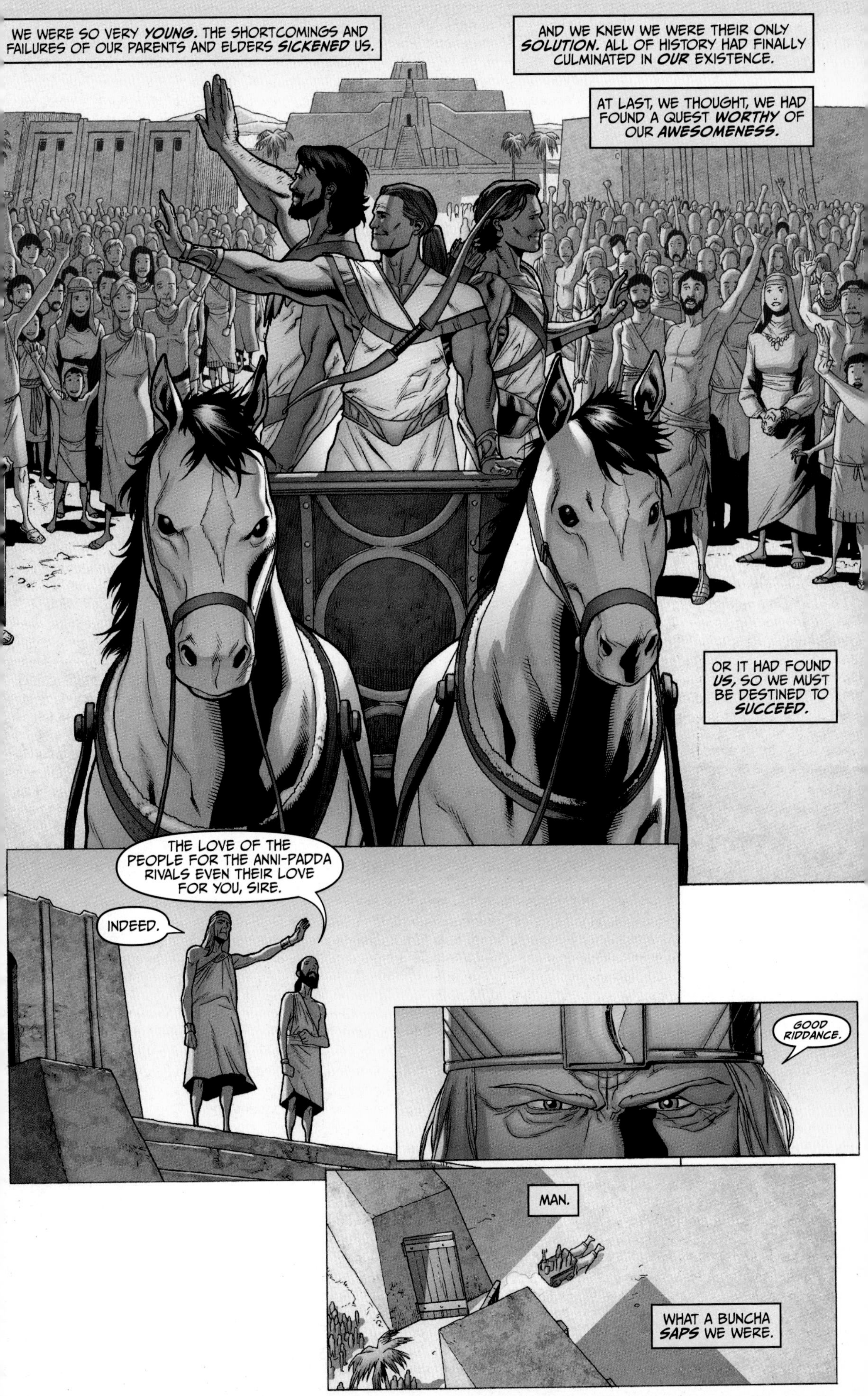
WE WERE SO VERY YOUNG. THE SHORTCOMINGS AND FAILURES OF OUR PARENTS AND ELDERS SICKENED US.
AND WE KNEW WE WERE THEIR ONLY SOLUTION. ALL OF HISTORY HAD FINALLY CULMINATED IN OUR EXISTENCE.
AT LAST, WE THOUGHT, WE HAD FOUND A QUEST WORTHY OF OUR AWESOMENESS.
OR IT HAD FOUND US, SO WE MUST BE DESTINED TO SUCCEED.
THE LOVE OF THE PEOPLE FOR THE ANNI-PADDA RIVALS EVEN THEIR LOVE FOR YOU, SIRE.
INDEED.
GOOD RIDDANCE.
MAN.
WHAT A BUNCHA SAPS WE WERE.

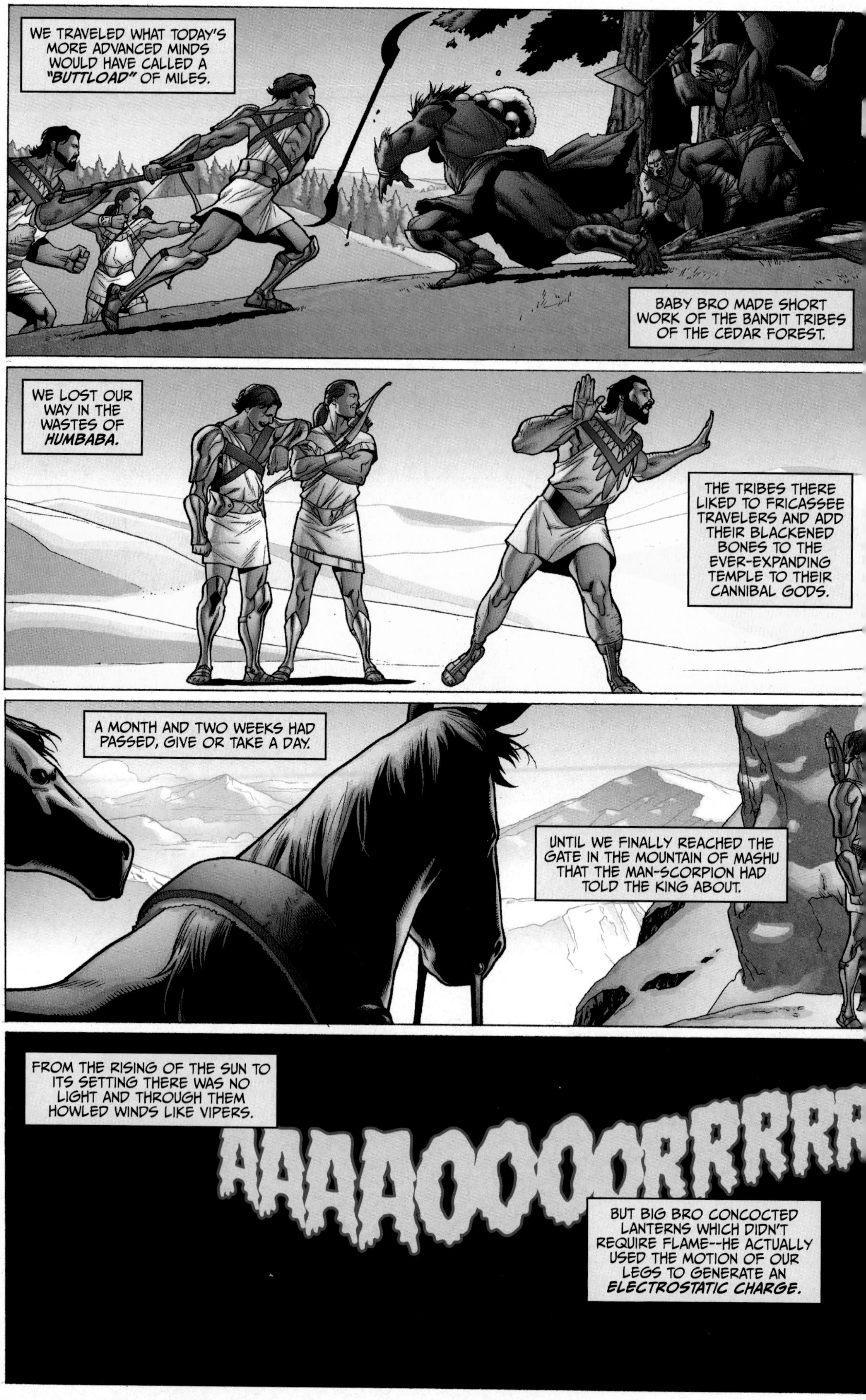
WE TRAVELED WHAT TODAY'S MORE ADVANCED MINDS WOULD HAVE CALLED A "BUTTLOAD" OF MILES.
BABY BRO MADE SHORT WORK OF THE BANDIT TRIBES OF THE CEDAR FOREST.
WE LOST OUR WAY IN THE WASTES OF HUMBABA.
THE TRIBES THERE LIKED TO FRICASSEE TRAVELERS AND ADD THEIR BLACKENED BONES TO THE EVER-EXPANDING TEMPLE TO THEIR CANNIBAL GODS.
A MONTH AND TWO WEEKS HAD PASSED, GIVE OR TAKE A DAY.
UNTIL WE FINALLY REACHED THE GATE IN THE MOUNTAIN OF MASHU THAT THE MAN-SCORPION HAD TOLD THE KING ABOUT.
FROM THE RISING OF THE SUN TO ITS SETTING THERE WAS NO LIGHT AND THROUGH THEM HOWLED WINDS LIKE VIPERS.
AAAAOOOORRRRR
BUT BIG BRO CONCOCTED LANTERNS WHICH DIDN'T REQUIRE FLAME--HE ACTUALLY USED THE MOTION OF OUR LEGS TO GENERATE AN ELECTROSTATIC CHARGE.

WE DIDN'T SPEAK THEIR WEIRD CASTANET TONGUE, BUT THE LANGUAGE OF *LIGHT DINNER THEATER* IS UNIVERSAL.

I SUFFICIENTLY AMUSED THEM THAT NOT ONLY DID THEY *NOT* CHAR-GRILL US, THEY SET US BACK ON THE RIGHT PATH AGAIN.

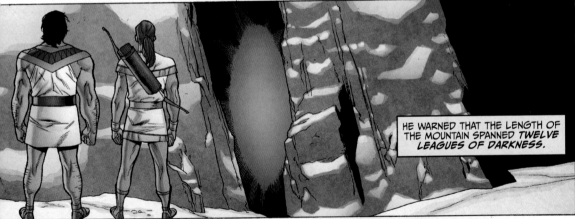

HE WARNED THAT THE LENGTH OF THE MOUNTAIN SPANNED *TWELVE LEAGUES OF DARKNESS.*

IVAR WAS WHAT YOU MIGHT CALL *"AHEAD OF HIS EPOCH."*

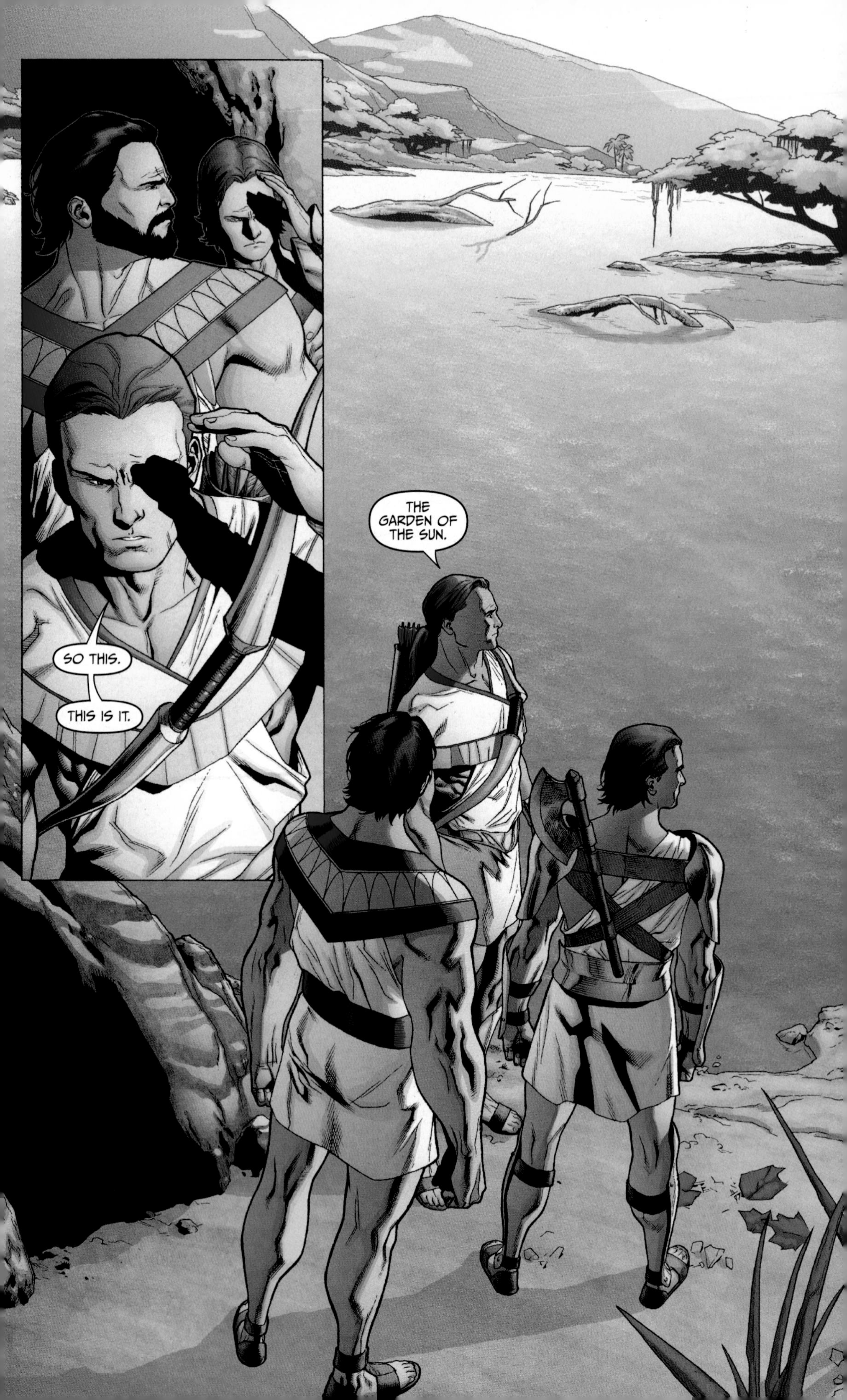
SO THIS.
THIS IS IT.
THE GARDEN OF THE SUN.

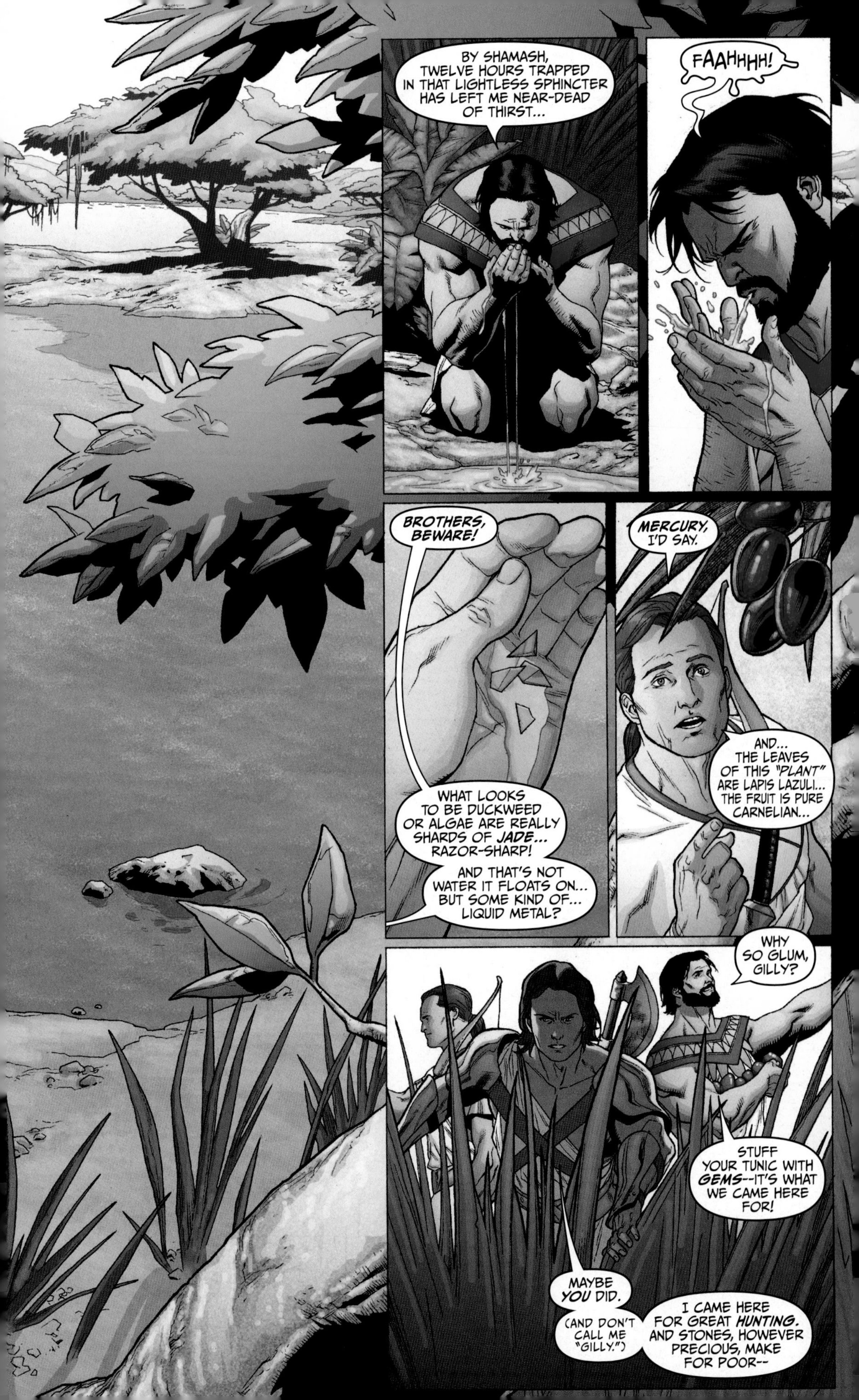
BY SHAMASH, TWELVE HOURS TRAPPED IN THAT LIGHTLESS SPHINCTER HAS LEFT ME NEAR-DEAD OF THIRST...
FAAHHHH!
BROTHERS, BEWARE!
WHAT LOOKS TO BE DUCKWEED OR ALGAE ARE REALLY SHARDS OF JADE... RAZOR-SHARP!
AND THAT'S NOT WATER IT FLOATS ON... BUT SOME KIND OF... LIQUID METAL?
MERCURY, I'D SAY.
AND... THE LEAVES OF THIS "PLANT" ARE LAPIS LAZULI... THE FRUIT IS PURE CARNELIAN...
WHY SO GLUM, GILLY?
STUFF YOUR TUNIC WITH GEMS--IT'S WHAT WE CAME HERE FOR!
MAYBE YOU DID.
(AND DON'T CALL ME "GILLY.")
I CAME HERE FOR GREAT HUNTING. AND STONES, HOWEVER PRECIOUS, MAKE FOR POOR--

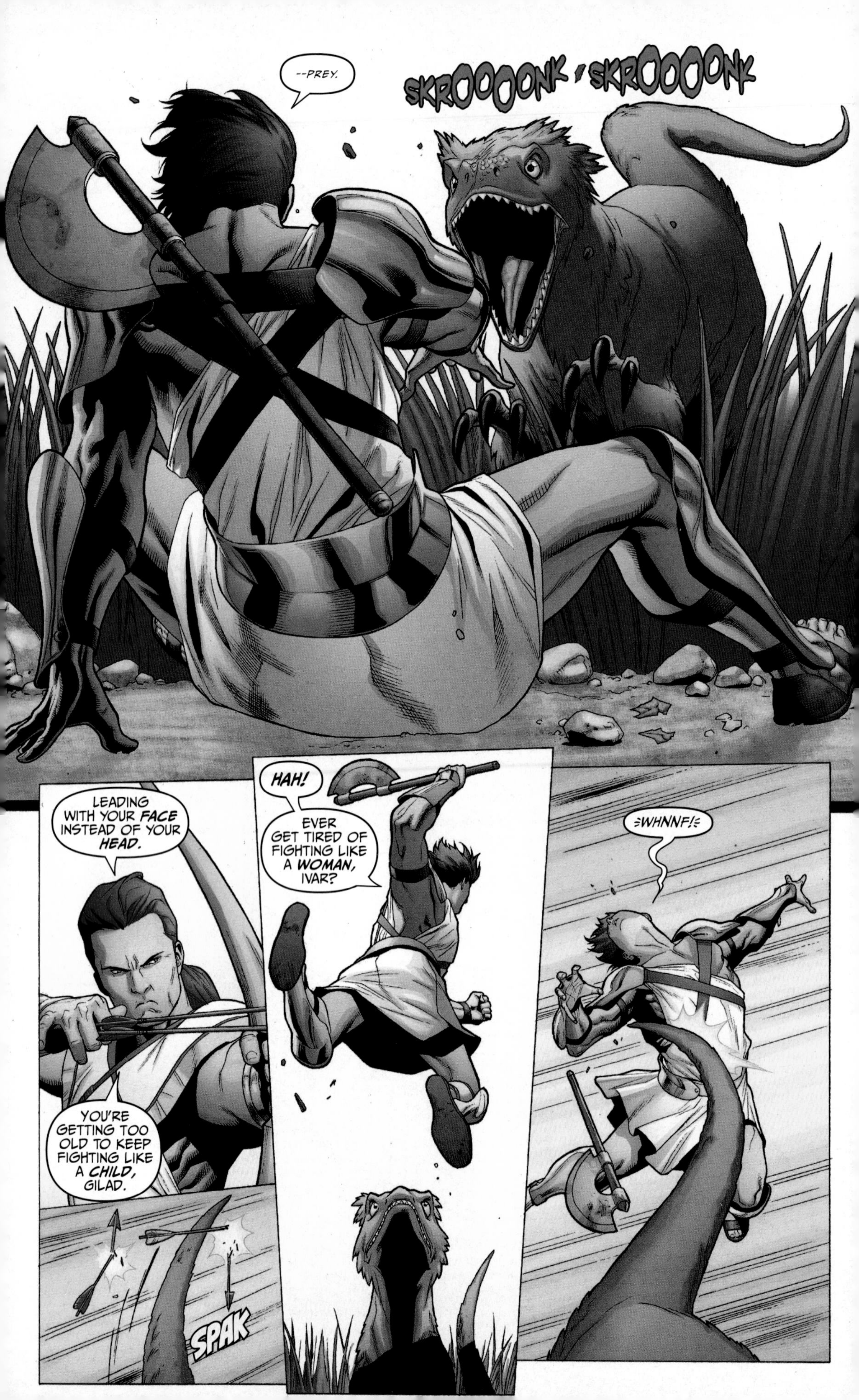
--PREY.
SKROOOOONK SKROOOOONK
LEADING WITH YOUR FACE INSTEAD OF YOUR HEAD.
YOU'RE GETTING TOO OLD TO KEEP FIGHTING LIKE A CHILD, GILAD.
SPAK
HAH!
EVER GET TIRED OF FIGHTING LIKE A WOMAN, IVAR?
WHNNF!

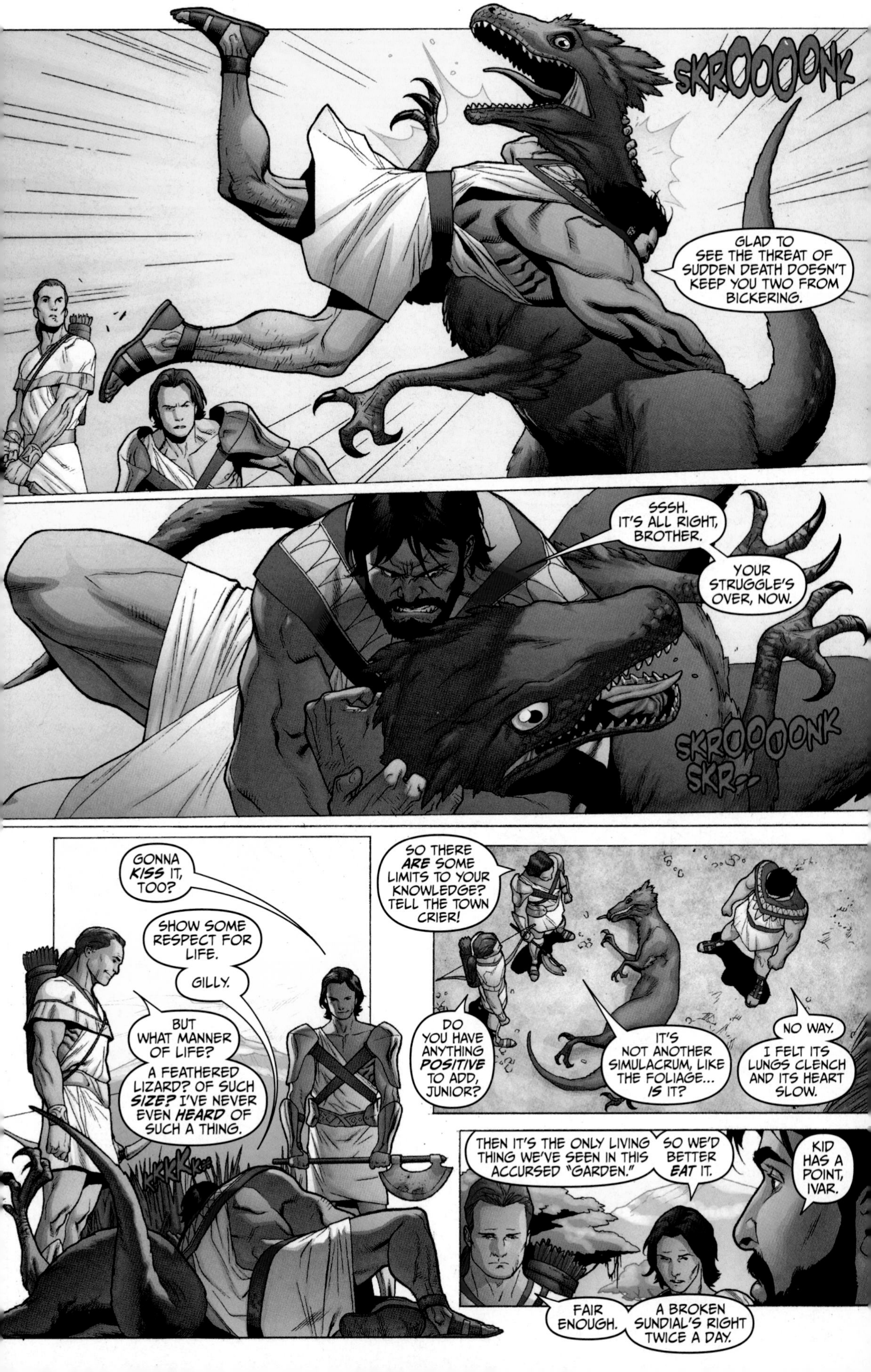
SKROOOONK
GLAD TO SEE THE THREAT OF SUDDEN DEATH DOESN'T KEEP YOU TWO FROM BICKERING.
SSSH. IT'S ALL RIGHT, BROTHER.
YOUR STRUGGLE'S OVER, NOW.
SKROOOONK SKR--
GONNA KISS IT, TOO?
SHOW SOME RESPECT FOR LIFE.
GILLY.
BUT WHAT MANNER OF LIFE?
A FEATHERED LIZARD? OF SUCH SIZE? I'VE NEVER EVEN HEARD OF SUCH A THING.
SO THERE ARE SOME LIMITS TO YOUR KNOWLEDGE? TELL THE TOWN CRIER!
DO YOU HAVE ANYTHING POSITIVE TO ADD, JUNIOR?
IT'S NOT ANOTHER SIMULACRUM, LIKE THE FOLIAGE... IS IT?
NO WAY.
I FELT ITS LUNGS CLENCH AND ITS HEART SLOW.
THEN IT'S THE ONLY LIVING THING WE'VE SEEN IN THIS ACCURSED "GARDEN."
SO WE'D BETTER EAT IT.
KID HAS A POINT, IVAR.
FAIR ENOUGH.
A BROKEN SUNDIAL'S RIGHT TWICE A DAY.

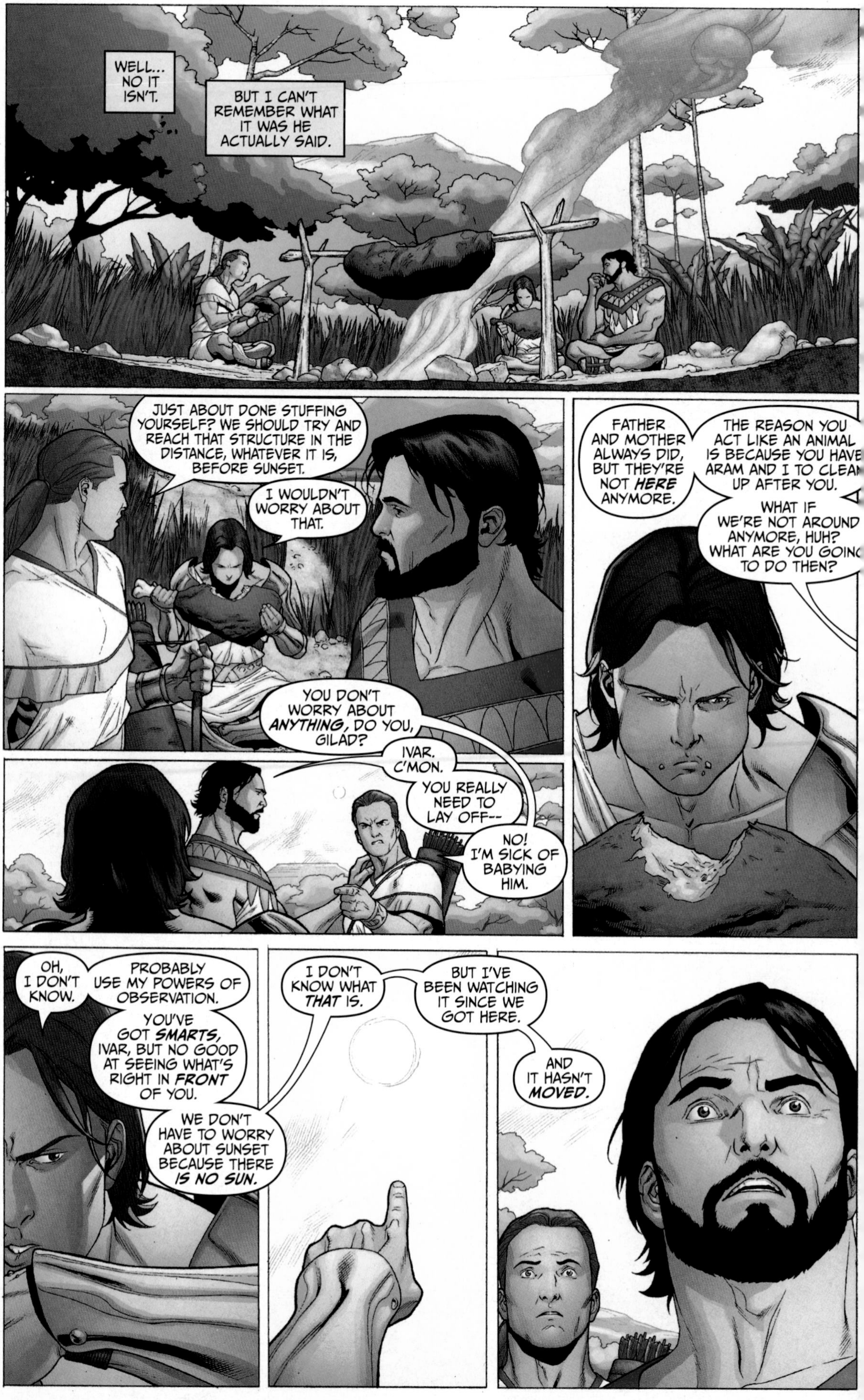
WELL... NO IT ISN'T.
BUT I CAN'T REMEMBER WHAT IT WAS HE ACTUALLY SAID.
JUST ABOUT DONE STUFFING YOURSELF? WE SHOULD TRY AND REACH THAT STRUCTURE IN THE DISTANCE, WHATEVER IT IS, BEFORE SUNSET.
I WOULDN'T WORRY ABOUT THAT.
YOU DON'T WORRY ABOUT ANYTHING, DO YOU, GILAD?
IVAR. C'MON.
YOU REALLY NEED TO LAY OFF--
NO! I'M SICK OF BABYING HIM.
FATHER AND MOTHER ALWAYS DID, BUT THEY'RE NOT HERE ANYMORE.
THE REASON YOU ACT LIKE AN ANIMAL IS BECAUSE YOU HAVE ARAM AND I TO CLEAN UP AFTER YOU.
WHAT IF WE'RE NOT AROUND ANYMORE, HUH? WHAT ARE YOU GOING TO DO THEN?
OH, I DON'T KNOW.
PROBABLY USE MY POWERS OF OBSERVATION.
YOU'VE GOT SMARTS, IVAR, BUT NO GOOD AT SEEING WHAT'S RIGHT IN FRONT OF YOU.
WE DON'T HAVE TO WORRY ABOUT SUNSET BECAUSE THERE IS NO SUN.
I DON'T KNOW WHAT THAT IS.
BUT I'VE BEEN WATCHING IT SINCE WE GOT HERE.
AND IT HASN'T MOVED.

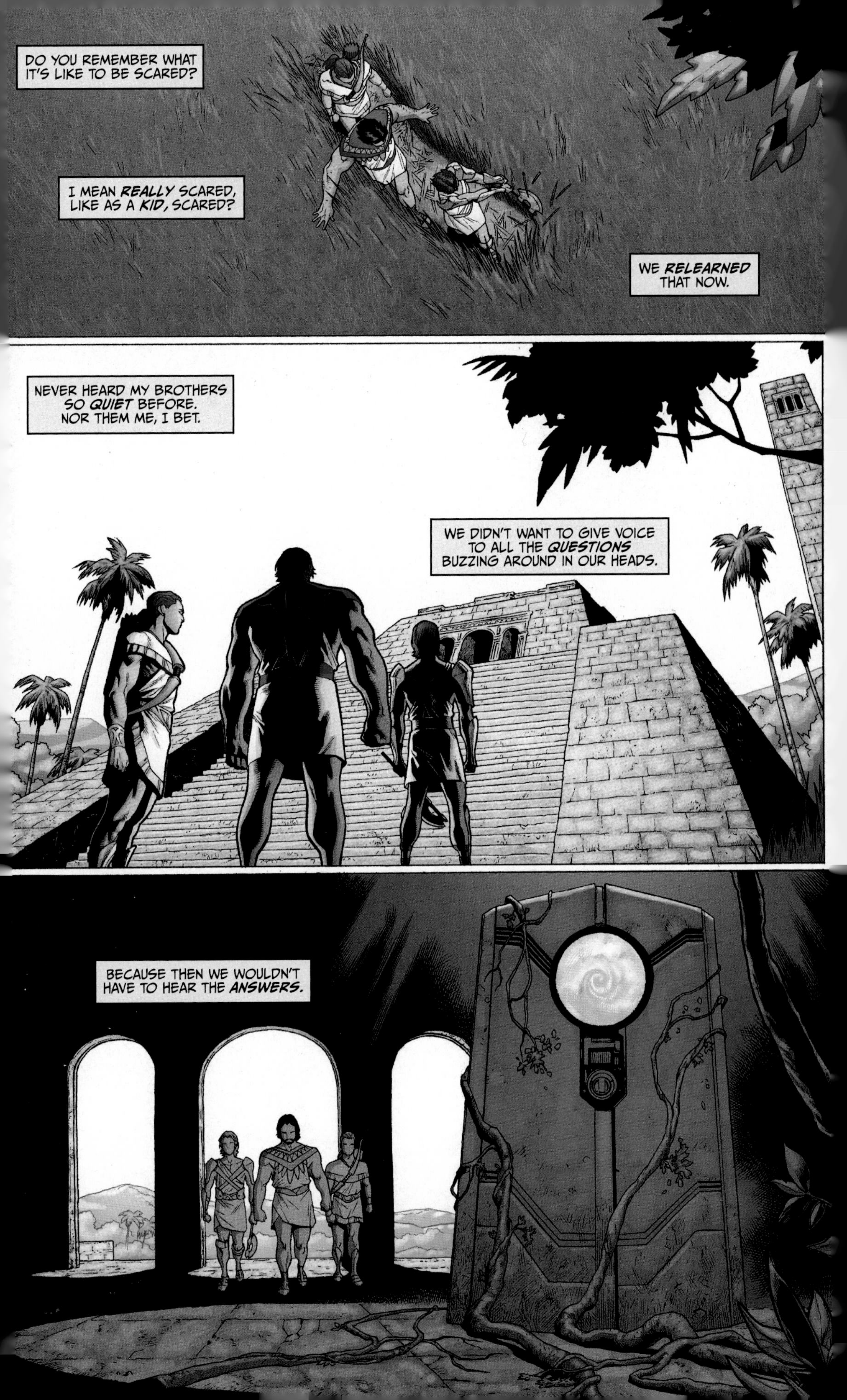
DO YOU REMEMBER WHAT IT'S LIKE TO BE SCARED?
I MEAN REALLY SCARED, LIKE AS A KID, SCARED?
WE RELEARNED THAT NOW.
NEVER HEARD MY BROTHERS SO QUIET BEFORE. NOR THEM ME, I BET.
WE DIDN'T WANT TO GIVE VOICE TO ALL THE QUESTIONS BUZZING AROUND IN OUR HEADS.
BECAUSE THEN WE WOULDN'T HAVE TO HEAR THE ANSWERS.

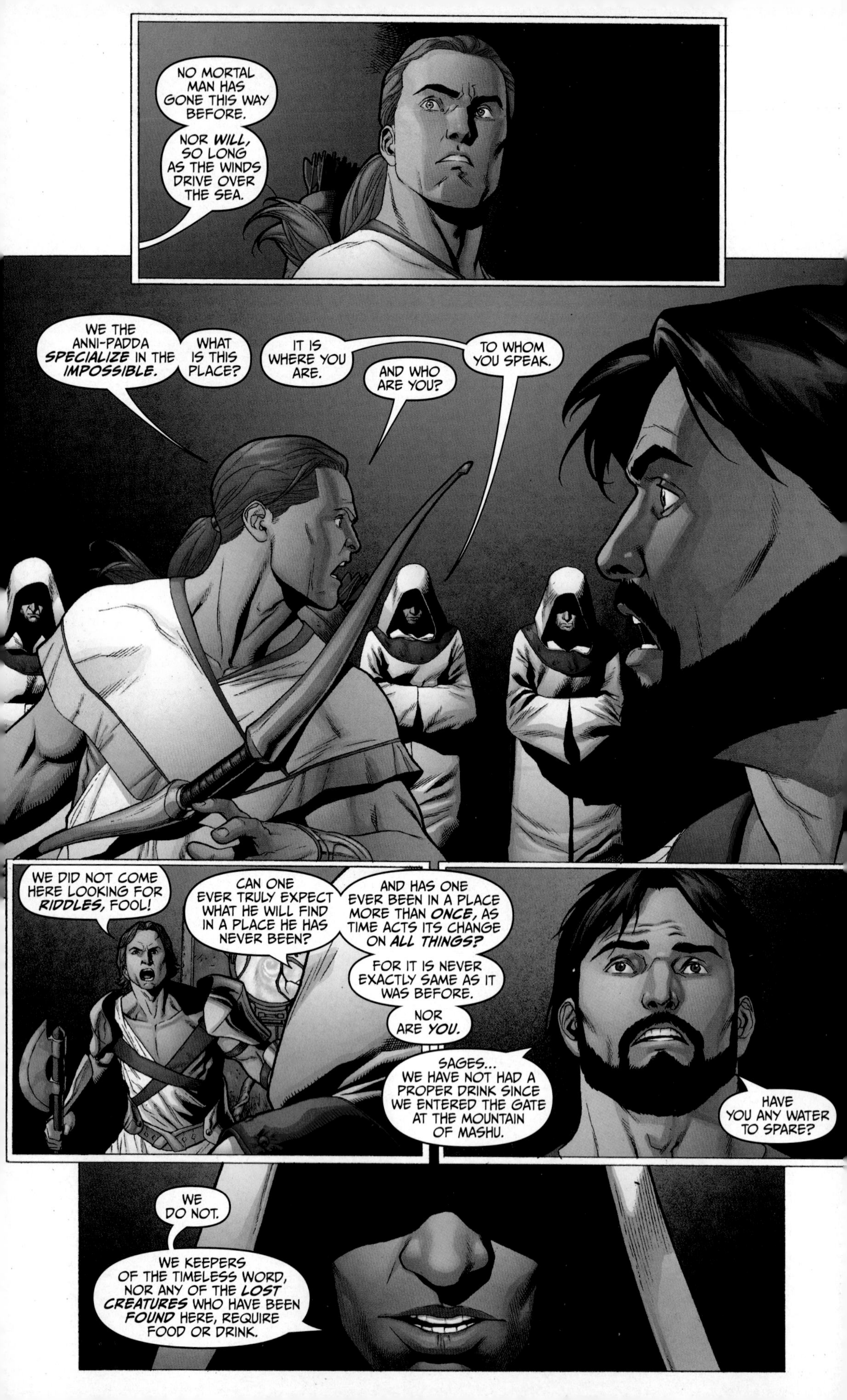
NO MORTAL MAN HAS GONE THIS WAY BEFORE.
NOR *WILL,* SO LONG AS THE WINDS DRIVE OVER THE SEA.
WE THE ANNI-PADDA *SPECIALIZE* IN THE *IMPOSSIBLE.*
WHAT IS THIS PLACE?
IT IS WHERE YOU ARE.
AND WHO ARE YOU?
TO WHOM YOU SPEAK.
WE DID NOT COME HERE LOOKING FOR *RIDDLES,* FOOL!
CAN ONE EVER TRULY EXPECT WHAT HE WILL FIND IN A PLACE HE HAS NEVER BEEN?
AND HAS ONE EVER BEEN IN A PLACE MORE THAN *ONCE,* AS TIME ACTS ITS CHANGE ON *ALL THINGS?*
FOR IT IS NEVER EXACTLY SAME AS IT WAS BEFORE.
NOR ARE *YOU.*
SAGES... WE HAVE NOT HAD A PROPER DRINK SINCE WE ENTERED THE GATE AT THE MOUNTAIN OF MASHU.
HAVE YOU ANY WATER TO SPARE?
WE DO NOT.
WE KEEPERS OF THE TIMELESS WORD, NOR ANY OF THE *LOST CREATURES* WHO HAVE BEEN *FOUND* HERE, REQUIRE FOOD OR DRINK.

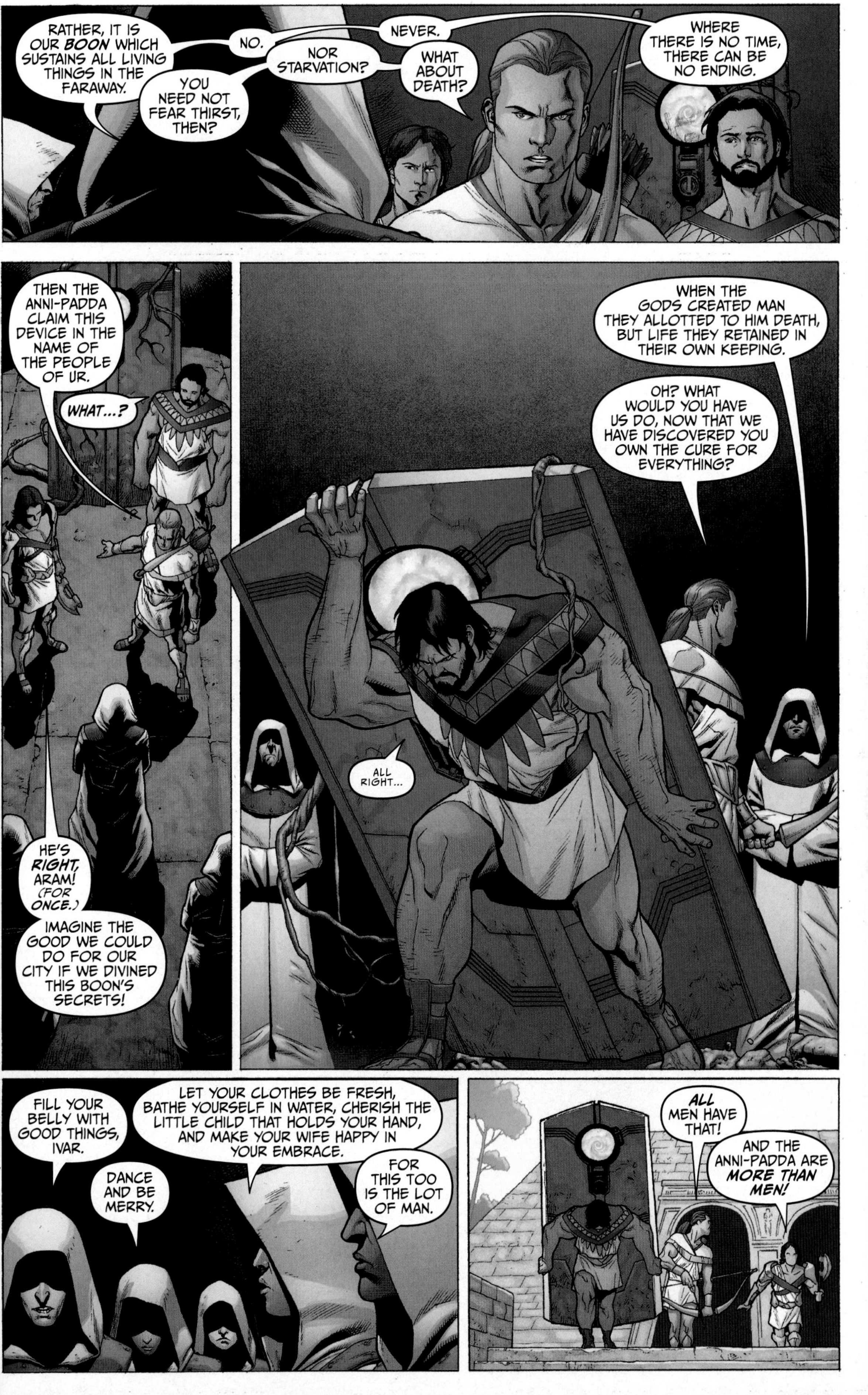
RATHER, IT IS OUR BOON WHICH SUSTAINS ALL LIVING THINGS IN THE FARAWAY.
YOU NEED NOT FEAR THIRST, THEN?
NO.
NOR STARVATION?
NEVER.
WHAT ABOUT DEATH?
WHERE THERE IS NO TIME, THERE CAN BE NO ENDING.
THEN THE ANNI-PADDA CLAIM THIS DEVICE IN THE NAME OF THE PEOPLE OF UR.
WHAT...?
HE'S RIGHT, ARAM! (FOR ONCE.)
IMAGINE THE GOOD WE COULD DO FOR OUR CITY IF WE DIVINED THIS BOON'S SECRETS!
WHEN THE GODS CREATED MAN THEY ALLOTTED TO HIM DEATH, BUT LIFE THEY RETAINED IN THEIR OWN KEEPING.
OH? WHAT WOULD YOU HAVE US DO, NOW THAT WE HAVE DISCOVERED YOU OWN THE CURE FOR EVERYTHING?
ALL RIGHT...
FILL YOUR BELLY WITH GOOD THINGS, IVAR.
DANCE AND BE MERRY.
LET YOUR CLOTHES BE FRESH, BATHE YOURSELF IN WATER, CHERISH THE LITTLE CHILD THAT HOLDS YOUR HAND, AND MAKE YOUR WIFE HAPPY IN YOUR EMBRACE.
FOR THIS TOO IS THE LOT OF MAN.
ALL MEN HAVE THAT!
AND THE ANNI-PADDA ARE MORE THAN MEN!

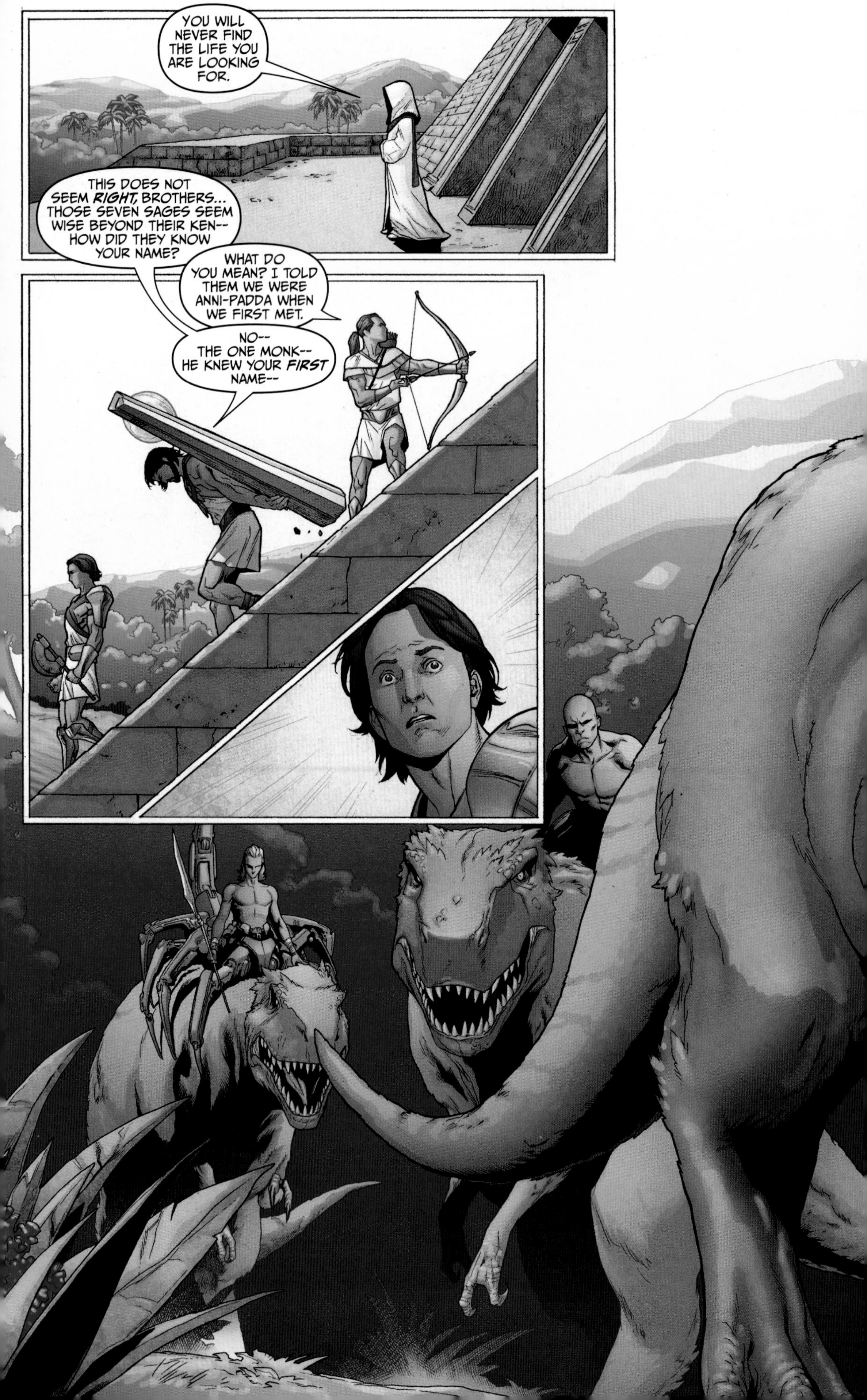
YOU WILL NEVER FIND THE LIFE YOU ARE LOOKING FOR.
THIS DOES NOT SEEM RIGHT, BROTHERS... THOSE SEVEN SAGES SEEM WISE BEYOND THEIR KEN-- HOW DID THEY KNOW YOUR NAME?
WHAT DO YOU MEAN? I TOLD THEM WE WERE ANNI-PADDA WHEN WE FIRST MET.
NO-- THE ONE MONK-- HE KNEW YOUR FIRST NAME--

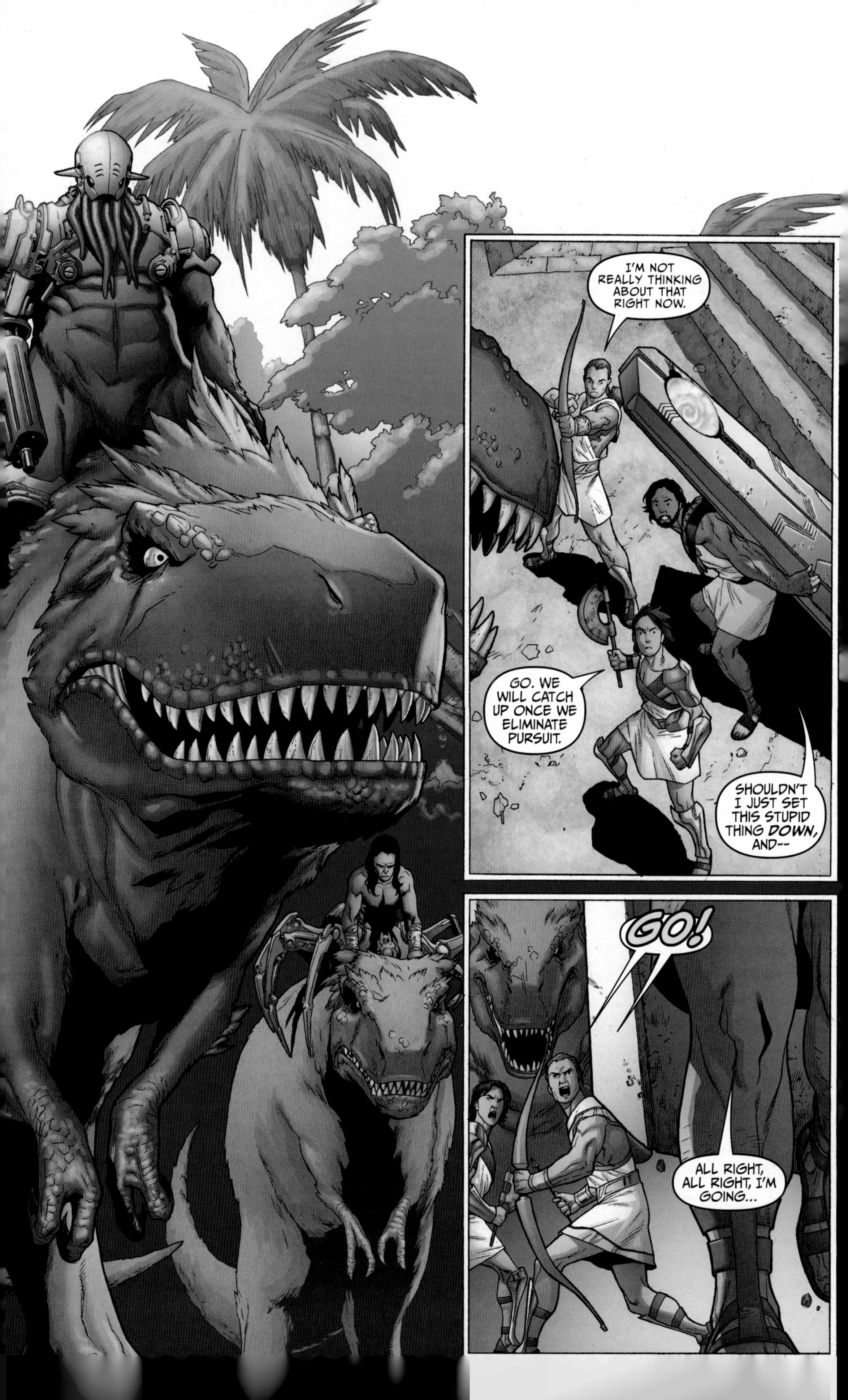
I'M NOT REALLY THINKING ABOUT THAT RIGHT NOW.
GO. WE WILL CATCH UP ONCE WE ELIMINATE PURSUIT.
SHOULDN'T I JUST SET THIS STUPID THING *DOWN*, AND--
GO!
ALL RIGHT, ALL RIGHT, I'M GOING...

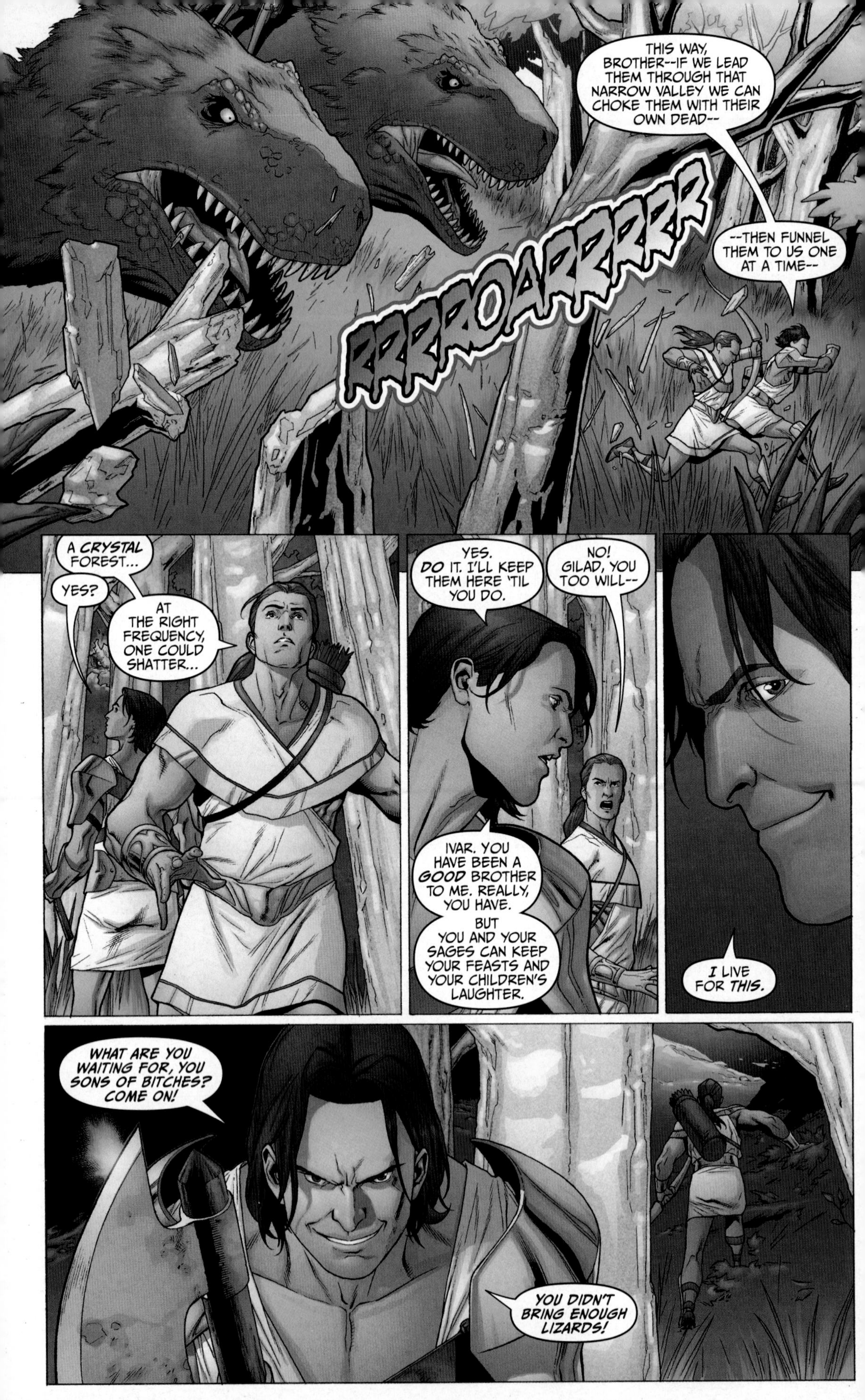
THIS WAY, BROTHER--IF WE LEAD THEM THROUGH THAT NARROW VALLEY WE CAN CHOKE THEM WITH THEIR OWN DEAD--
RRRROARRRRR
--THEN FUNNEL THEM TO US ONE AT A TIME--
A CRYSTAL FOREST...
YES?
AT THE RIGHT FREQUENCY, ONE COULD SHATTER...
YES. DO IT. I'LL KEEP THEM HERE 'TIL YOU DO.
NO! GILAD, YOU TOO WILL--
IVAR. YOU HAVE BEEN A GOOD BROTHER TO ME. REALLY, YOU HAVE.
BUT YOU AND YOUR SAGES CAN KEEP YOUR FEASTS AND YOUR CHILDREN'S LAUGHTER.
I LIVE FOR THIS.
WHAT ARE YOU WAITING FOR, YOU SONS OF BITCHES? COME ON!
YOU DIDN'T BRING ENOUGH LIZARDS!

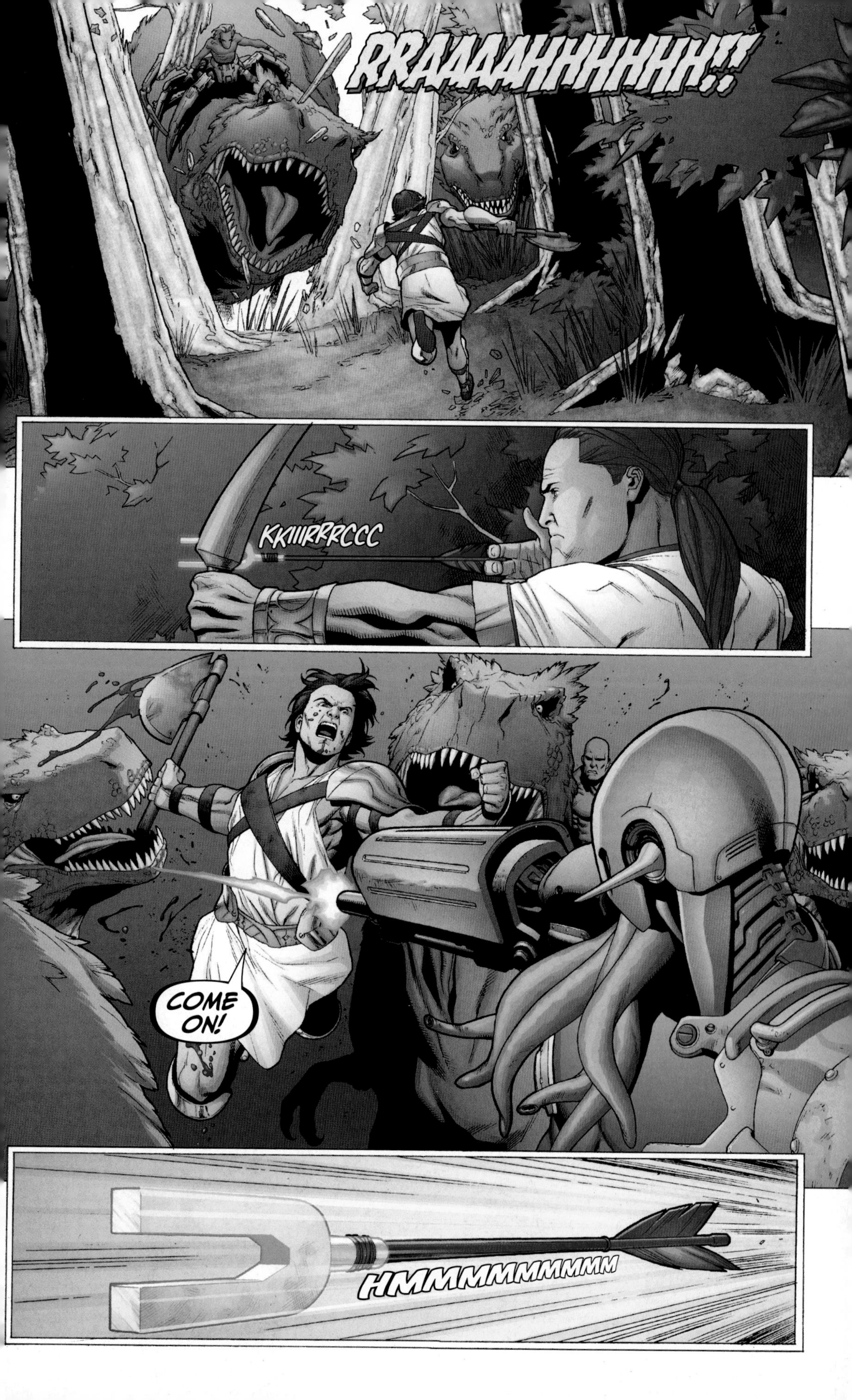
RRAAAAHHHHHH!!
KKIIIRRRCCC
COME ON!
HMMMMMMMMM

BY SHAMASH--!

IVAR... WHAT...

HE DIED. SAVING YOU. AND ME.

HE WAS MY LITTLE BROTHER. IT WAS MY JOB TO *PROTECT* HIM. I...I DIDN'T DO THAT. I--

GILAD WAS A *BORN WARRIOR.* HE LOVED WHAT HE DID. YOU CAN'T--

IS THIS *IT?* IS THIS ALL WE *HAVE* IN LIFE? TO STRIVE AND CONQUER, ONLY TO LOSE IT ALL IN THE END?

NO. PERHAPS *OTHER* MEN ARE BOUND BY THIS. BUT THE ANNI-PADDA ARE *NOT* OTHER MEN!

WE *WILL* RETURN TO UR! I *WILL* UNDERSTAND THE INNER WORKINGS OF THIS BOON--

--AGAIN WILL I SE MY DEAR BROTHE WITH MY EYES!

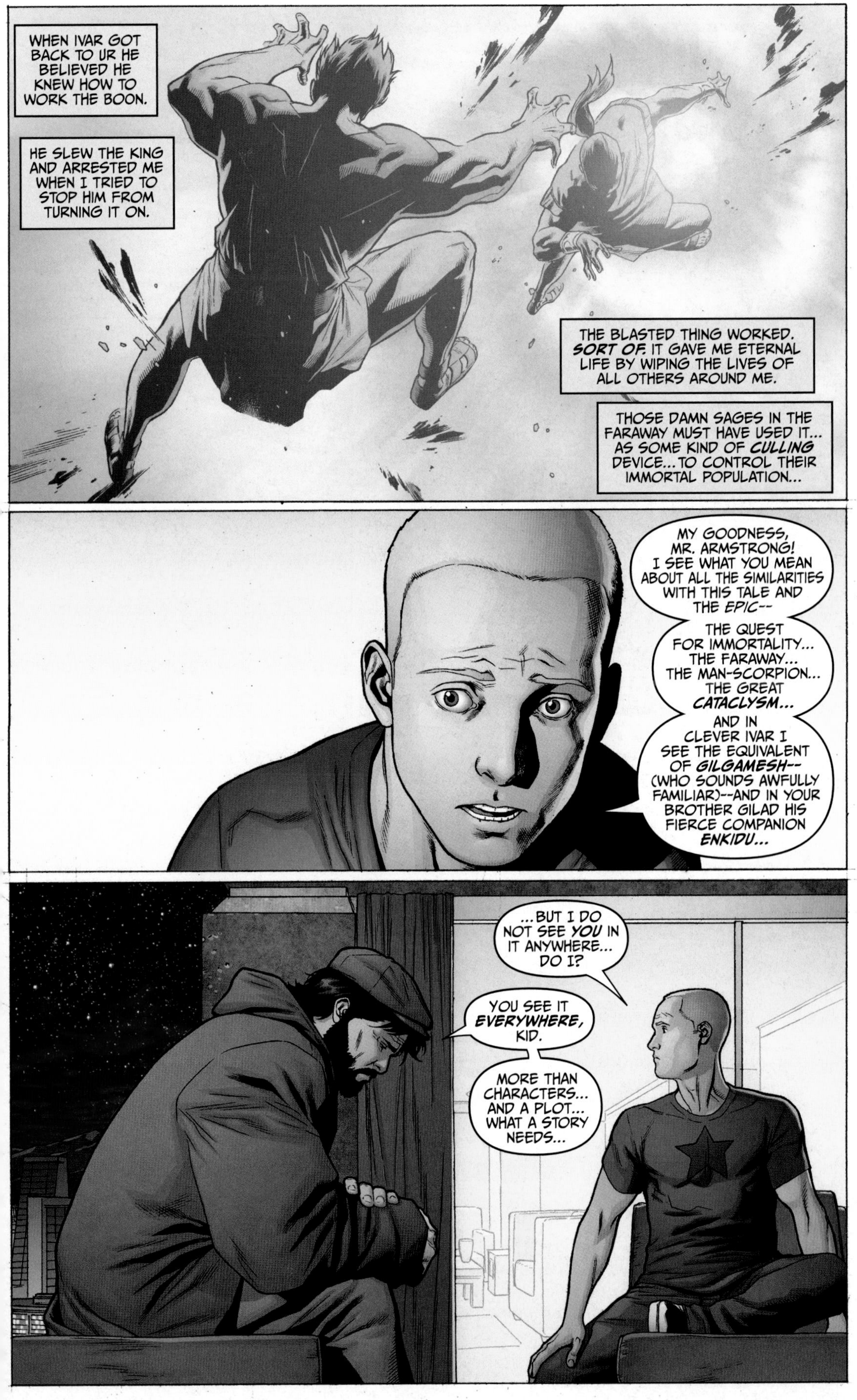

WHEN IVAR GOT BACK TO UR HE BELIEVED HE KNEW HOW TO WORK THE BOON.
HE SLEW THE KING AND ARRESTED ME WHEN I TRIED TO STOP HIM FROM TURNING IT ON.
THE BLASTED THING WORKED. ***SORT OF.*** IT GAVE ME ETERNAL LIFE BY WIPING THE LIVES OF ALL OTHERS AROUND ME.
THOSE DAMN SAGES IN THE FARAWAY MUST HAVE USED IT... AS SOME KIND OF ***CULLING*** DEVICE...TO CONTROL THEIR IMMORTAL POPULATION...
MY GOODNESS, MR. ARMSTRONG! I SEE WHAT YOU MEAN ABOUT ALL THE SIMILARITIES WITH THIS TALE AND THE *EPIC*--
THE QUEST FOR IMMORTALITY... THE FARAWAY... THE MAN-SCORPION... THE GREAT ***CATACLYSM...***
AND IN CLEVER IVAR I SEE THE EQUIVALENT OF ***GILGAMESH***--(WHO SOUNDS AWFULLY FAMILIAR)--AND IN YOUR BROTHER GILAD HIS FIERCE COMPANION ***ENKIDU...***
...BUT I DO NOT SEE ***YOU*** IN IT ANYWHERE... DO I?
YOU SEE IT ***EVERYWHERE,*** KID.
MORE THAN CHARACTERS... AND A PLOT... WHAT A STORY NEEDS...

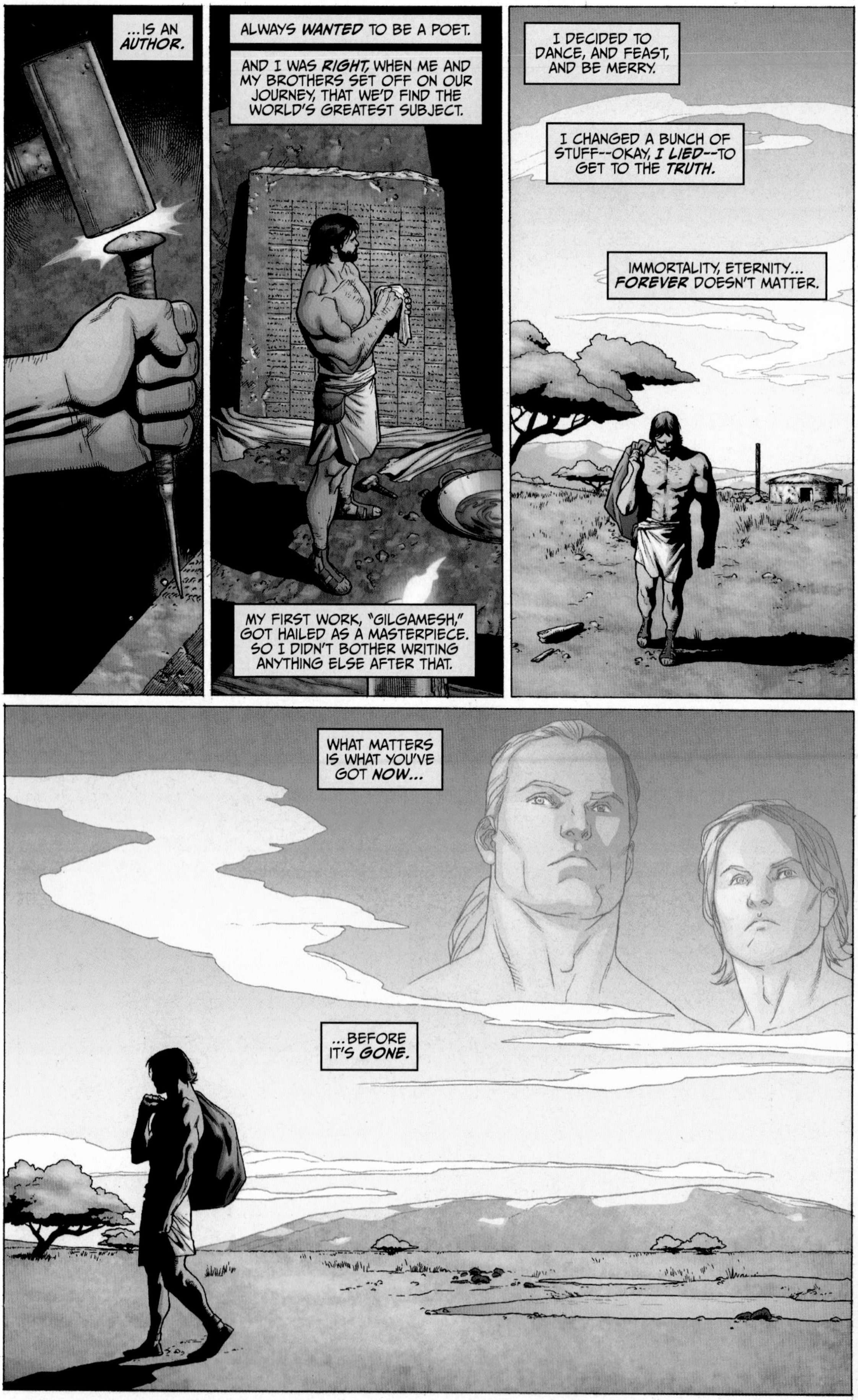
...IS AN AUTHOR.
ALWAYS WANTED TO BE A POET.
AND I WAS RIGHT, WHEN ME AND MY BROTHERS SET OFF ON OUR JOURNEY, THAT WE'D FIND THE WORLD'S GREATEST SUBJECT.
MY FIRST WORK, "GILGAMESH," GOT HAILED AS A MASTERPIECE. SO I DIDN'T BOTHER WRITING ANYTHING ELSE AFTER THAT.
I DECIDED TO DANCE, AND FEAST, AND BE MERRY.
I CHANGED A BUNCH OF STUFF--OKAY, I LIED--TO GET TO THE TRUTH.
IMMORTALITY, ETERNITY... FOREVER DOESN'T MATTER.
WHAT MATTERS IS WHAT YOU'VE GOT NOW...
...BEFORE IT'S GONE.

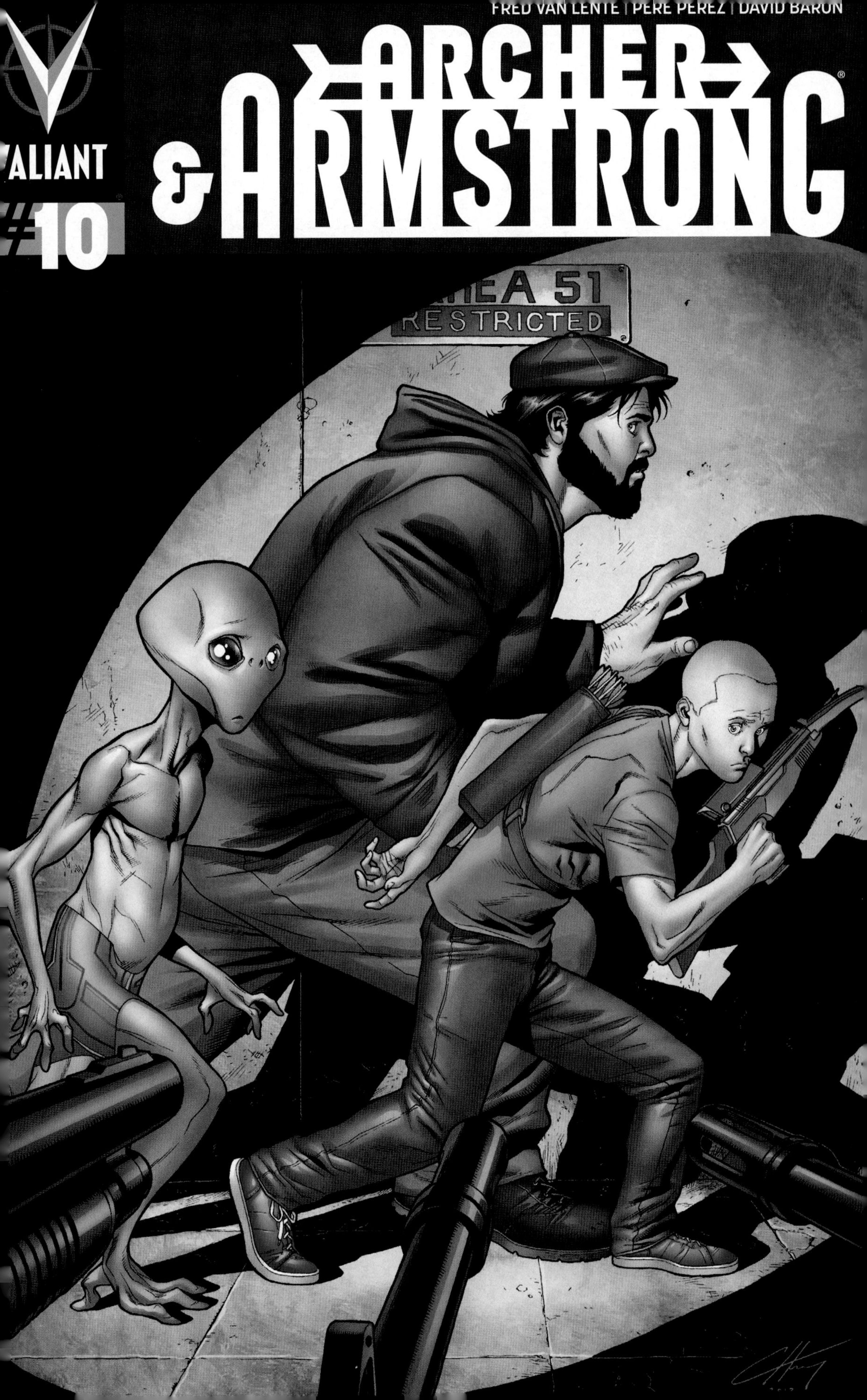
FRED VAN LENTE | PERE PEREZ | DAVID BARON
VALIANT
#10
ARCHER & ARMSTRONG
RESTRICTED

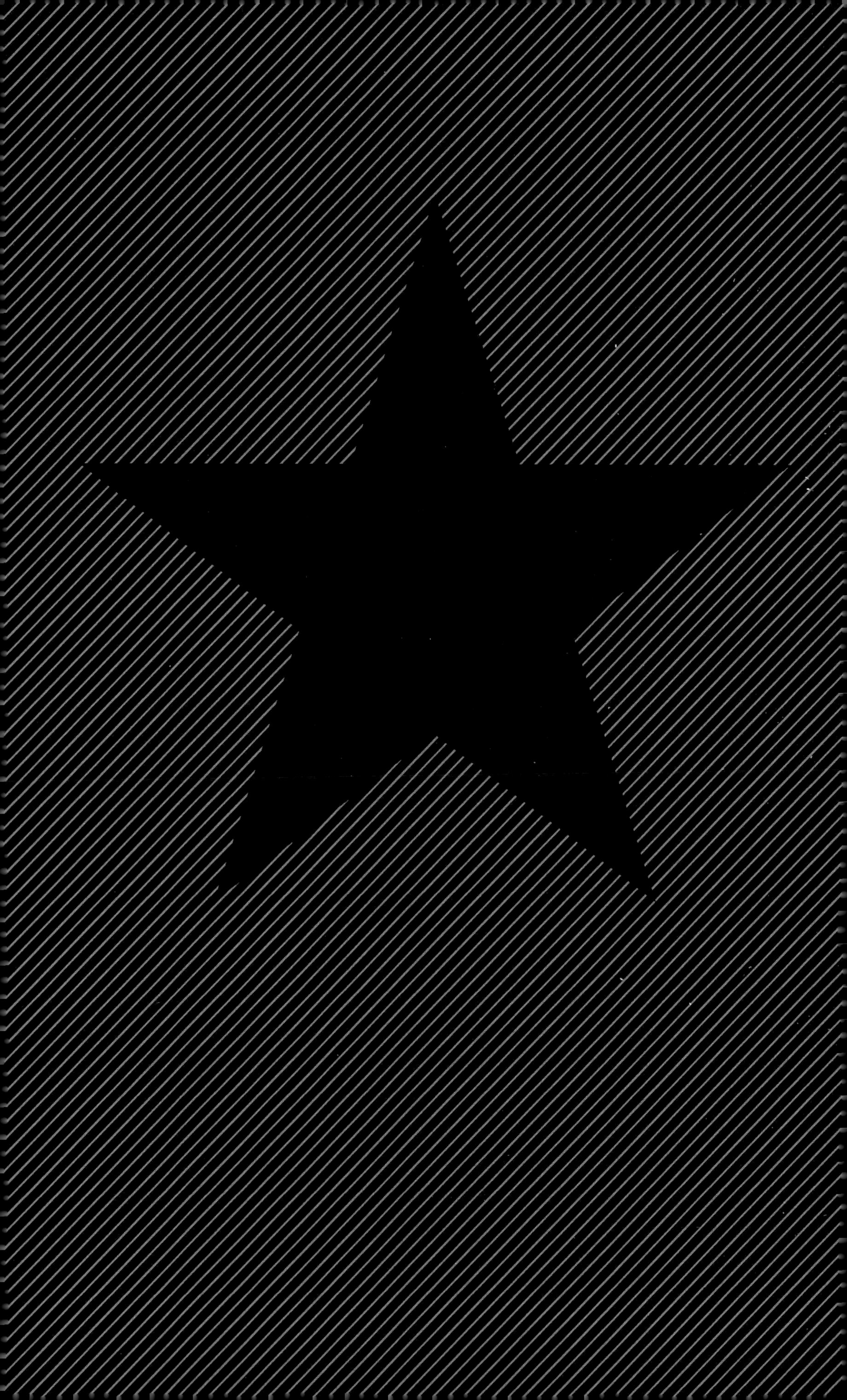

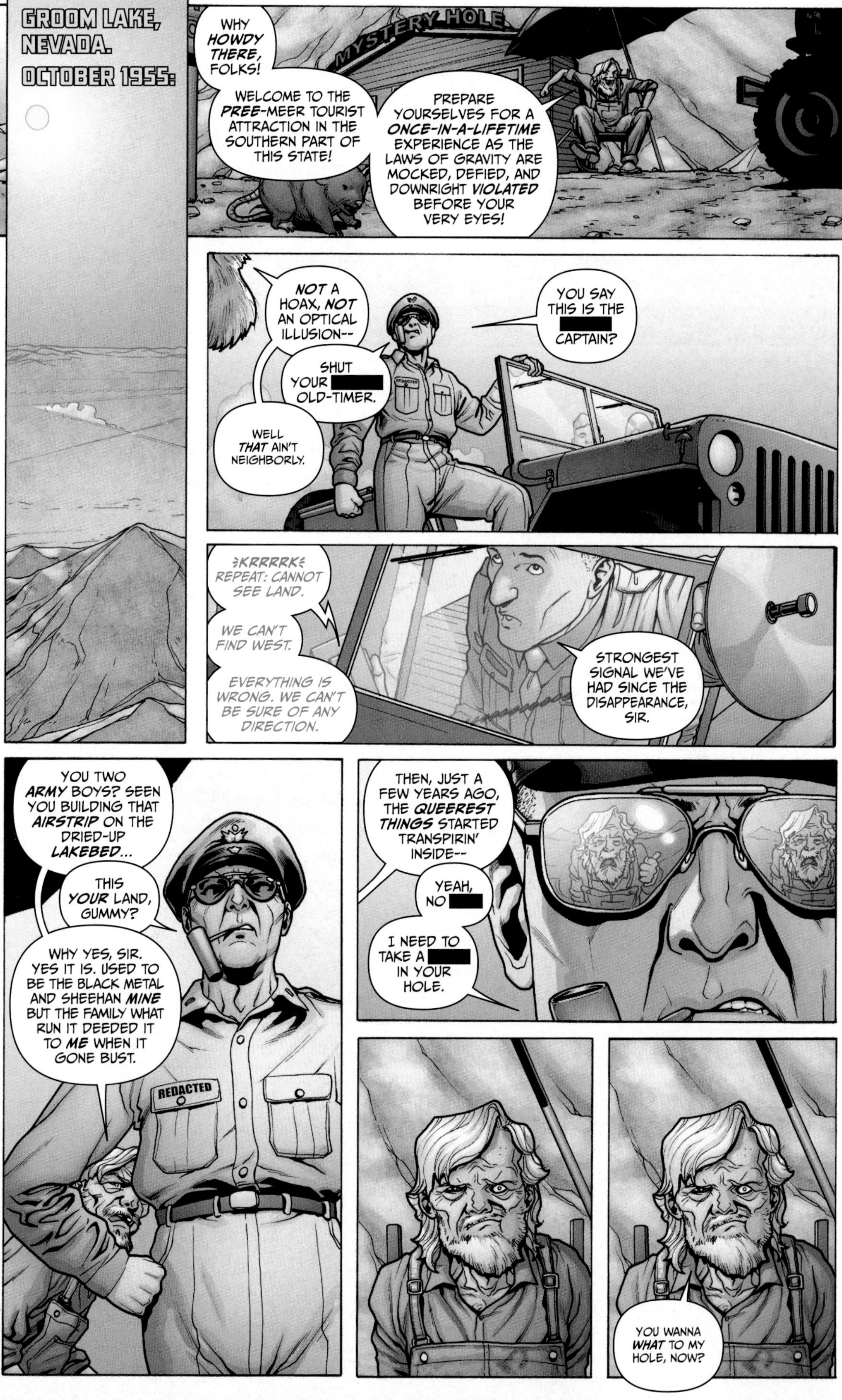
GROOM LAKE, NEVADA.
OCTOBER 1955:
MYSTERY HOLE
WHY HOWDY THERE, FOLKS!
WELCOME TO THE PREE-MEER TOURIST ATTRACTION IN THE SOUTHERN PART OF THIS STATE!
PREPARE YOURSELVES FOR A ONCE-IN-A-LIFETIME EXPERIENCE AS THE LAWS OF GRAVITY ARE MOCKED, DEFIED, AND DOWNRIGHT VIOLATED BEFORE YOUR VERY EYES!
NOT A HOAX, NOT AN OPTICAL ILLUSION--
YOU SAY THIS IS THE [redacted] CAPTAIN?
SHUT YOUR [redacted] OLD-TIMER.
REDACTED
WELL THAT AIN'T NEIGHBORLY.
KRRRRK REPEAT: CANNOT SEE LAND.
WE CAN'T FIND WEST.
EVERYTHING IS WRONG. WE CAN'T BE SURE OF ANY DIRECTION.
STRONGEST SIGNAL WE'VE HAD SINCE THE DISAPPEARANCE, SIR.
YOU TWO ARMY BOYS? SEEN YOU BUILDING THAT AIRSTRIP ON THE DRIED-UP LAKEBED...
THIS YOUR LAND, GUMMY?
WHY YES, SIR. YES IT IS. USED TO BE THE BLACK METAL AND SHEEHAN MINE BUT THE FAMILY WHAT RUN IT DEEDED IT TO ME WHEN IT GONE BUST.
REDACTED
THEN, JUST A FEW YEARS AGO, THE QUEEREST THINGS STARTED TRANSPIRIN' INSIDE--
YEAH, NO [redacted]
I NEED TO TAKE A [redacted] IN YOUR HOLE.
YOU WANNA WHAT TO MY HOLE, NOW?

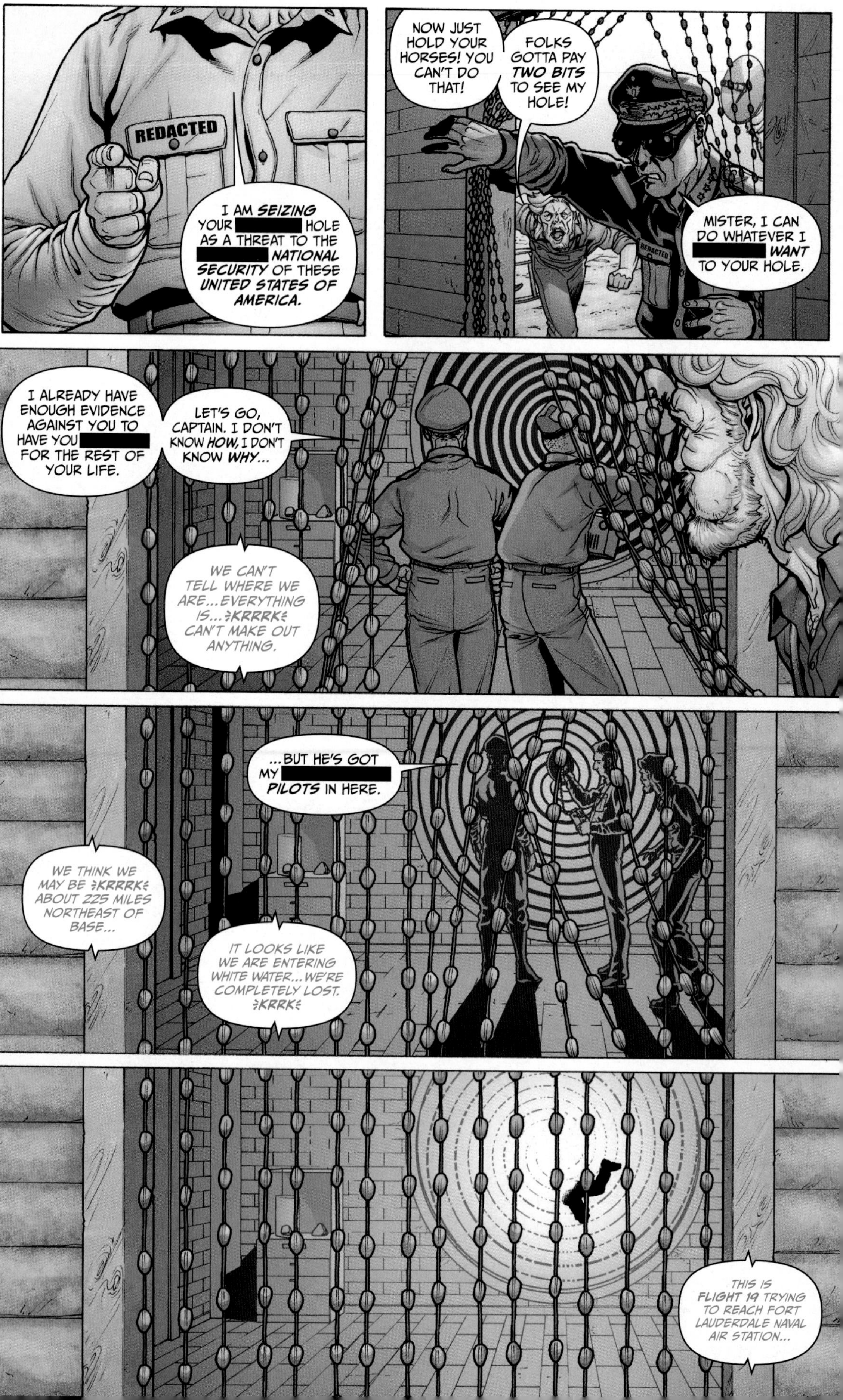
REDACTED
I AM SEIZING YOUR [redacted] HOLE AS A THREAT TO THE [redacted] NATIONAL SECURITY OF THESE UNITED STATES OF AMERICA.
NOW JUST HOLD YOUR HORSES! YOU CAN'T DO THAT!
FOLKS GOTTA PAY TWO BITS TO SEE MY HOLE!
REDACTED
MISTER, I CAN DO WHATEVER I [redacted] WANT TO YOUR HOLE.
I ALREADY HAVE ENOUGH EVIDENCE AGAINST YOU TO HAVE YOU [redacted] FOR THE REST OF YOUR LIFE.
LET'S GO, CAPTAIN. I DON'T KNOW HOW, I DON'T KNOW WHY...
WE CAN'T TELL WHERE WE ARE...EVERYTHING IS... KRRRK CAN'T MAKE OUT ANYTHING.
...BUT HE'S GOT MY [redacted] PILOTS IN HERE.
WE THINK WE MAY BE KRRRK ABOUT 225 MILES NORTHEAST OF BASE...
IT LOOKS LIKE WE ARE ENTERING WHITE WATER...WE'RE COMPLETELY LOST. KRRK
THIS IS FLIGHT 19 TRYING TO REACH FORT LAUDERDALE NAVAL AIR STATION...

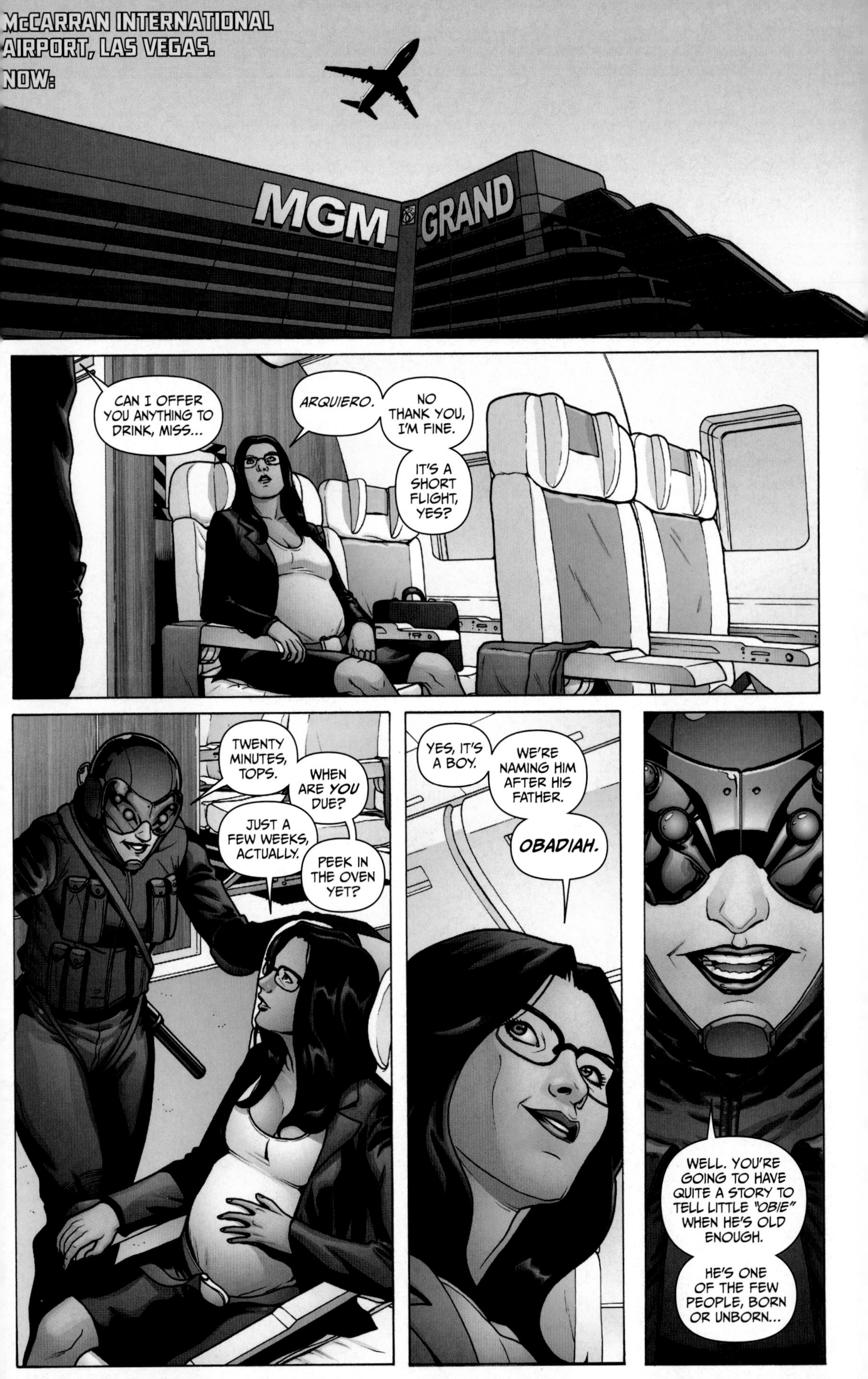
McCARRAN INTERNATIONAL AIRPORT, LAS VEGAS.
NOW:
MGM GRAND
CAN I OFFER YOU ANYTHING TO DRINK, MISS...
ARQUIERO.
NO THANK YOU, I'M FINE.
IT'S A SHORT FLIGHT, YES?
TWENTY MINUTES, TOPS.
WHEN ARE YOU DUE?
JUST A FEW WEEKS, ACTUALLY.
PEEK IN THE OVEN YET?
YES, IT'S A BOY.
WE'RE NAMING HIM AFTER HIS FATHER.
OBADIAH.
WELL. YOU'RE GOING TO HAVE QUITE A STORY TO TELL LITTLE "OBIE" WHEN HE'S OLD ENOUGH.
HE'S ONE OF THE FEW PEOPLE, BORN OR UNBORN...

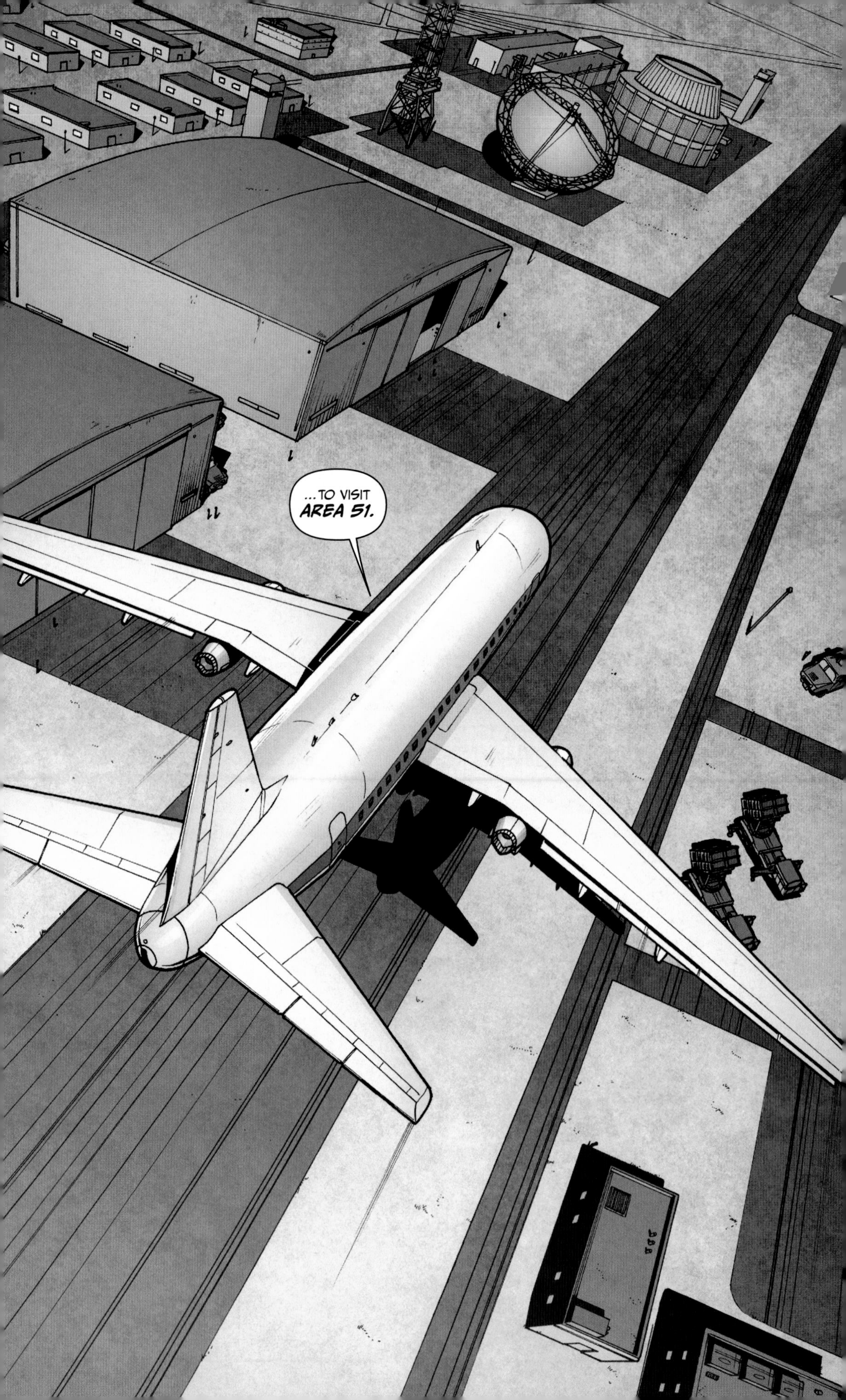
...TO VISIT
AREA 51.

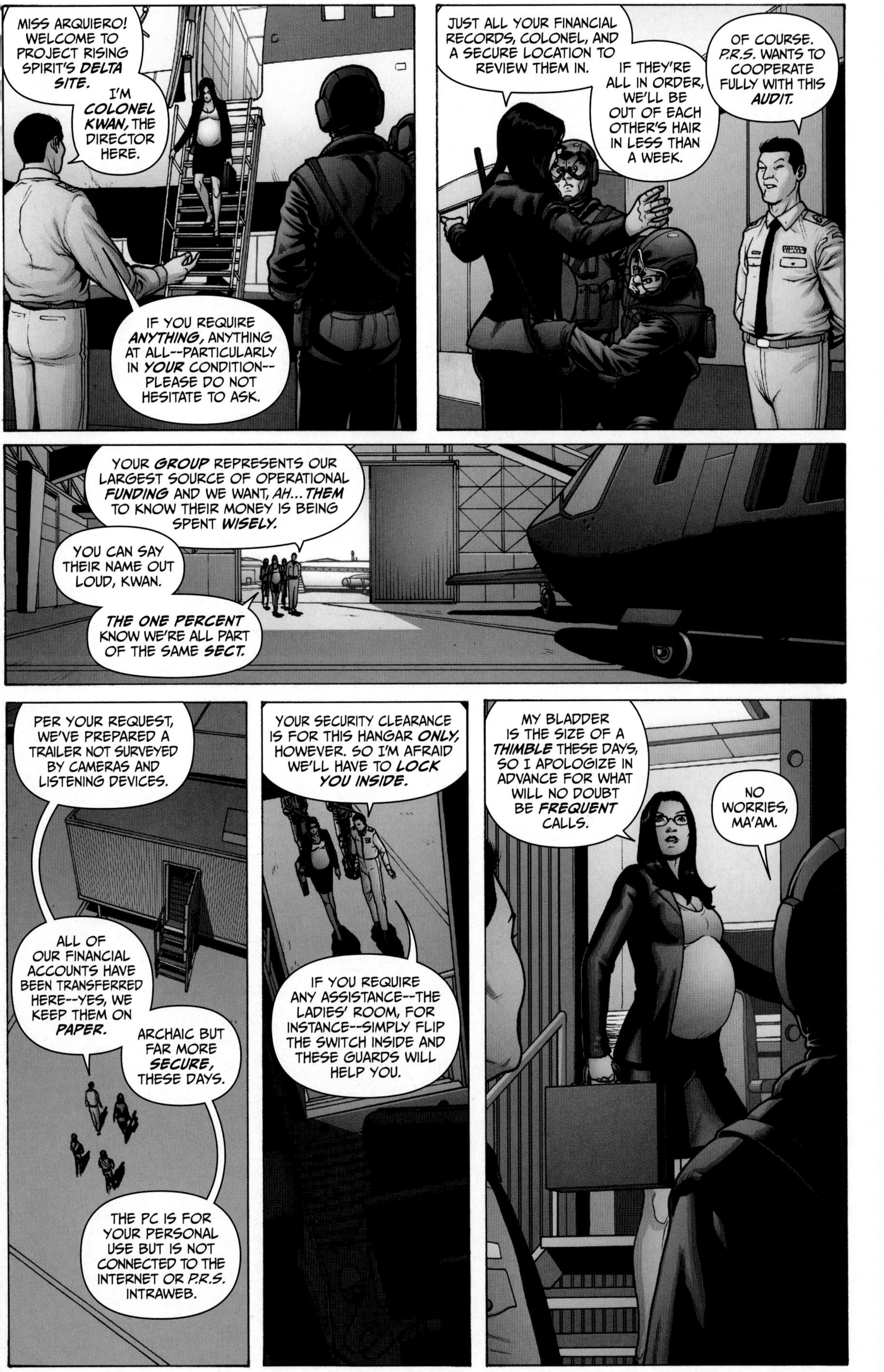
MISS ARQUIERO! WELCOME TO PROJECT RISING SPIRIT'S DELTA SITE.
I'M COLONEL KWAN, THE DIRECTOR HERE.
IF YOU REQUIRE ANYTHING, ANYTHING AT ALL--PARTICULARLY IN YOUR CONDITION--PLEASE DO NOT HESITATE TO ASK.
JUST ALL YOUR FINANCIAL RECORDS, COLONEL, AND A SECURE LOCATION TO REVIEW THEM IN.
IF THEY'RE ALL IN ORDER, WE'LL BE OUT OF EACH OTHER'S HAIR IN LESS THAN A WEEK.
OF COURSE. P.R.S. WANTS TO COOPERATE FULLY WITH THIS AUDIT.
YOUR GROUP REPRESENTS OUR LARGEST SOURCE OF OPERATIONAL FUNDING AND WE WANT, AH... THEM TO KNOW THEIR MONEY IS BEING SPENT WISELY.
YOU CAN SAY THEIR NAME OUT LOUD, KWAN.
THE ONE PERCENT KNOW WE'RE ALL PART OF THE SAME SECT.
PER YOUR REQUEST, WE'VE PREPARED A TRAILER NOT SURVEYED BY CAMERAS AND LISTENING DEVICES.
ALL OF OUR FINANCIAL ACCOUNTS HAVE BEEN TRANSFERRED HERE--YES, WE KEEP THEM ON PAPER.
ARCHAIC BUT FAR MORE SECURE, THESE DAYS.
THE PC IS FOR YOUR PERSONAL USE BUT IS NOT CONNECTED TO THE INTERNET OR P.R.S. INTRAWEB.
YOUR SECURITY CLEARANCE IS FOR THIS HANGAR ONLY, HOWEVER. SO I'M AFRAID WE'LL HAVE TO LOCK YOU INSIDE.
IF YOU REQUIRE ANY ASSISTANCE--THE LADIES' ROOM, FOR INSTANCE--SIMPLY FLIP THE SWITCH INSIDE AND THESE GUARDS WILL HELP YOU.
MY BLADDER IS THE SIZE OF A THIMBLE THESE DAYS, SO I APOLOGIZE IN ADVANCE FOR WHAT WILL NO DOUBT BE FREQUENT CALLS.
NO WORRIES, MA'AM.

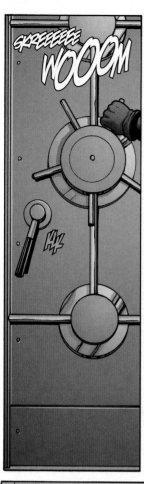
SKREEEEEE
WOOOM
HK

RRRIP

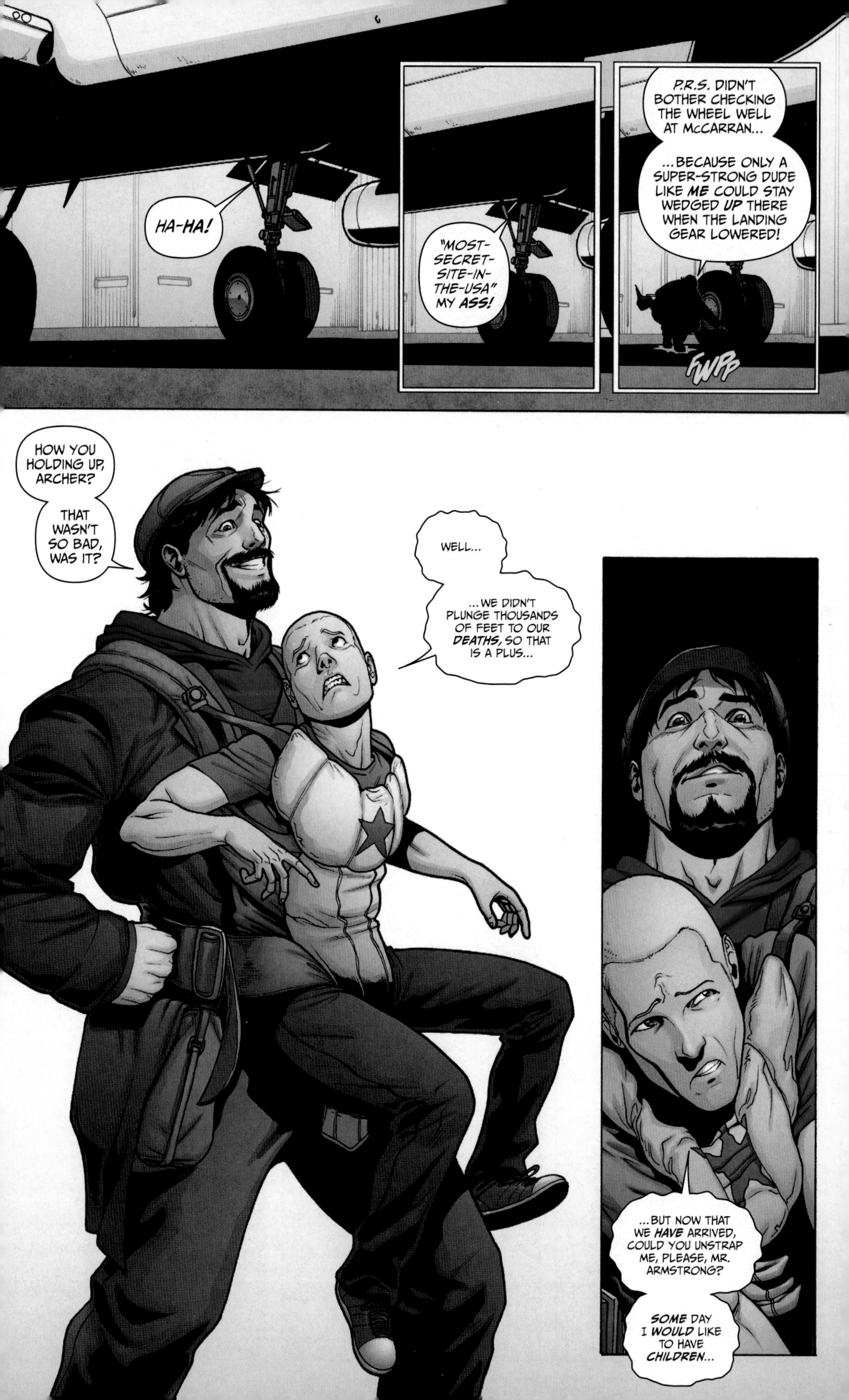
HA-HA!
"MOST-SECRET-SITE-IN-THE-USA" MY ASS!
P.R.S. DIDN'T BOTHER CHECKING THE WHEEL WELL AT McCARRAN...
...BECAUSE ONLY A SUPER-STRONG DUDE LIKE ME COULD STAY WEDGED UP THERE WHEN THE LANDING GEAR LOWERED!
FWPP
HOW YOU HOLDING UP, ARCHER?
THAT WASN'T SO BAD, WAS IT?
WELL...
...WE DIDN'T PLUNGE THOUSANDS OF FEET TO OUR DEATHS, SO THAT IS A PLUS...
...BUT NOW THAT WE HAVE ARRIVED, COULD YOU UNSTRAP ME, PLEASE, MR. ARMSTRONG?
SOME DAY I WOULD LIKE TO HAVE CHILDREN...

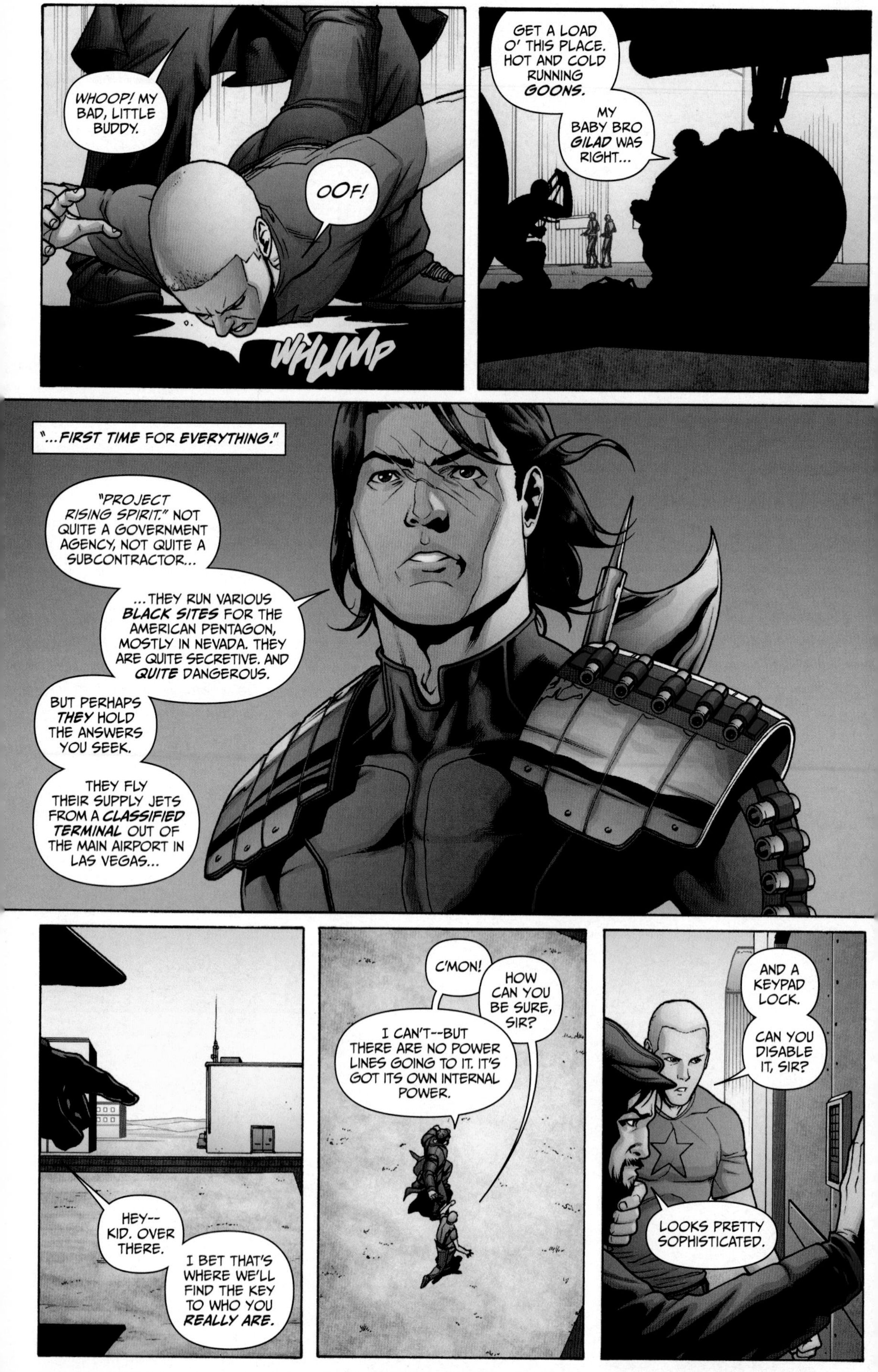
WHOOP! MY BAD, LITTLE BUDDY.
OOF!
WHUMP
GET A LOAD O' THIS PLACE. HOT AND COLD RUNNING GOONS.
MY BABY BRO GILAD WAS RIGHT...
"...FIRST TIME FOR EVERYTHING."
"PROJECT RISING SPIRIT." NOT QUITE A GOVERNMENT AGENCY, NOT QUITE A SUBCONTRACTOR...
...THEY RUN VARIOUS BLACK SITES FOR THE AMERICAN PENTAGON, MOSTLY IN NEVADA. THEY ARE QUITE SECRETIVE. AND QUITE DANGEROUS.
BUT PERHAPS THEY HOLD THE ANSWERS YOU SEEK.
THEY FLY THEIR SUPPLY JETS FROM A CLASSIFIED TERMINAL OUT OF THE MAIN AIRPORT IN LAS VEGAS...
HEY-- KID. OVER THERE.
I BET THAT'S WHERE WE'LL FIND THE KEY TO WHO YOU REALLY ARE.
C'MON!
HOW CAN YOU BE SURE, SIR?
I CAN'T--BUT THERE ARE NO POWER LINES GOING TO IT. IT'S GOT ITS OWN INTERNAL POWER.
AND A KEYPAD LOCK.
CAN YOU DISABLE IT, SIR?
LOOKS PRETTY SOPHISTICATED.

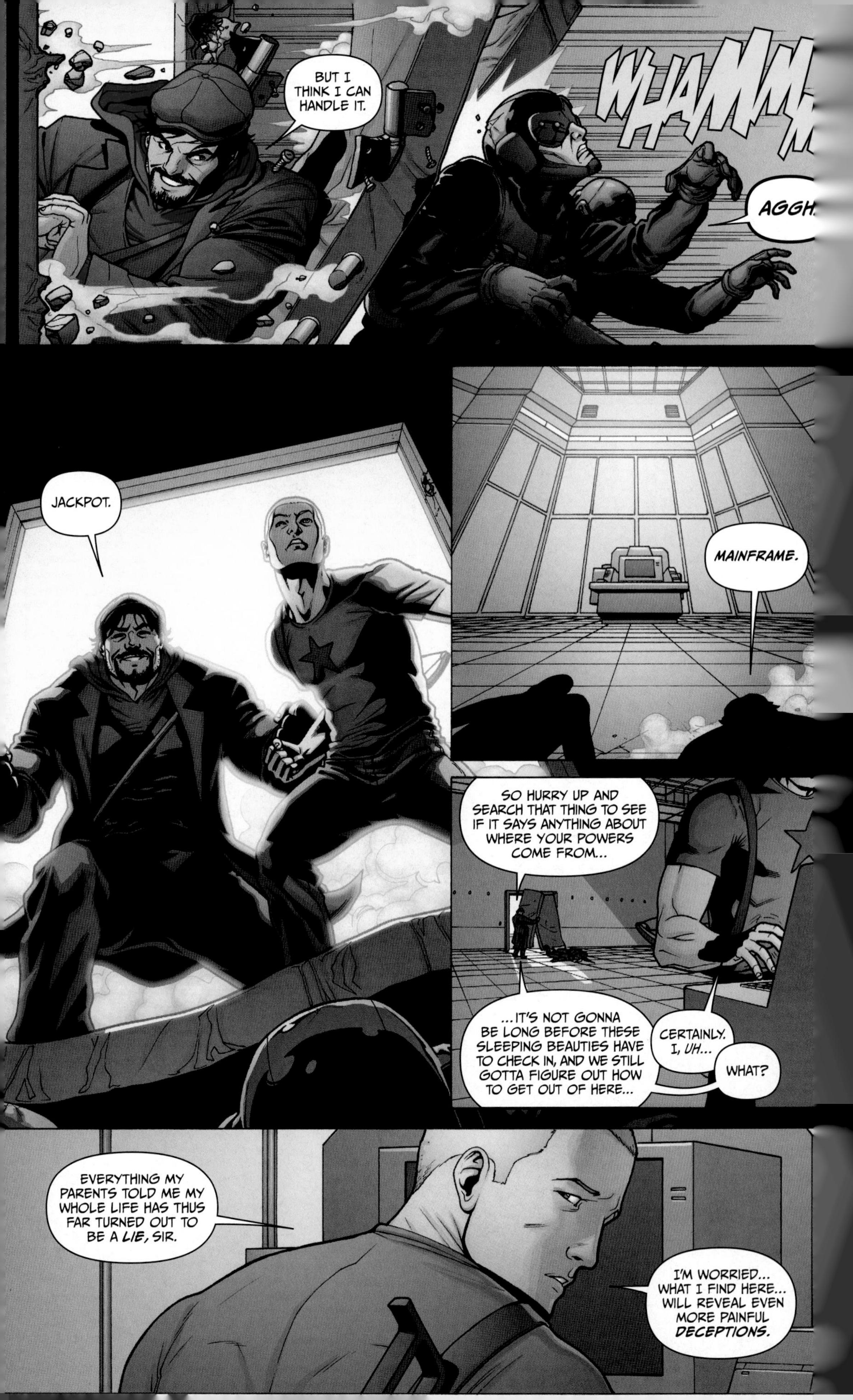
BUT I THINK I CAN HANDLE IT.
WHAMMM
AGGH
JACKPOT.
MAINFRAME.
SO HURRY UP AND SEARCH THAT THING TO SEE IF IT SAYS ANYTHING ABOUT WHERE YOUR POWERS COME FROM...
...IT'S NOT GONNA BE LONG BEFORE THESE SLEEPING BEAUTIES HAVE TO CHECK IN, AND WE STILL GOTTA FIGURE OUT HOW TO GET OUT OF HERE...
CERTAINLY. I, UH...
WHAT?
EVERYTHING MY PARENTS TOLD ME MY WHOLE LIFE HAS THUS FAR TURNED OUT TO BE A LIE, SIR.
I'M WORRIED... WHAT I FIND HERE... WILL REVEAL EVEN MORE PAINFUL DECEPTIONS.

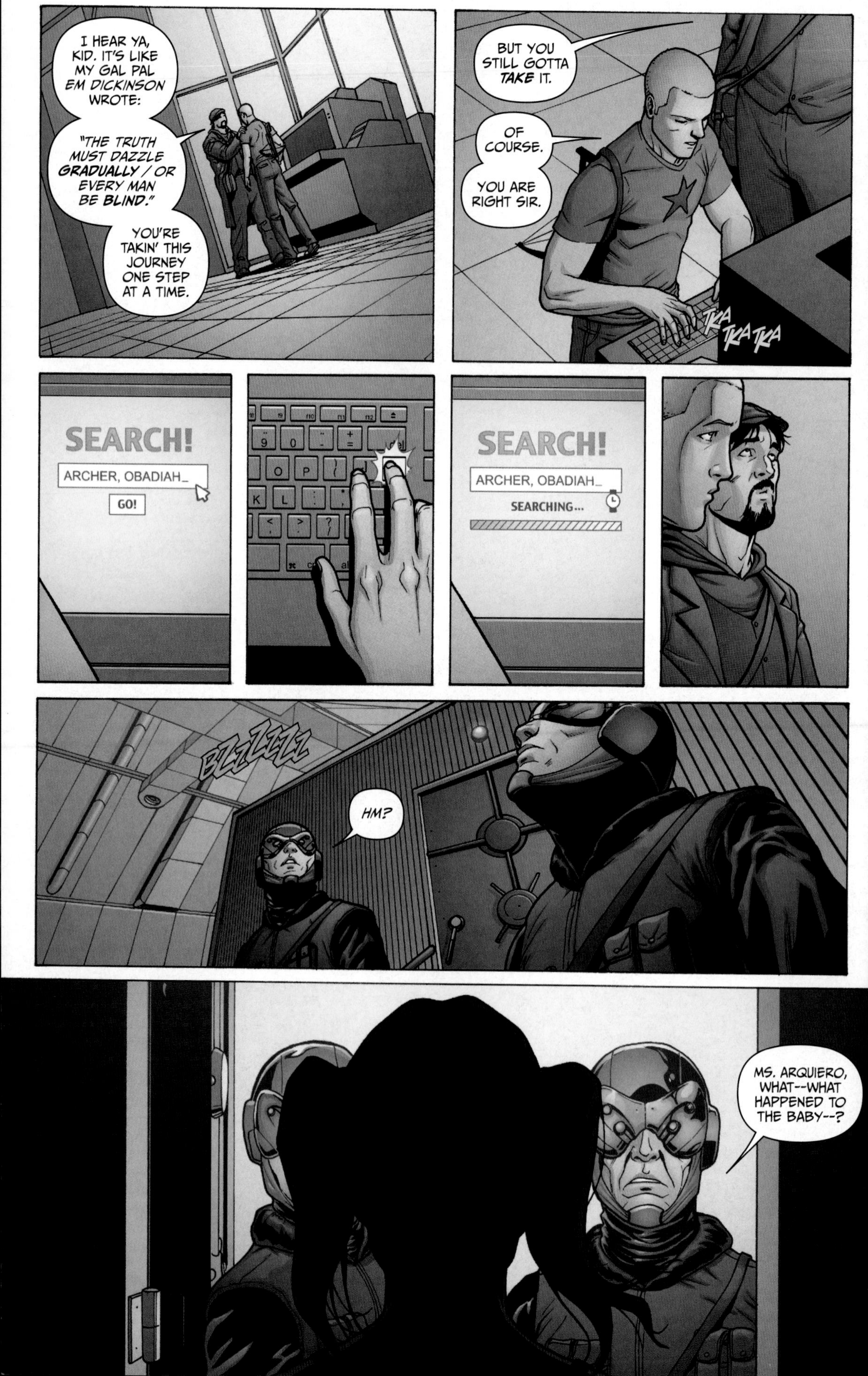
I HEAR YA, KID. IT'S LIKE MY GAL PAL EM DICKINSON WROTE:
"THE TRUTH MUST DAZZLE GRADUALLY / OR EVERY MAN BE BLIND."
YOU'RE TAKIN' THIS JOURNEY ONE STEP AT A TIME.
BUT YOU STILL GOTTA TAKE IT.
OF COURSE.
YOU ARE RIGHT SIR.
TKA TKA TKA TKA
SEARCH!
ARCHER, OBADIAH_
GO!
SEARCH!
ARCHER, OBADIAH_
SEARCHING...
BZZZZZZ
HM?
MS. ARQUIERO, WHAT--WHAT HAPPENED TO THE BABY--?

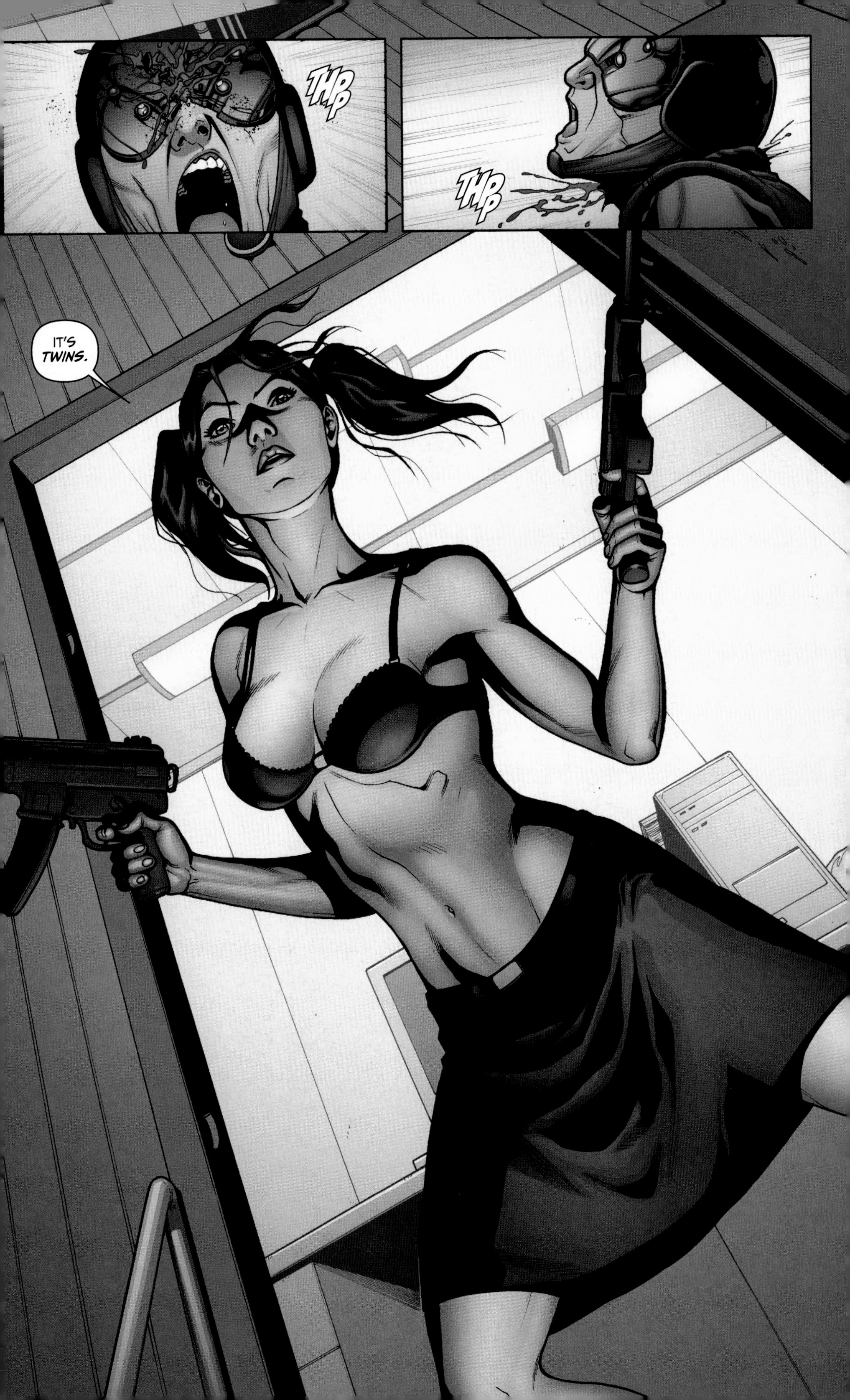

THPP
THPP
IT'S TWINS.

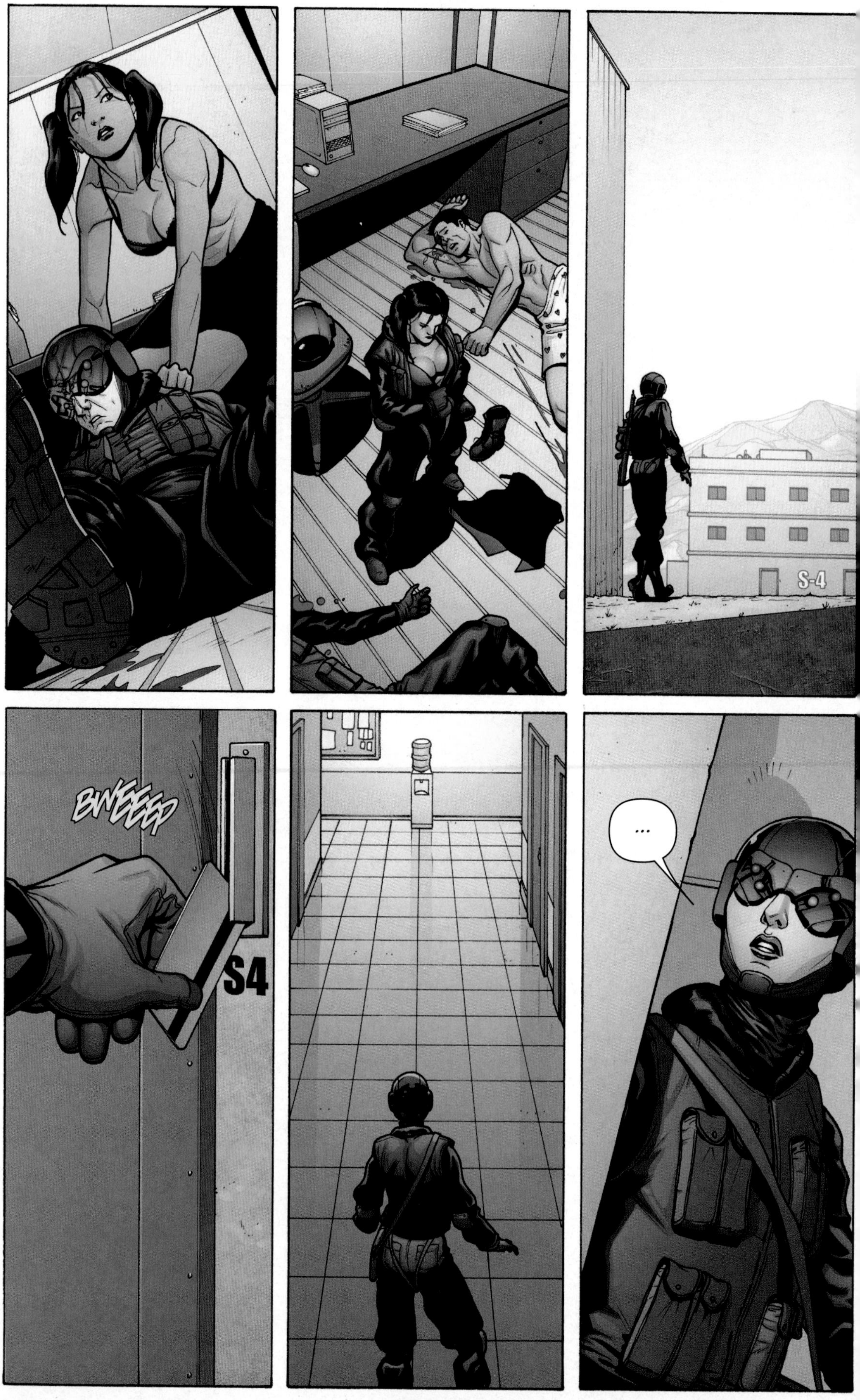
S-4
BWEEEP
S4
...

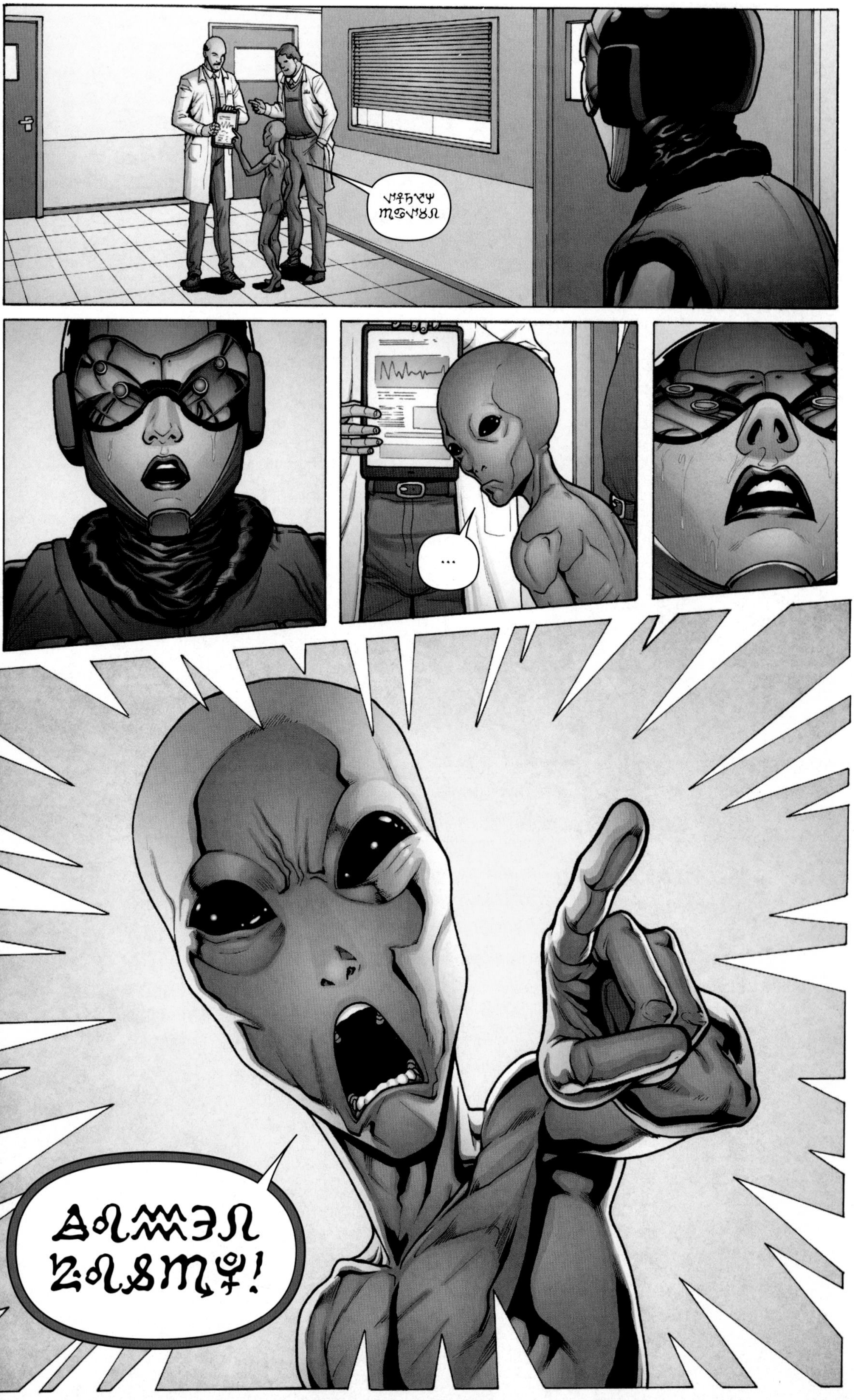
...

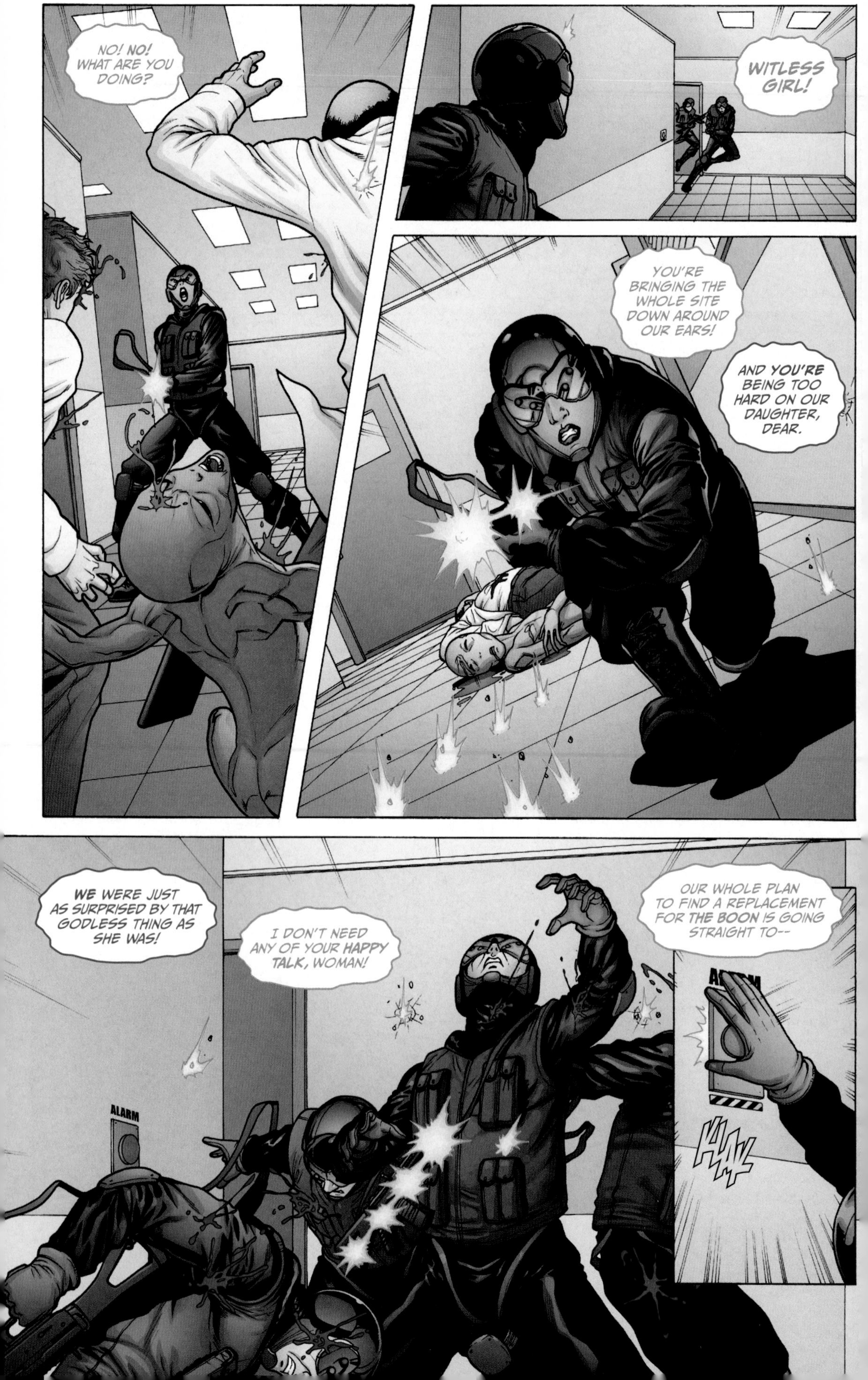

NO! NO! WHAT ARE YOU DOING?
WITLESS GIRL!
YOU'RE BRINGING THE WHOLE SITE DOWN AROUND OUR EARS!
AND YOU'RE BEING TOO HARD ON OUR DAUGHTER, DEAR.
WE WERE JUST AS SURPRISED BY THAT GODLESS THING AS SHE WAS!
I DON'T NEED ANY OF YOUR HAPPY TALK, WOMAN!
OUR WHOLE PLAN TO FIND A REPLACEMENT FOR THE BOON IS GOING STRAIGHT TO--
ALARM

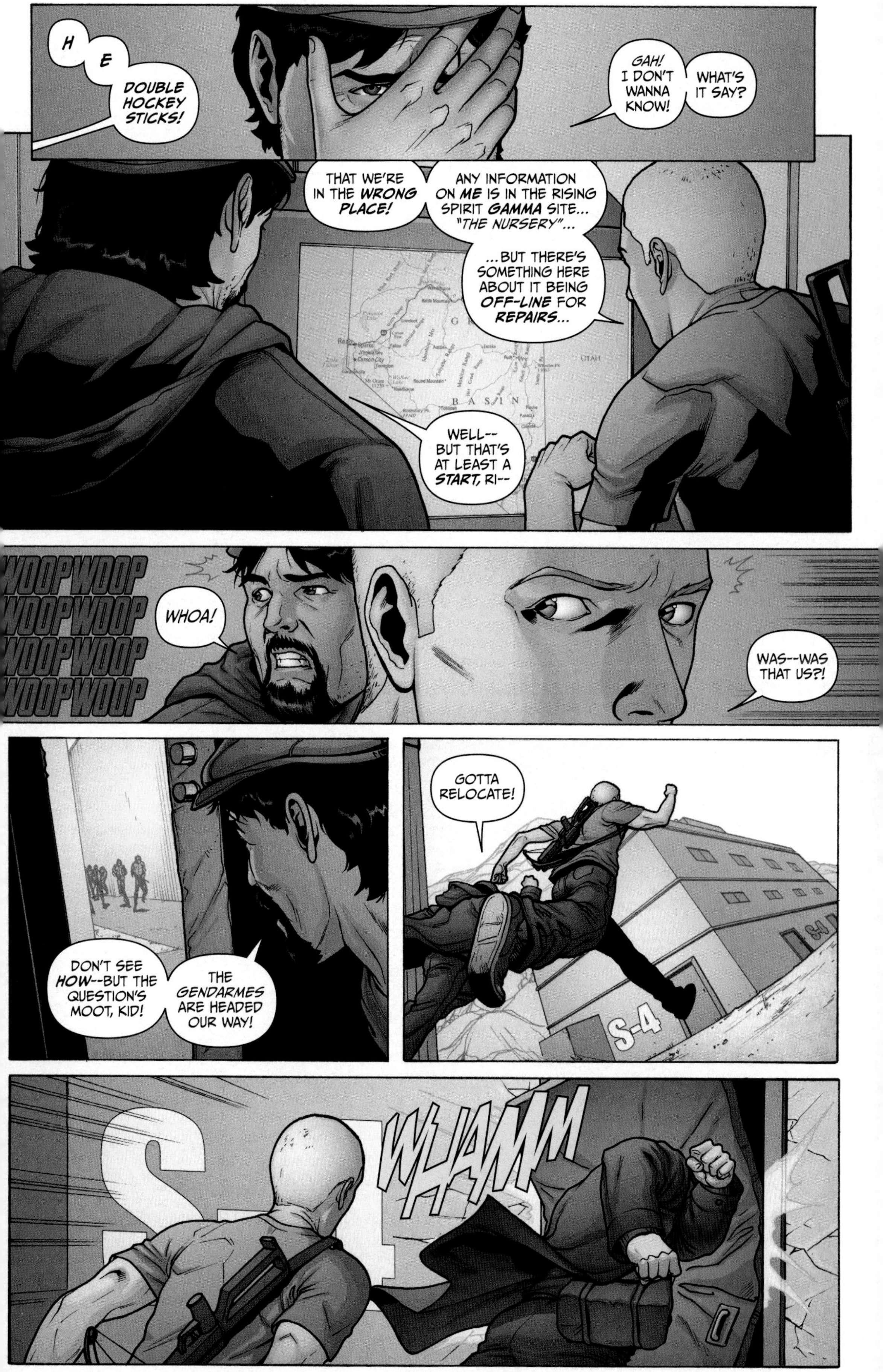
H
E
DOUBLE HOCKEY STICKS!
GAH! I DON'T WANNA KNOW!
WHAT'S IT SAY?
THAT WE'RE IN THE WRONG PLACE!
ANY INFORMATION ON ME IS IN THE RISING SPIRIT GAMMA SITE... "THE NURSERY"...
...BUT THERE'S SOMETHING HERE ABOUT IT BEING OFF-LINE FOR REPAIRS...
WELL-- BUT THAT'S AT LEAST A START, RI--
UTAH
BASIN
WOOPWOOP WOOPWOOP WOOPWOOP WOOPWOOP
WHOA!
WAS--WAS THAT US?!
DON'T SEE HOW--BUT THE QUESTION'S MOOT, KID!
THE GENDARMES ARE HEADED OUR WAY!
GOTTA RELOCATE!
S-4
S-4
WHAMM

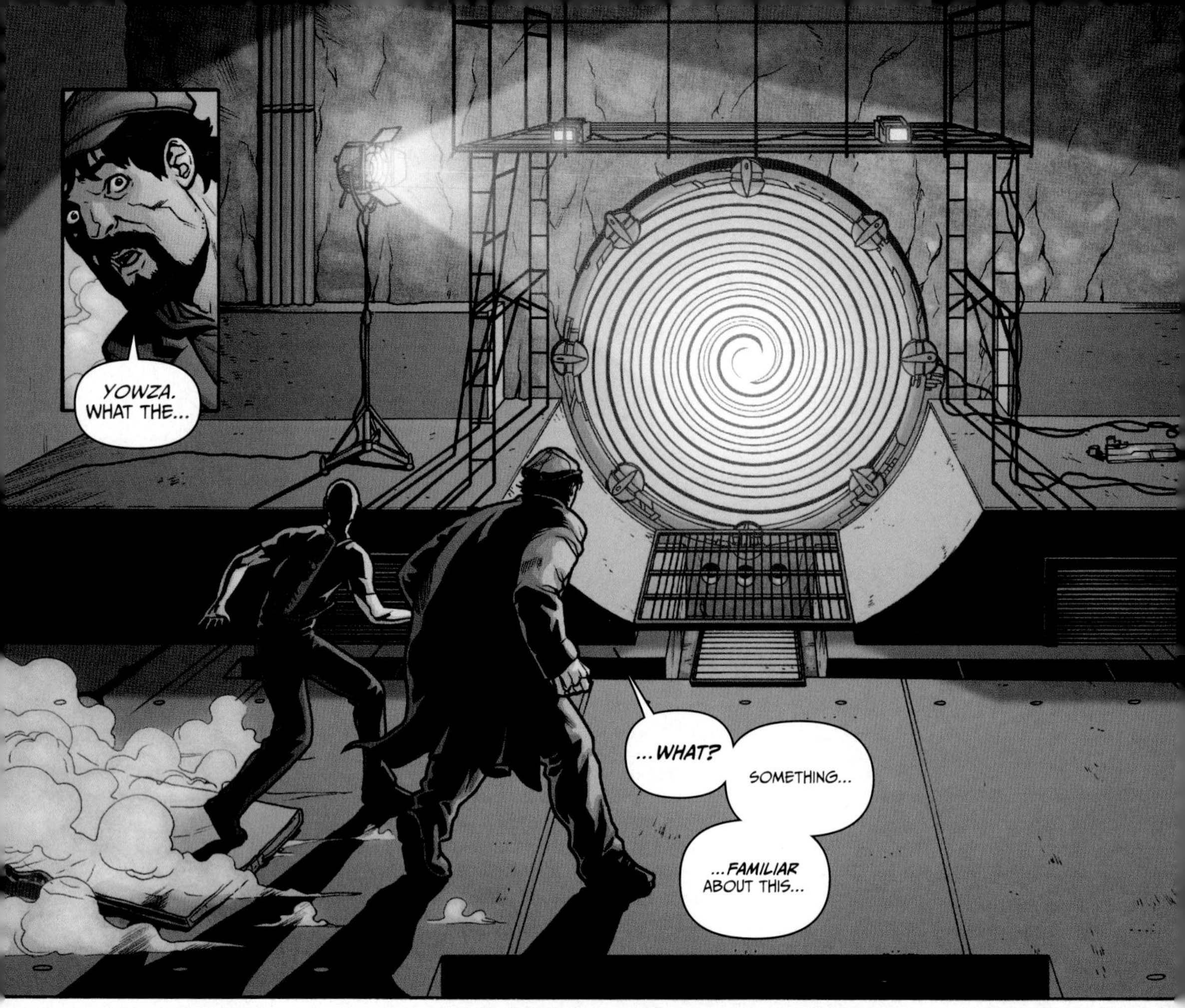
YOWZA. WHAT THE...
...WHAT?
SOMETHING...
...FAMILIAR ABOUT THIS...

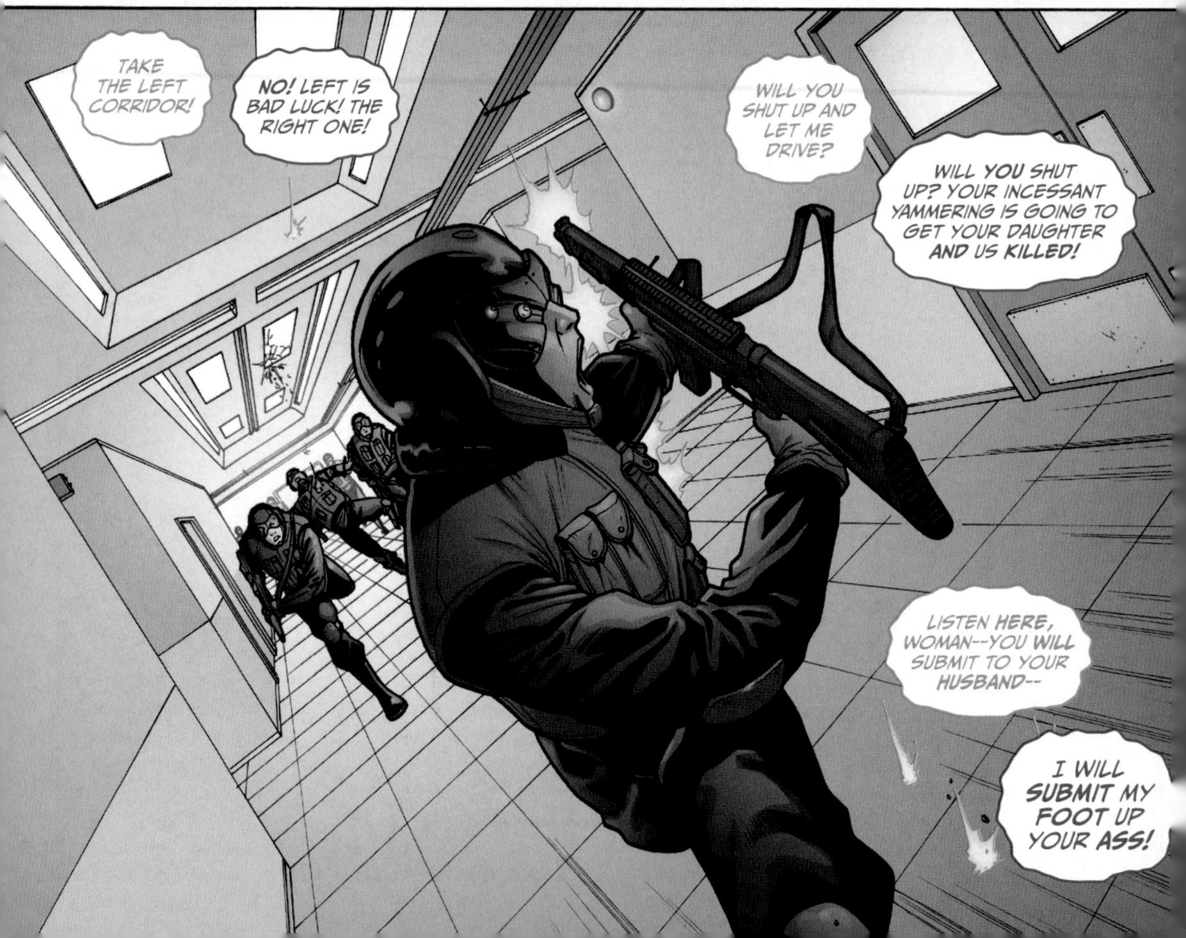
TAKE THE LEFT CORRIDOR!
NO! LEFT IS BAD LUCK! THE RIGHT ONE!
WILL YOU SHUT UP AND LET ME DRIVE?
WILL YOU SHUT UP? YOUR INCESSANT YAMMERING IS GOING TO GET YOUR DAUGHTER AND US KILLED!
LISTEN HERE, WOMAN--YOU WILL SUBMIT TO YOUR HUSBAND--
I WILL SUBMIT MY FOOT UP YOUR ASS!

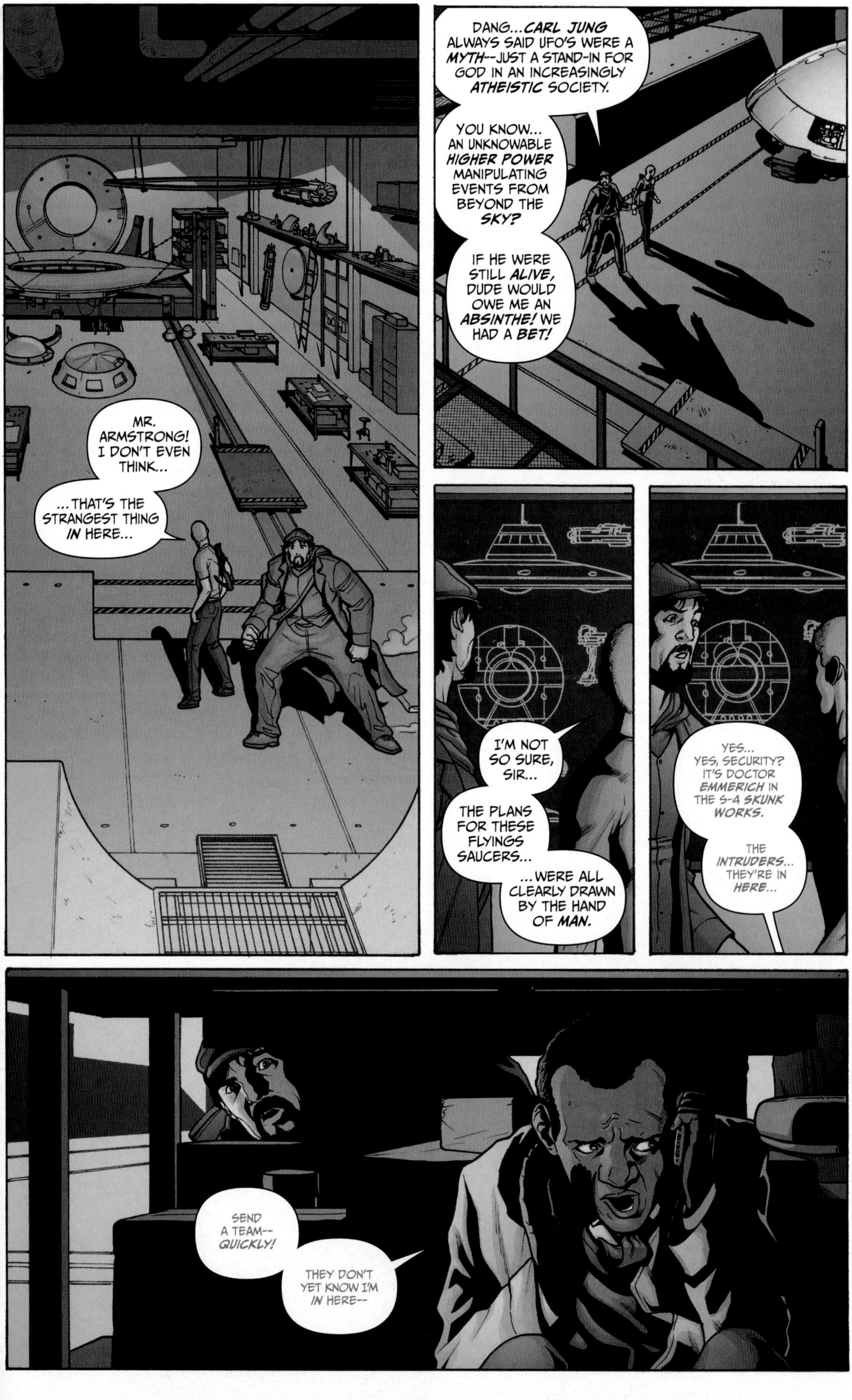
MR. ARMSTRONG! I DON'T EVEN THINK...
...THAT'S THE STRANGEST THING IN HERE...
DANG...CARL JUNG ALWAYS SAID UFO'S WERE A MYTH--JUST A STAND-IN FOR GOD IN AN INCREASINGLY ATHEISTIC SOCIETY.
YOU KNOW... AN UNKNOWABLE HIGHER POWER MANIPULATING EVENTS FROM BEYOND THE SKY?
IF HE WERE STILL ALIVE, DUDE WOULD OWE ME AN ABSINTHE! WE HAD A BET!
I'M NOT SO SURE, SIR...
THE PLANS FOR THESE FLYINGS SAUCERS...
...WERE ALL CLEARLY DRAWN BY THE HAND OF MAN.
YES... YES, SECURITY? IT'S DOCTOR EMMERICH IN THE S-4 SKUNK WORKS.
THE INTRUDERS... THEY'RE IN HERE...
SEND A TEAM-- QUICKLY!
THEY DON'T YET KNOW I'M IN HERE--

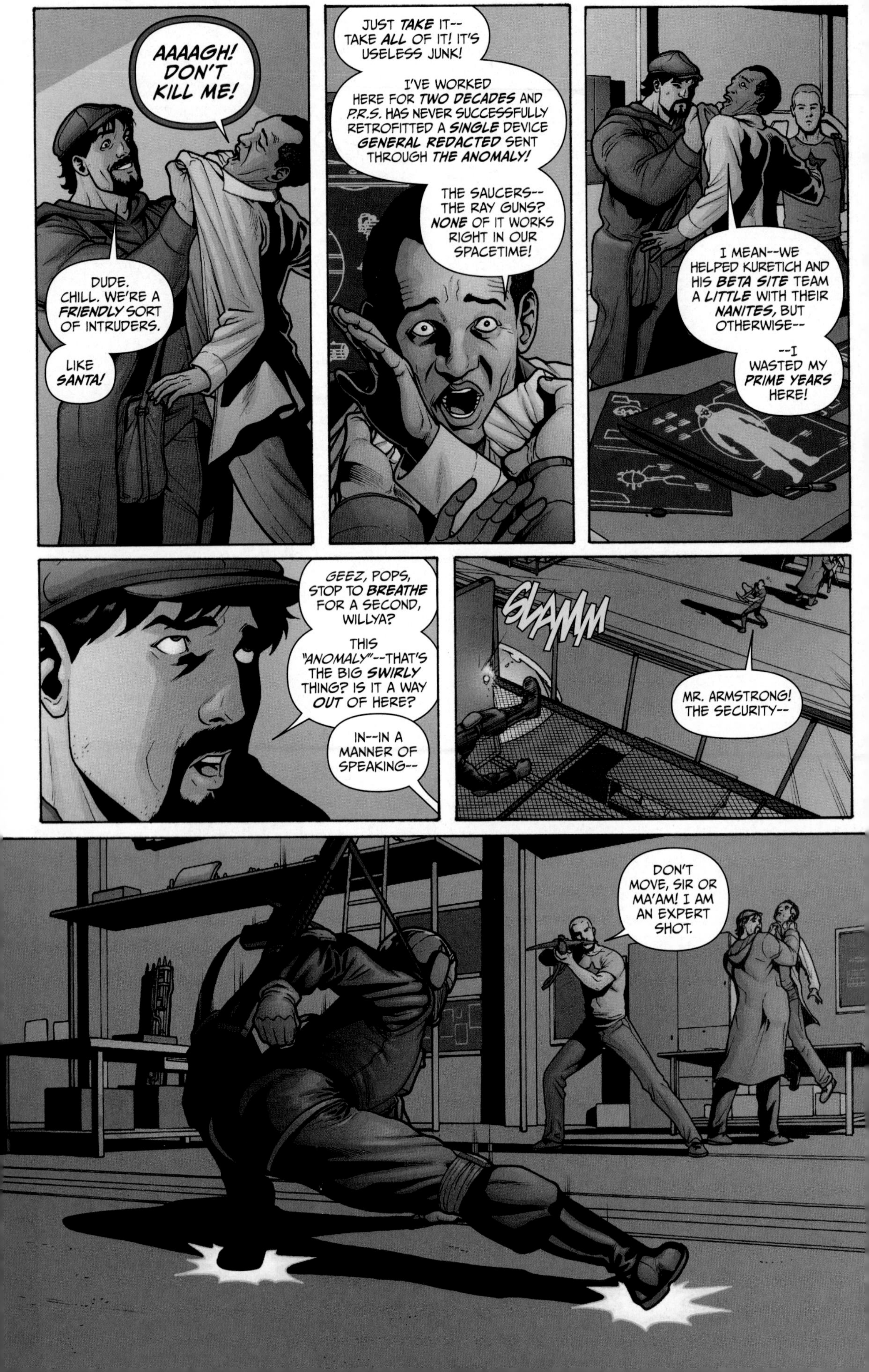
AAAAGH! DON'T KILL ME!
DUDE. CHILL. WE'RE A FRIENDLY SORT OF INTRUDERS.
LIKE SANTA!
JUST TAKE IT--TAKE ALL OF IT! IT'S USELESS JUNK!
I'VE WORKED HERE FOR TWO DECADES AND P.R.S. HAS NEVER SUCCESSFULLY RETROFITTED A SINGLE DEVICE GENERAL REDACTED SENT THROUGH THE ANOMALY!
THE SAUCERS--THE RAY GUNS? NONE OF IT WORKS RIGHT IN OUR SPACETIME!
I MEAN--WE HELPED KURETICH AND HIS BETA SITE TEAM A LITTLE WITH THEIR NANITES, BUT OTHERWISE--
--I WASTED MY PRIME YEARS HERE!
GEEZ, POPS, STOP TO BREATHE FOR A SECOND, WILLYA?
THIS "ANOMALY"--THAT'S THE BIG SWIRLY THING? IS IT A WAY OUT OF HERE?
IN--IN A MANNER OF SPEAKING--
SLAMM
MR. ARMSTRONG! THE SECURITY--
DON'T MOVE, SIR OR MA'AM! I AM AN EXPERT SHOT.

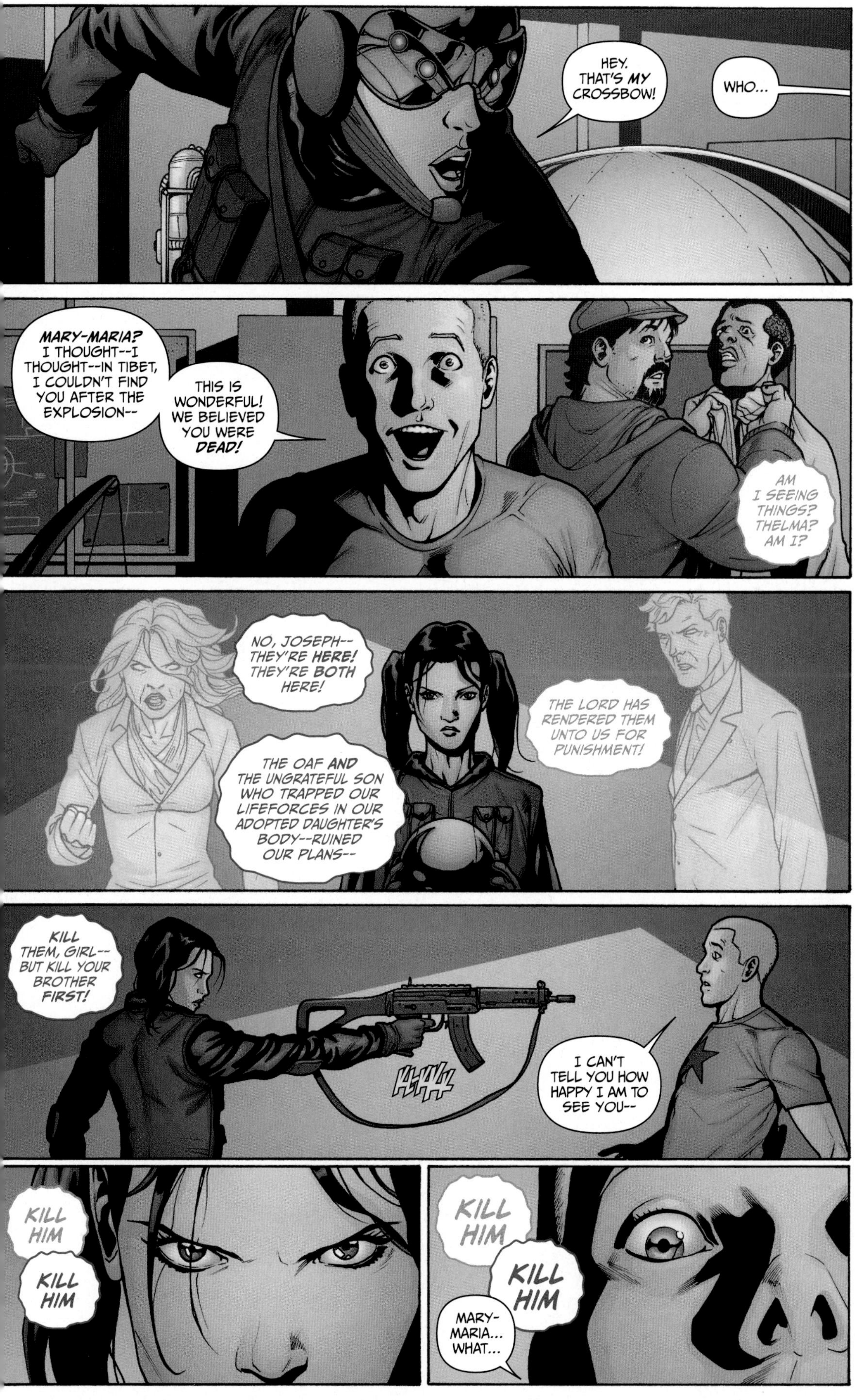
HEY. THAT'S MY CROSSBOW!
WHO...
MARY-MARIA? I THOUGHT--I THOUGHT--IN TIBET, I COULDN'T FIND YOU AFTER THE EXPLOSION--
THIS IS WONDERFUL! WE BELIEVED YOU WERE DEAD!
AM I SEEING THINGS? THELMA? AM I?
NO, JOSEPH--THEY'RE HERE! THEY'RE BOTH HERE!
THE LORD HAS RENDERED THEM UNTO US FOR PUNISHMENT!
THE OAF AND THE UNGRATEFUL SON WHO TRAPPED OUR LIFEFORCES IN OUR ADOPTED DAUGHTER'S BODY--RUINED OUR PLANS--
KILL THEM, GIRL--BUT KILL YOUR BROTHER FIRST!
I CAN'T TELL YOU HOW HAPPY I AM TO SEE YOU--
KILL HIM
KILL HIM
KILL HIM
KILL HIM
MARY-MARIA... WHAT...

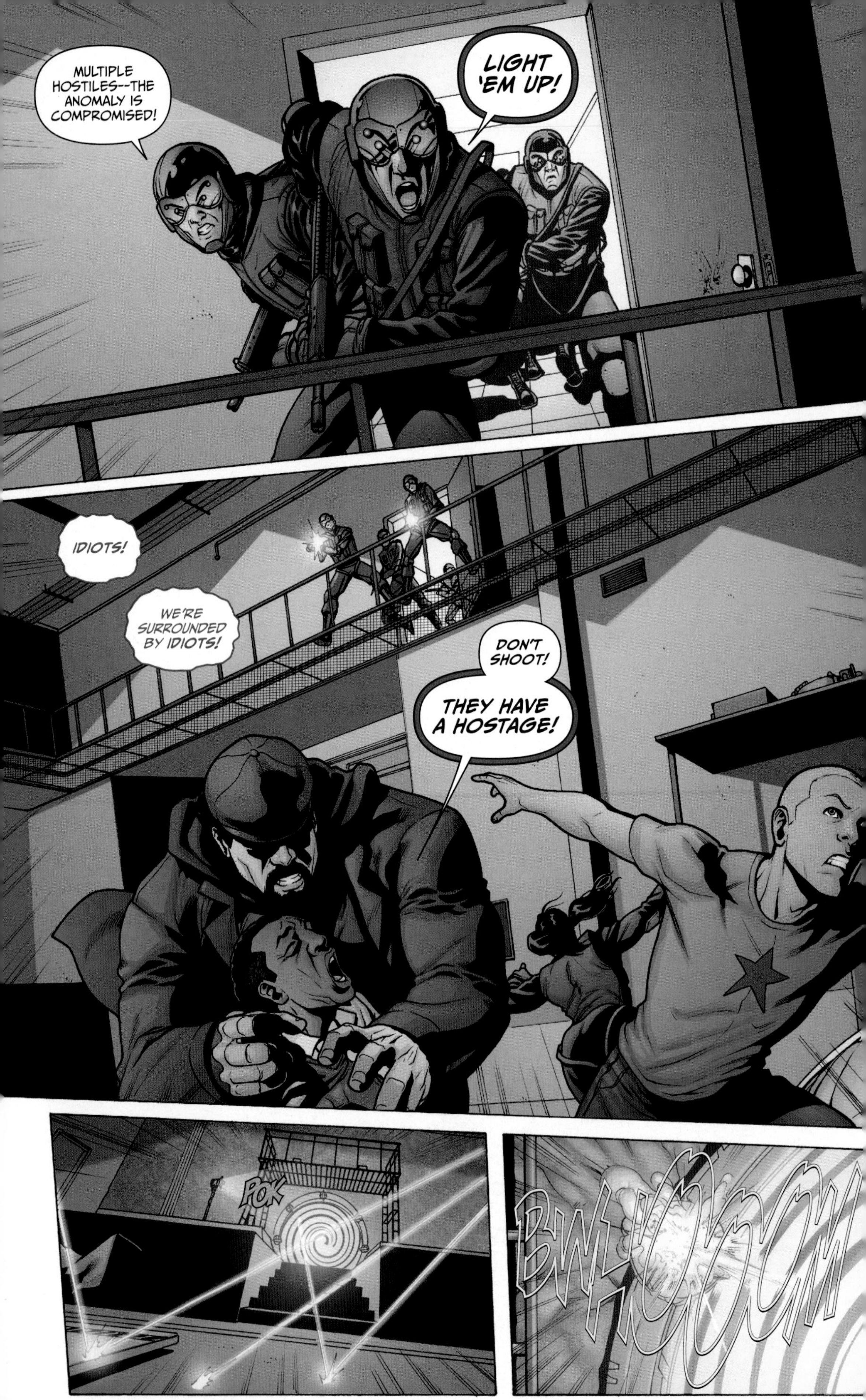
MULTIPLE HOSTILES--THE ANOMALY IS COMPROMISED!
LIGHT 'EM UP!
IDIOTS!
WE'RE SURROUNDED BY IDIOTS!
DON'T SHOOT!
THEY HAVE A HOSTAGE!
POK
BWUOOOM

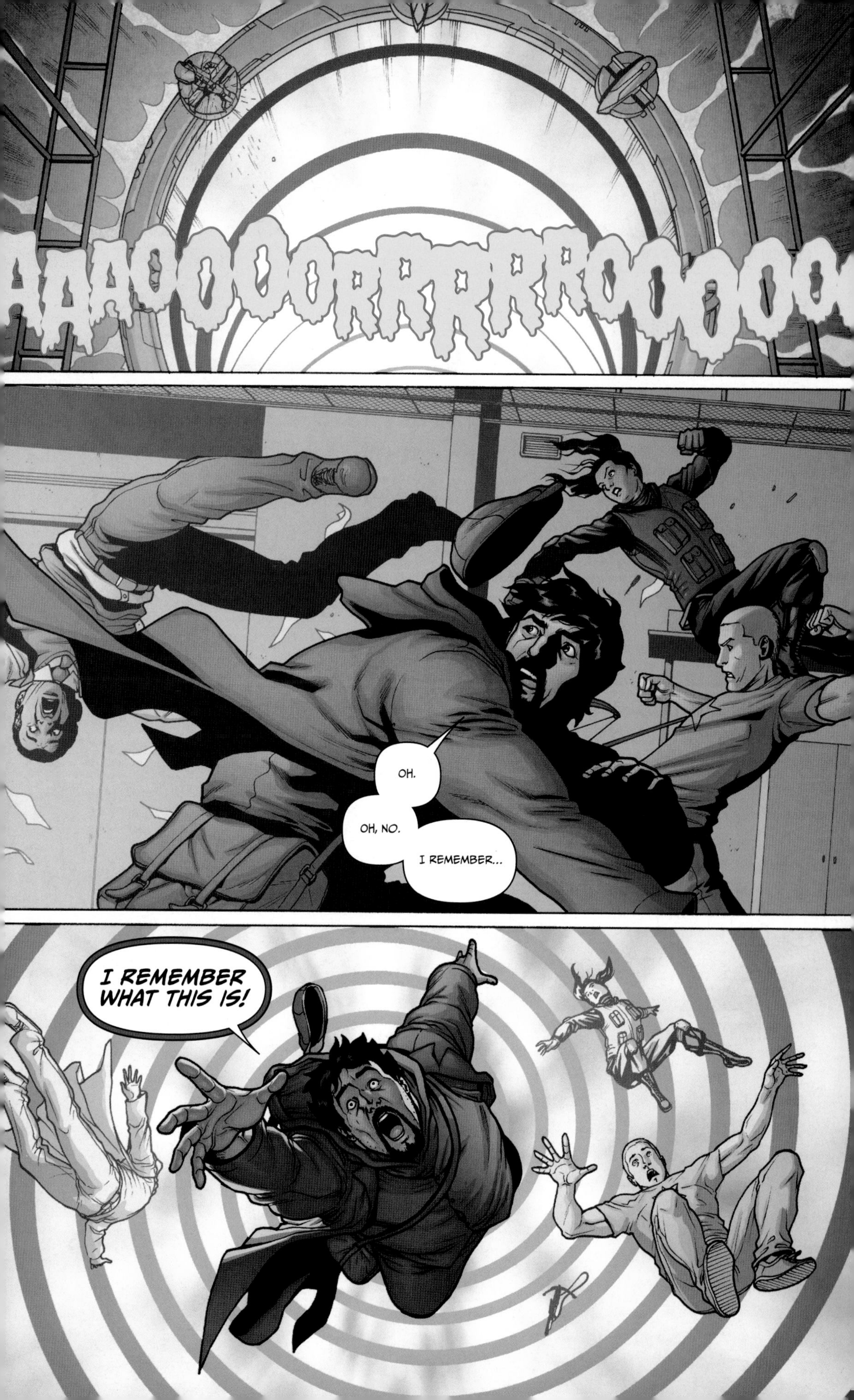
AAAOOOORRRRROOOOO
OH.
OH, NO.
I REMEMBER...
I REMEMBER WHAT THIS IS!

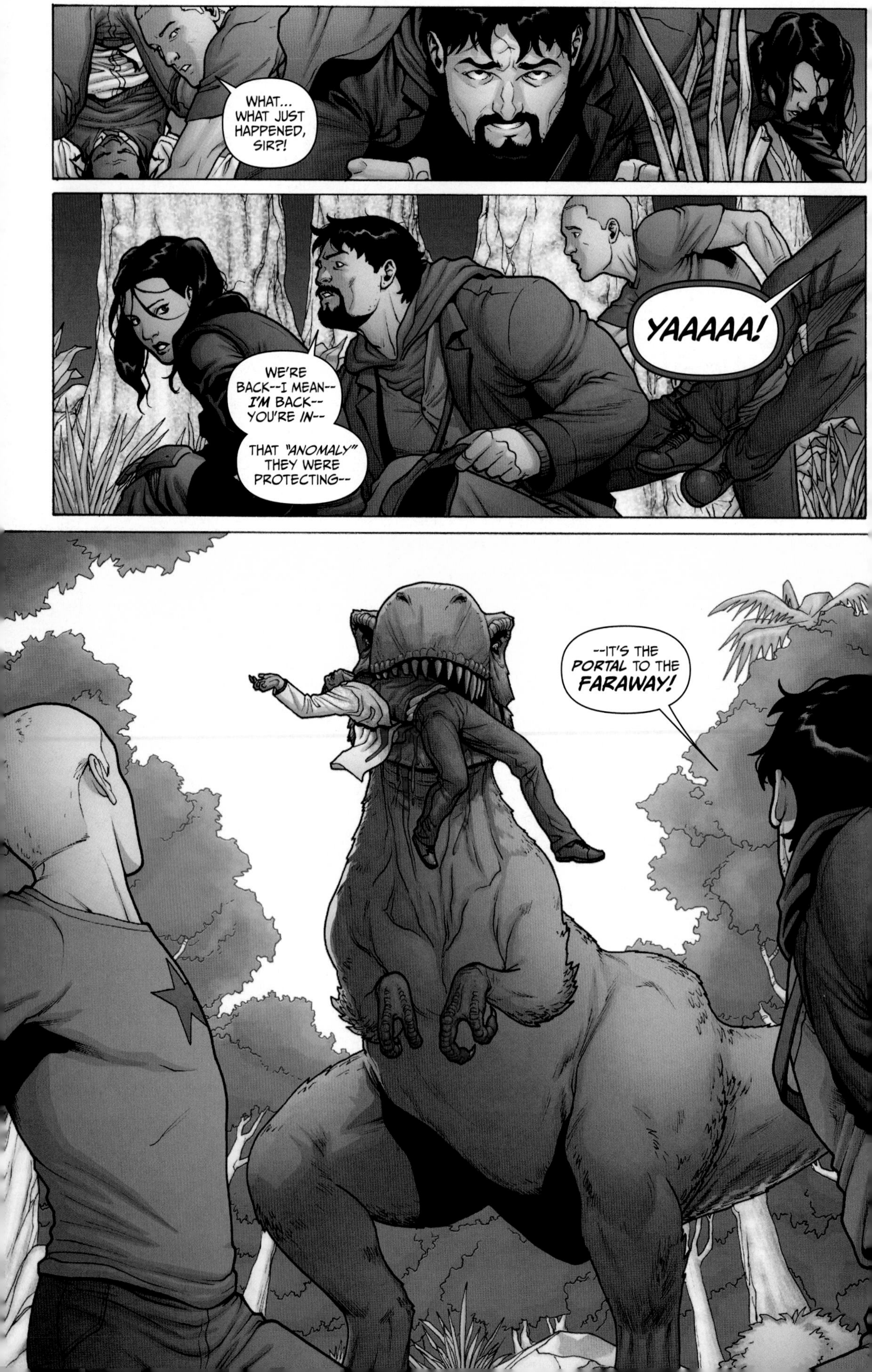
WHAT... WHAT JUST HAPPENED, SIR?!
WE'RE BACK--I MEAN-- I'M BACK-- YOU'RE IN--
THAT "ANOMALY" THEY WERE PROTECTING--
YAAAAA!
--IT'S THE PORTAL TO THE FARAWAY!

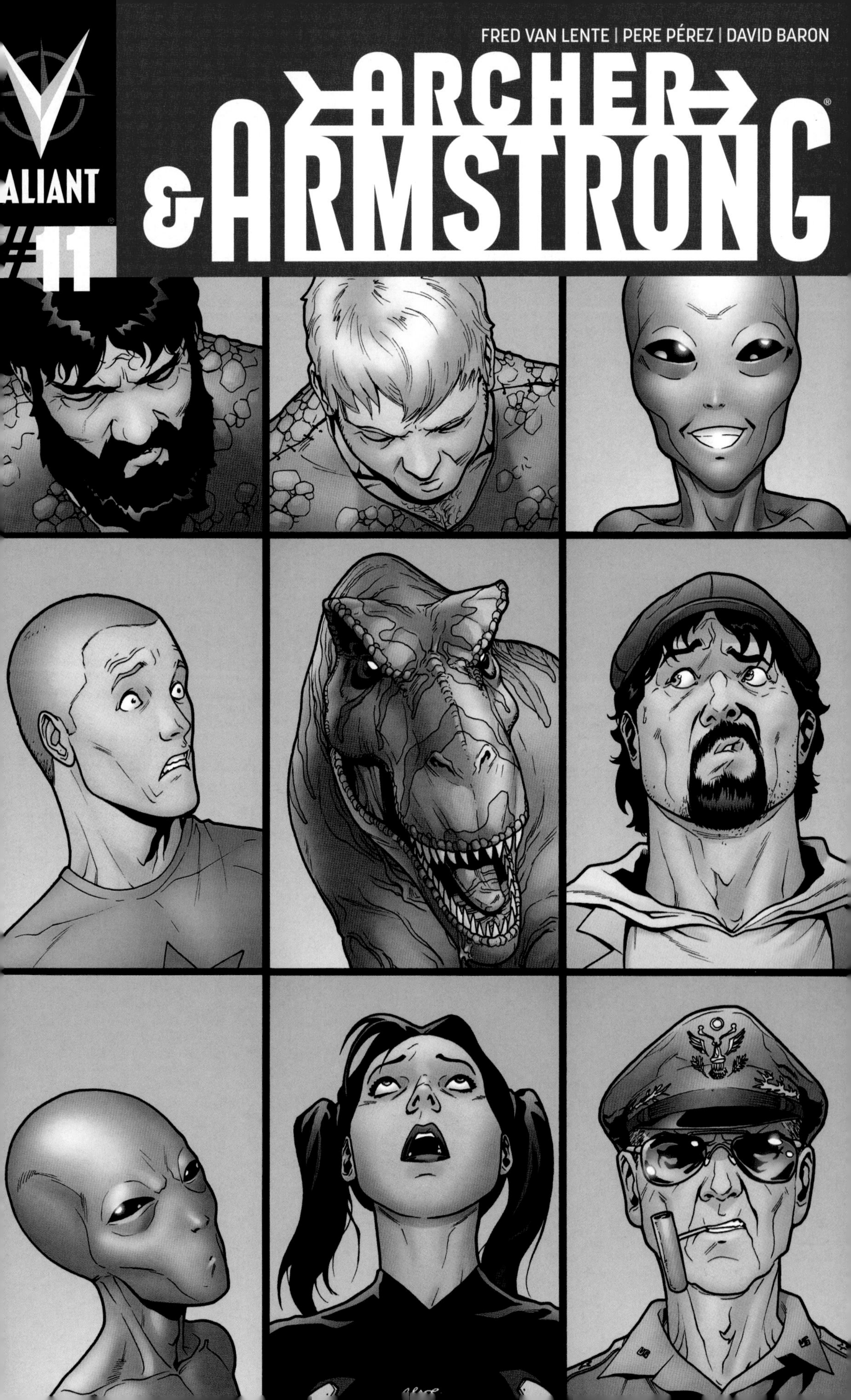
FRED VAN LENTE | PERE PÉREZ | DAVID BARON
ARCHER & ARMSTRONG
#11
VALIANT

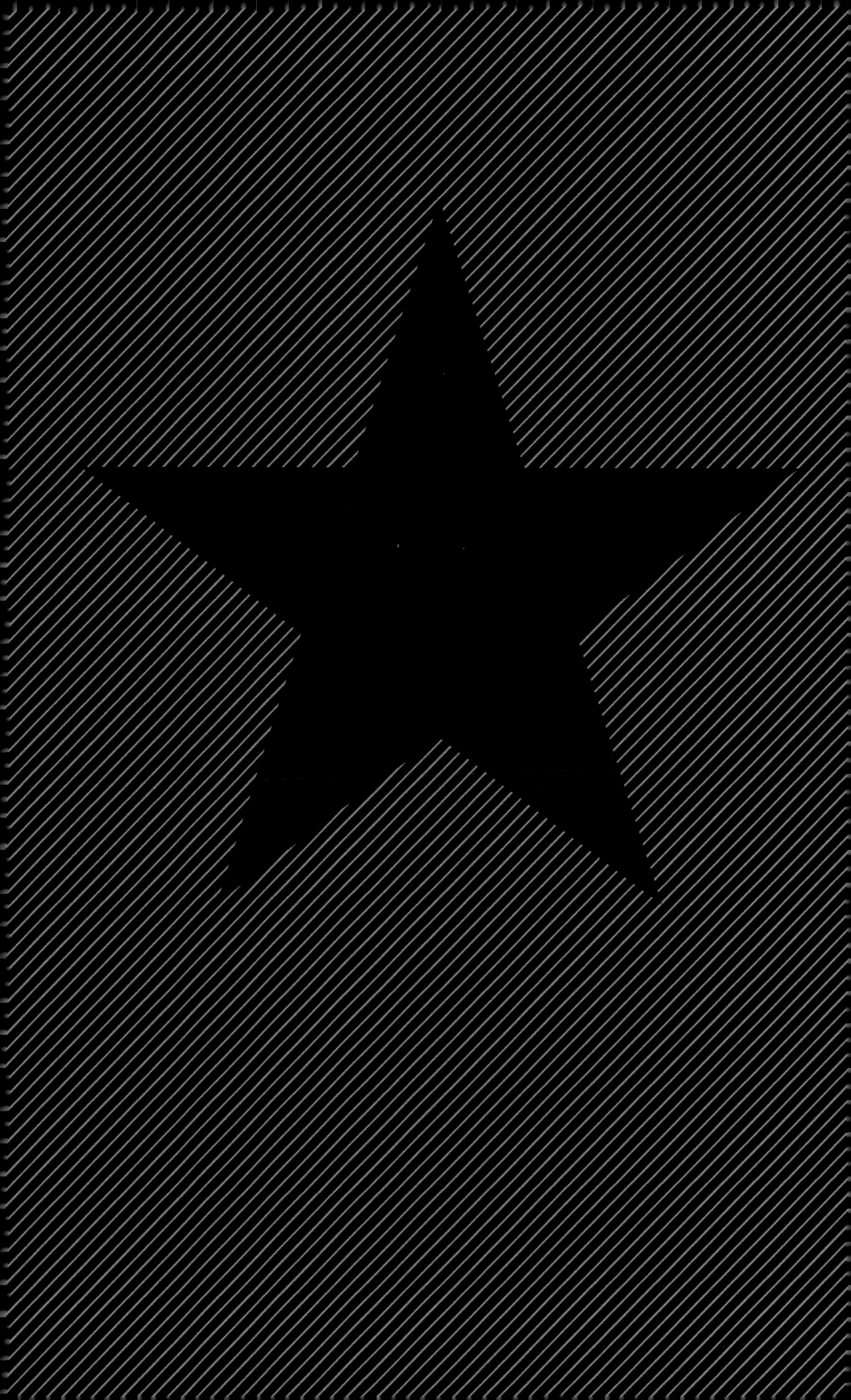

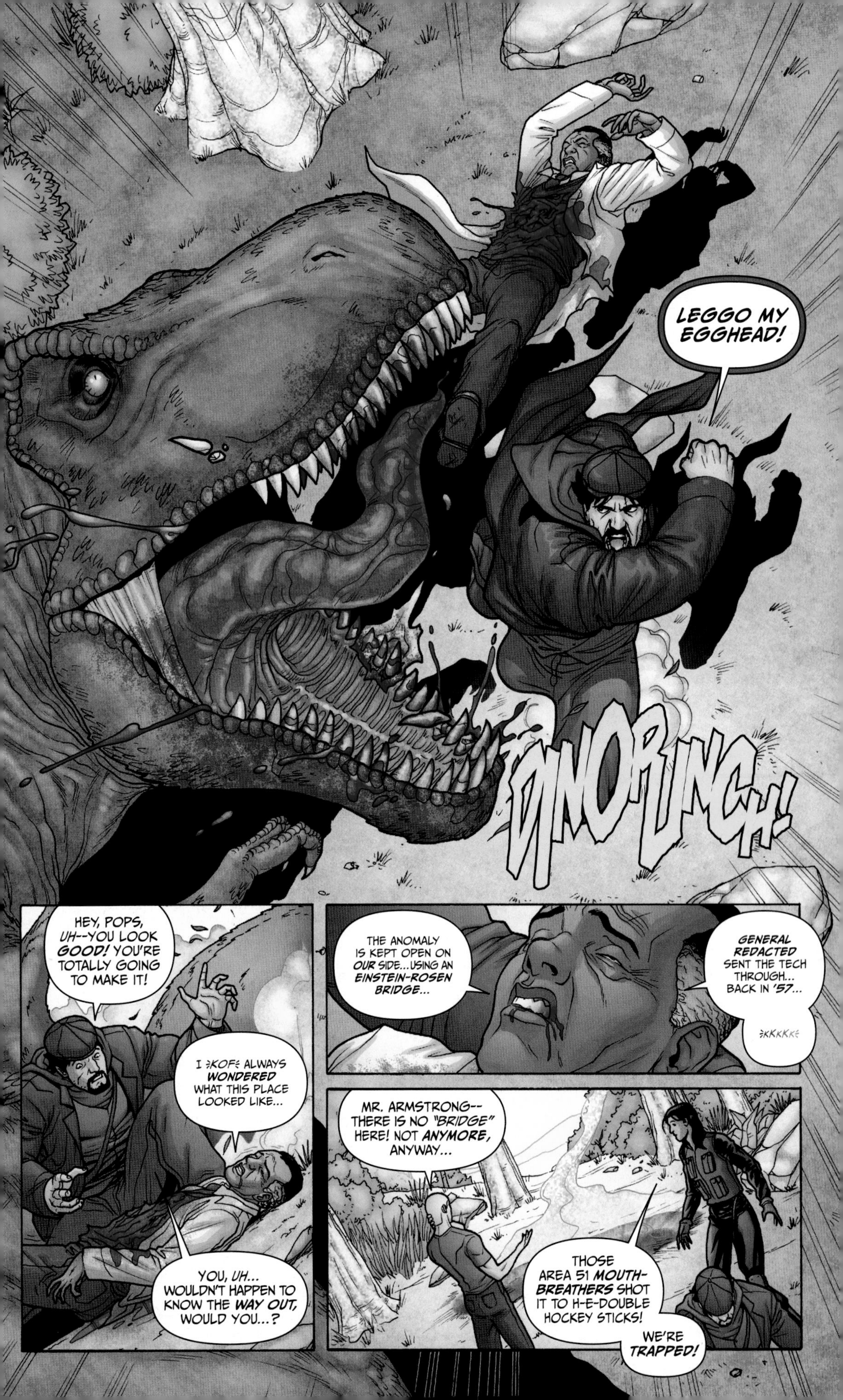

LEGGO MY EGGHEAD!
DINOCRUNCH!
HEY, POPS, UH--YOU LOOK GOOD! YOU'RE TOTALLY GOING TO MAKE IT!
I KOF ALWAYS WONDERED WHAT THIS PLACE LOOKED LIKE...
YOU, UH... WOULDN'T HAPPEN TO KNOW THE WAY OUT, WOULD YOU...?
THE ANOMALY IS KEPT OPEN ON OUR SIDE...USING AN EINSTEIN-ROSEN BRIDGE...
GENERAL REDACTED SENT THE TECH THROUGH... BACK IN '57...
KKKKK
MR. ARMSTRONG--THERE IS NO "BRIDGE" HERE! NOT ANYMORE, ANYWAY...
THOSE AREA 51 MOUTH-BREATHERS SHOT IT TO H-E-DOUBLE HOCKEY STICKS!
WE'RE TRAPPED!

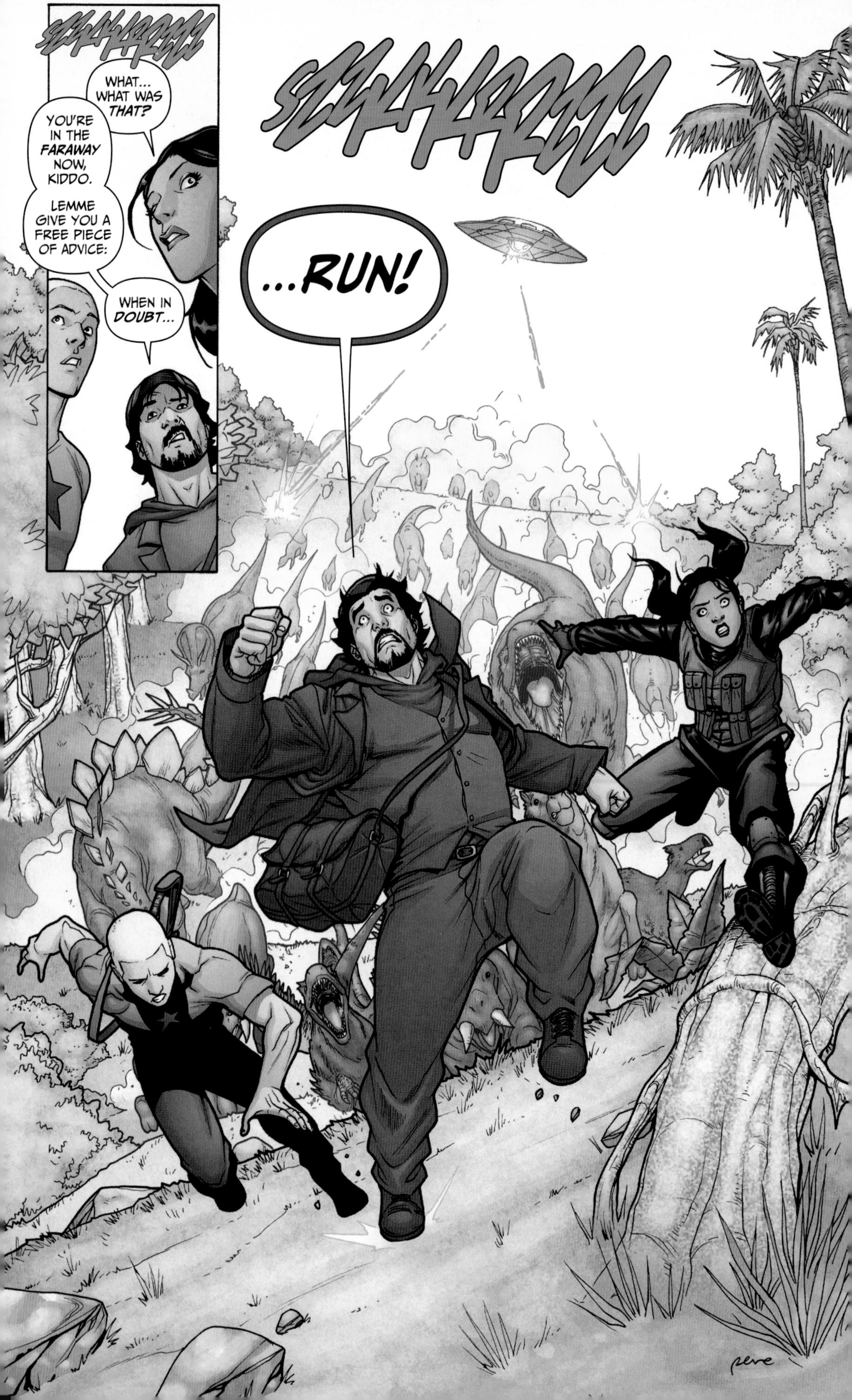
WHAT... WHAT WAS THAT?
YOU'RE IN THE FARAWAY NOW, KIDDO.
LEMME GIVE YOU A FREE PIECE OF ADVICE:
WHEN IN DOUBT...
...RUN!

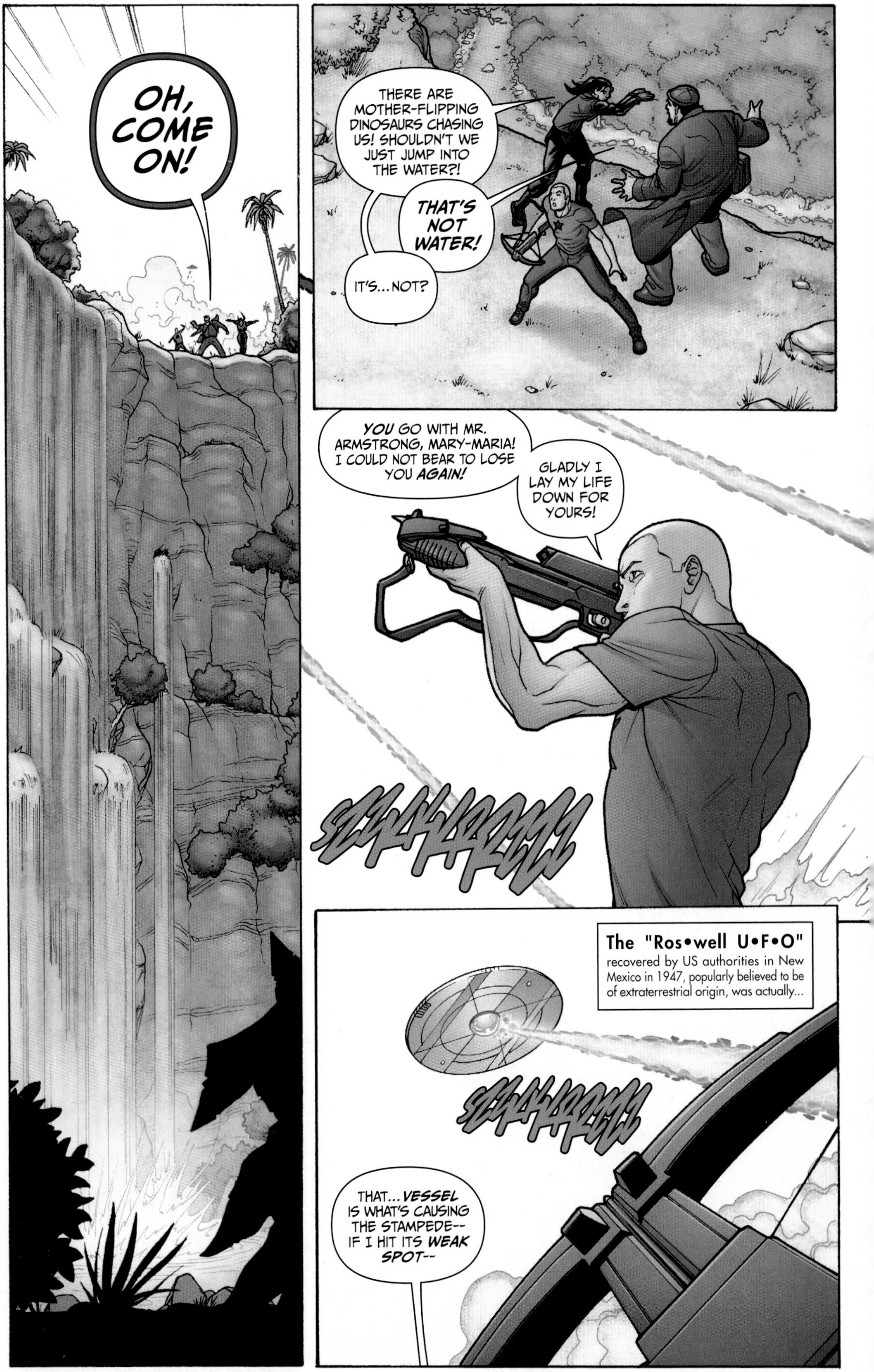
OH, COME ON!
THERE ARE MOTHER-FLIPPING DINOSAURS CHASING US! SHOULDN'T WE JUST JUMP INTO THE WATER?!
THAT'S NOT WATER!
IT'S...NOT?
YOU GO WITH MR. ARMSTRONG, MARY-MARIA! I COULD NOT BEAR TO LOSE YOU AGAIN!
GLADLY I LAY MY LIFE DOWN FOR YOURS!
The "Ros•well U•F•O" recovered by US authorities in New Mexico in 1947, popularly believed to be of extraterrestrial origin, was actually...
THAT...VESSEL IS WHAT'S CAUSING THE STAMPEDE-- IF I HIT ITS WEAK SPOT--

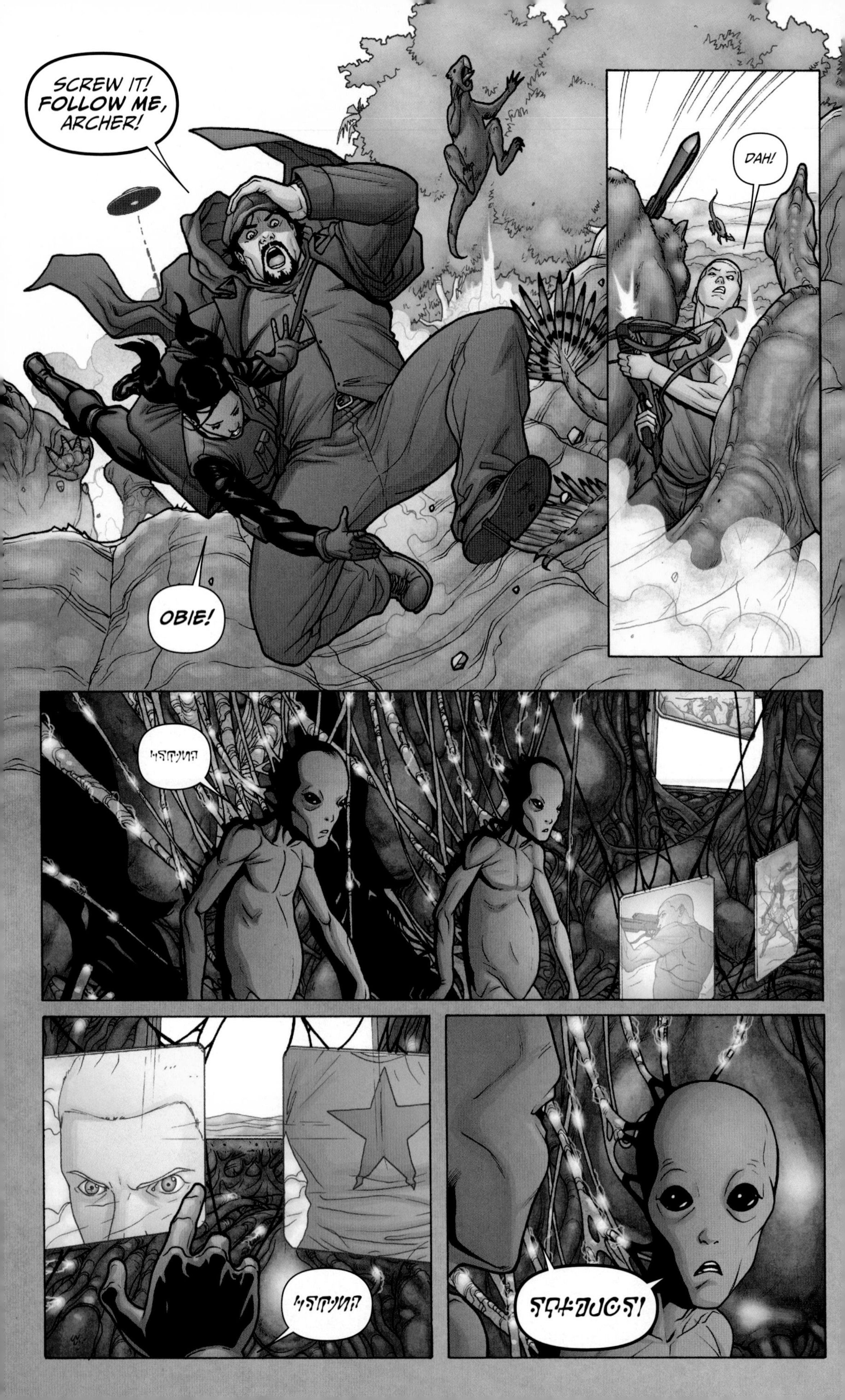
SCREW IT! FOLLOW ME, ARCHER!
DAH!
OBIE!

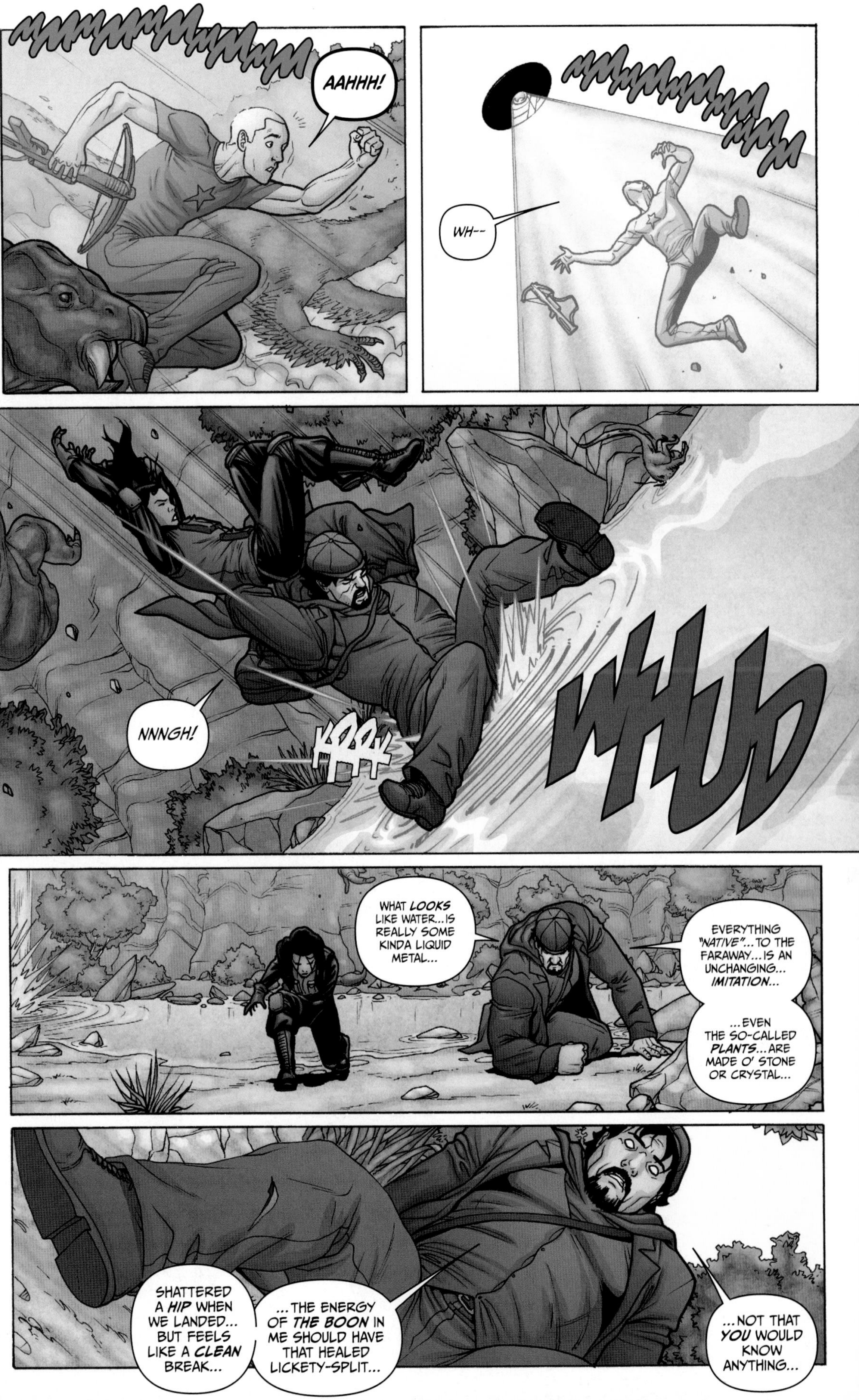
AAHHH!
WH--
NNNGH!
WHUD
WHAT *LOOKS* LIKE WATER...IS REALLY SOME KINDA LIQUID METAL...
EVERYTHING *"NATIVE"*...TO THE FARAWAY...IS AN UNCHANGING... *IMITATION*...
...EVEN THE SO-CALLED *PLANTS*...ARE MADE O' STONE OR CRYSTAL...
SHATTERED A *HIP* WHEN WE LANDED... BUT FEELS LIKE A *CLEAN* BREAK...
...THE ENERGY OF *THE BOON* IN ME SHOULD HAVE THAT HEALED LICKETY-SPLIT...
...NOT THAT *YOU* WOULD KNOW ANYTHING...

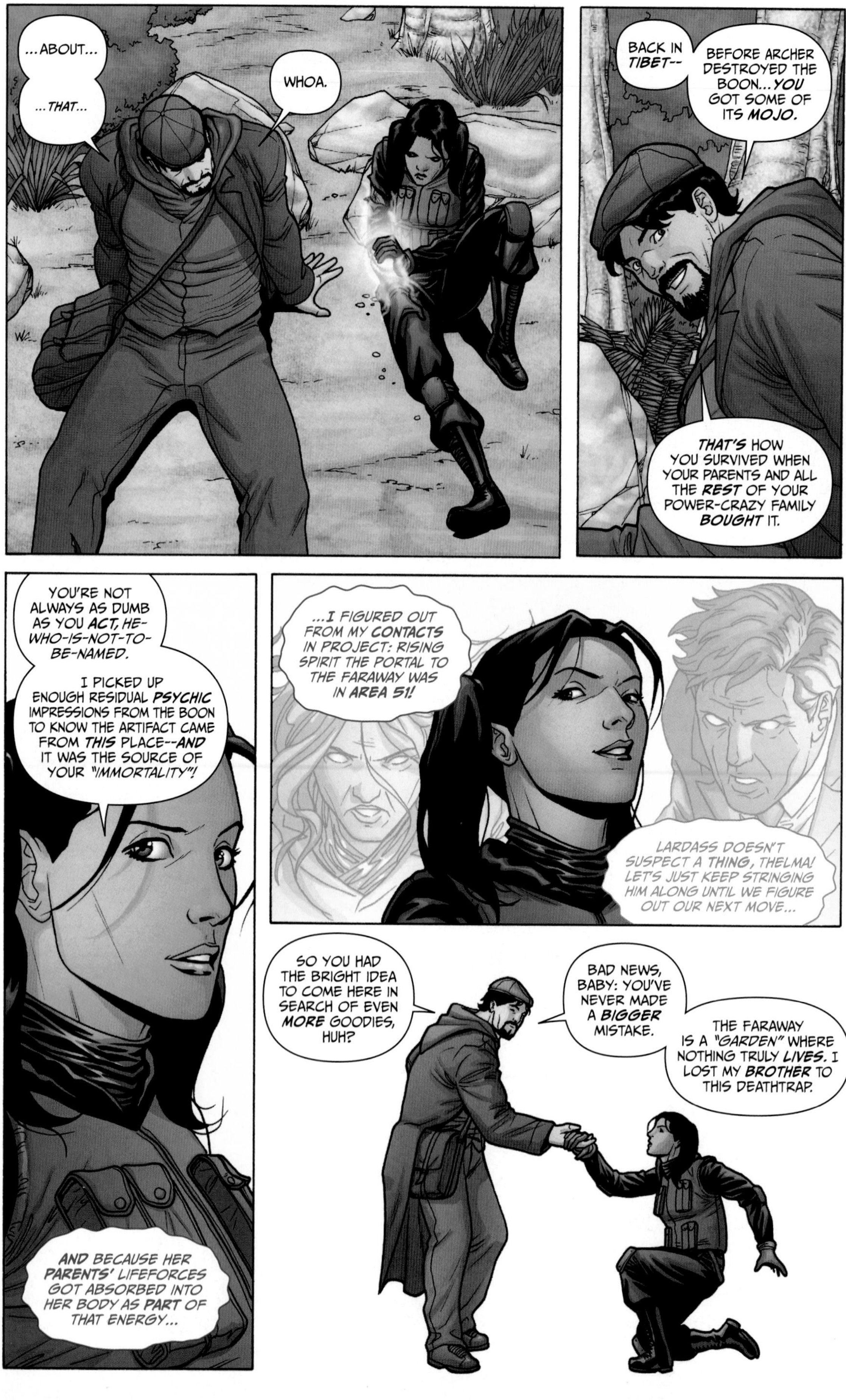
...ABOUT...
...THAT...
WHOA.
BACK IN TIBET--
BEFORE ARCHER DESTROYED THE BOON...YOU GOT SOME OF ITS MOJO.
THAT'S HOW YOU SURVIVED WHEN YOUR PARENTS AND ALL THE REST OF YOUR POWER-CRAZY FAMILY BOUGHT IT.
YOU'RE NOT ALWAYS AS DUMB AS YOU ACT, HE-WHO-IS-NOT-TO-BE-NAMED.
I PICKED UP ENOUGH RESIDUAL PSYCHIC IMPRESSIONS FROM THE BOON TO KNOW THE ARTIFACT CAME FROM THIS PLACE--AND IT WAS THE SOURCE OF YOUR "IMMORTALITY"!
AND BECAUSE HER PARENTS' LIFEFORCES GOT ABSORBED INTO HER BODY AS PART OF THAT ENERGY...
...I FIGURED OUT FROM MY CONTACTS IN PROJECT: RISING SPIRIT THE PORTAL TO THE FARAWAY WAS IN AREA 51!
LARDASS DOESN'T SUSPECT A THING, THELMA! LET'S JUST KEEP STRINGING HIM ALONG UNTIL WE FIGURE OUT OUR NEXT MOVE...
SO YOU HAD THE BRIGHT IDEA TO COME HERE IN SEARCH OF EVEN MORE GOODIES, HUH?
BAD NEWS, BABY: YOU'VE NEVER MADE A BIGGER MISTAKE.
THE FARAWAY IS A "GARDEN" WHERE NOTHING TRULY LIVES. I LOST MY BROTHER TO THIS DEATHTRAP.

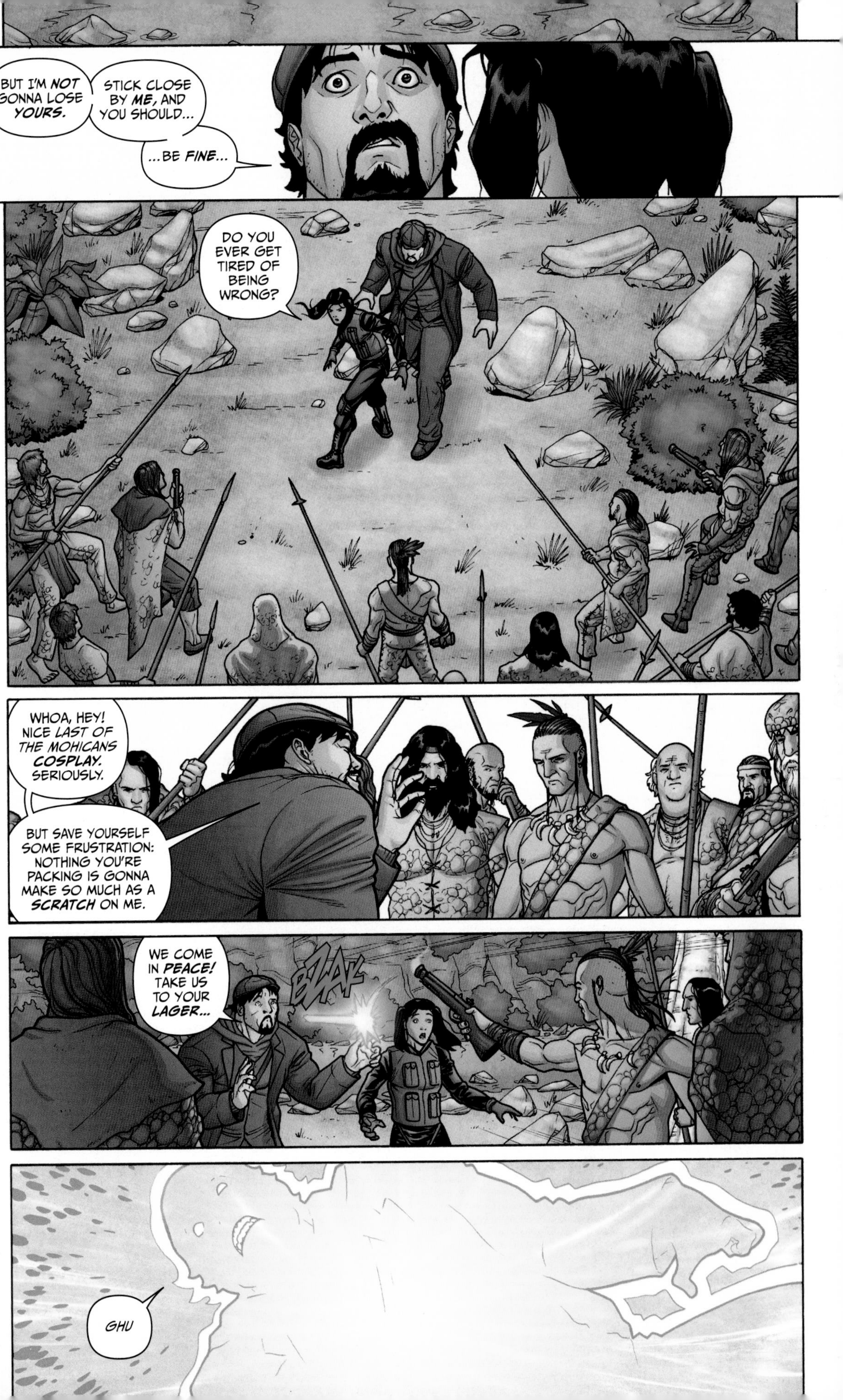
BUT I'M NOT GONNA LOSE YOURS.
STICK CLOSE BY ME, AND YOU SHOULD...
...BE FINE...
DO YOU EVER GET TIRED OF BEING WRONG?
WHOA, HEY! NICE LAST OF THE MOHICANS COSPLAY. SERIOUSLY.
BUT SAVE YOURSELF SOME FRUSTRATION: NOTHING YOU'RE PACKING IS GONNA MAKE SO MUCH AS A SCRATCH ON ME.
WE COME IN PEACE! TAKE US TO YOUR LAGER...
BZAK
GHU

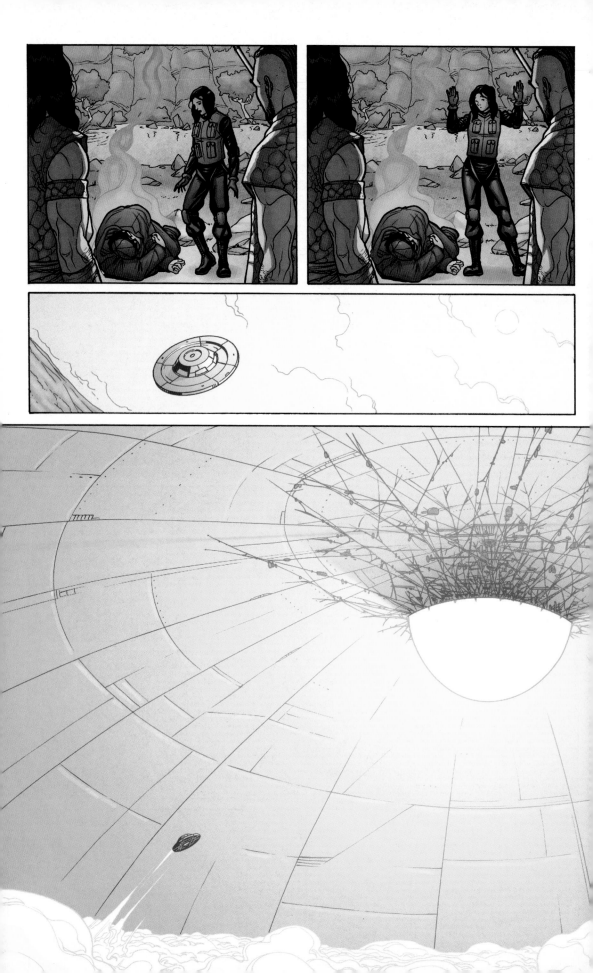

SSSHHHUNK

ᔕᕽᕼᕽᒍᕼᒍ⊢ᔕᕽ

ᒍᕽᕼ⊢ᒍᒍᔕᕽ⊢!

MY QUESTION FOR YOU IS REAL *SIMPLE*, SKINNY:

WHY?

WHY? WHY *WHAT* WHY?

KRRAKLL

AAHHH!

DON'T YOU ANSWER *MY* QUESTIONS WITH *MORE* QUESTIONS,

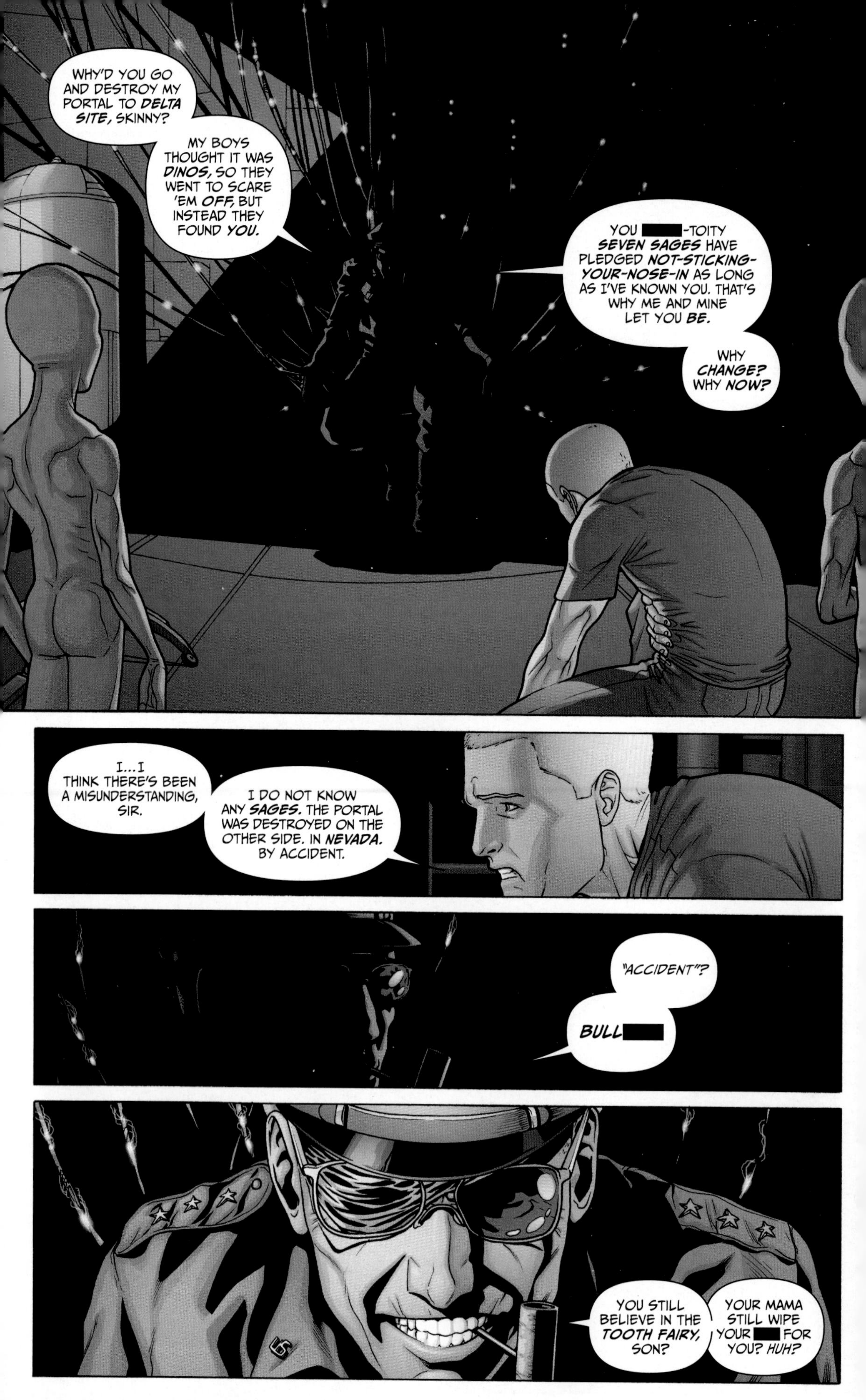
WHY'D YOU GO AND DESTROY MY PORTAL TO DELTA SITE, SKINNY?
MY BOYS THOUGHT IT WAS DINOS, SO THEY WENT TO SCARE 'EM OFF, BUT INSTEAD THEY FOUND YOU.
YOU [redacted]-TOITY SEVEN SAGES HAVE PLEDGED NOT-STICKING-YOUR-NOSE-IN AS LONG AS I'VE KNOWN YOU. THAT'S WHY ME AND MINE LET YOU BE.
WHY CHANGE? WHY NOW?
I...I THINK THERE'S BEEN A MISUNDERSTANDING, SIR.
I DO NOT KNOW ANY SAGES. THE PORTAL WAS DESTROYED ON THE OTHER SIDE. IN NEVADA. BY ACCIDENT.
"ACCIDENT"?
BULL[redacted]
YOU STILL BELIEVE IN THE TOOTH FAIRY, SON?
YOUR MAMA STILL WIPE YOUR [redacted] FOR YOU? HUH?

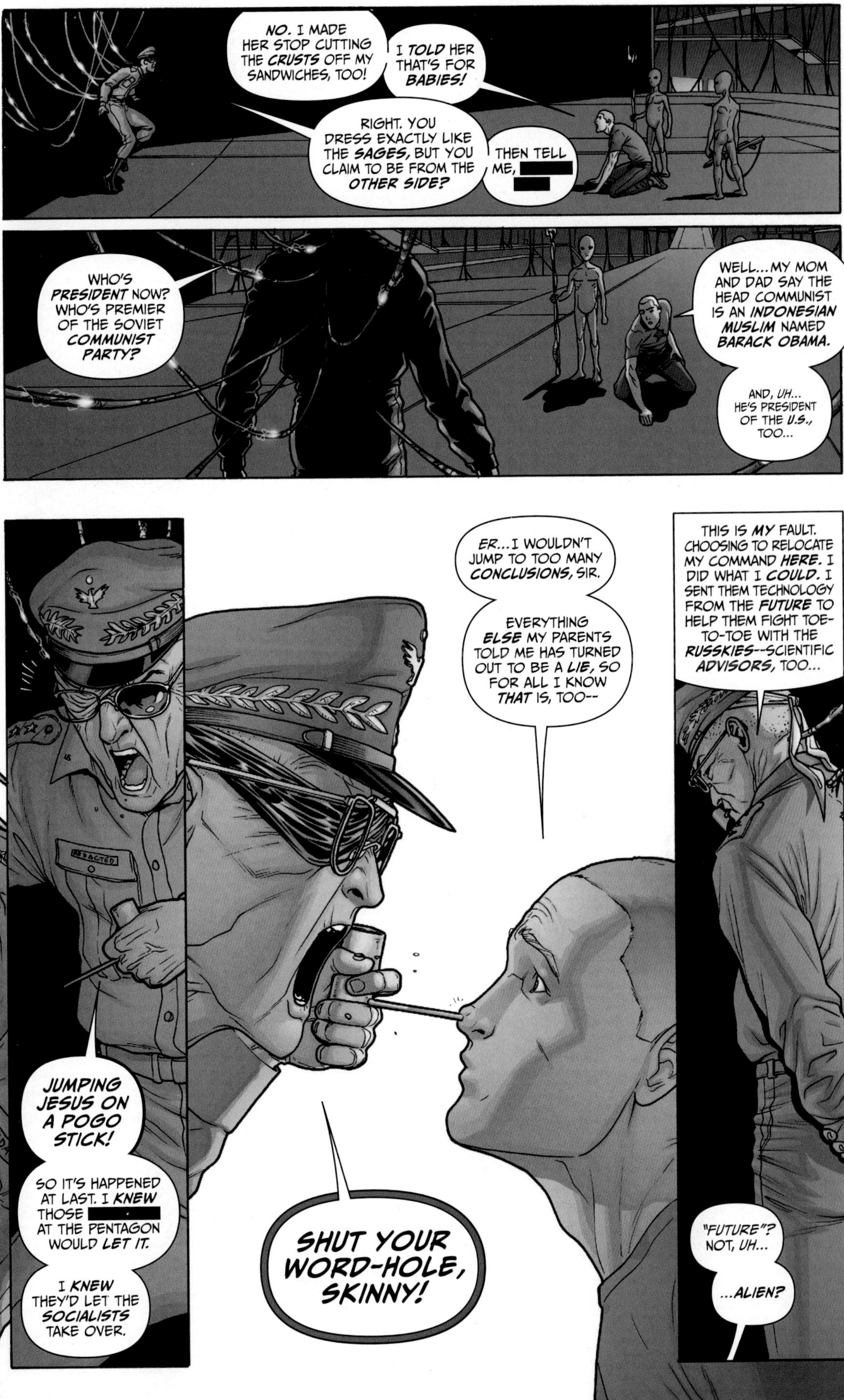
NO. I MADE HER STOP CUTTING THE CRUSTS OFF MY SANDWICHES, TOO!
I TOLD HER THAT'S FOR BABIES!
RIGHT. YOU DRESS EXACTLY LIKE THE SAGES, BUT YOU CLAIM TO BE FROM THE OTHER SIDE?
THEN TELL ME, [redacted]
WHO'S PRESIDENT NOW? WHO'S PREMIER OF THE SOVIET COMMUNIST PARTY?
WELL... MY MOM AND DAD SAY THE HEAD COMMUNIST IS AN INDONESIAN MUSLIM NAMED BARACK OBAMA.
AND, UH... HE'S PRESIDENT OF THE U.S., TOO...
ER... I WOULDN'T JUMP TO TOO MANY CONCLUSIONS, SIR.
EVERYTHING ELSE MY PARENTS TOLD ME HAS TURNED OUT TO BE A LIE, SO FOR ALL I KNOW THAT IS, TOO--
THIS IS MY FAULT. CHOOSING TO RELOCATE MY COMMAND HERE. I DID WHAT I COULD. I SENT THEM TECHNOLOGY FROM THE FUTURE TO HELP THEM FIGHT TOE-TO-TOE WITH THE RUSSKIES--SCIENTIFIC ADVISORS, TOO...
JUMPING JESUS ON A POGO STICK!
SO IT'S HAPPENED AT LAST. I KNEW THOSE [redacted] AT THE PENTAGON WOULD LET IT.
I KNEW THEY'D LET THE SOCIALISTS TAKE OVER.
SHUT YOUR WORD-HOLE, SKINNY!
"FUTURE"? NOT, UH...
...ALIEN?

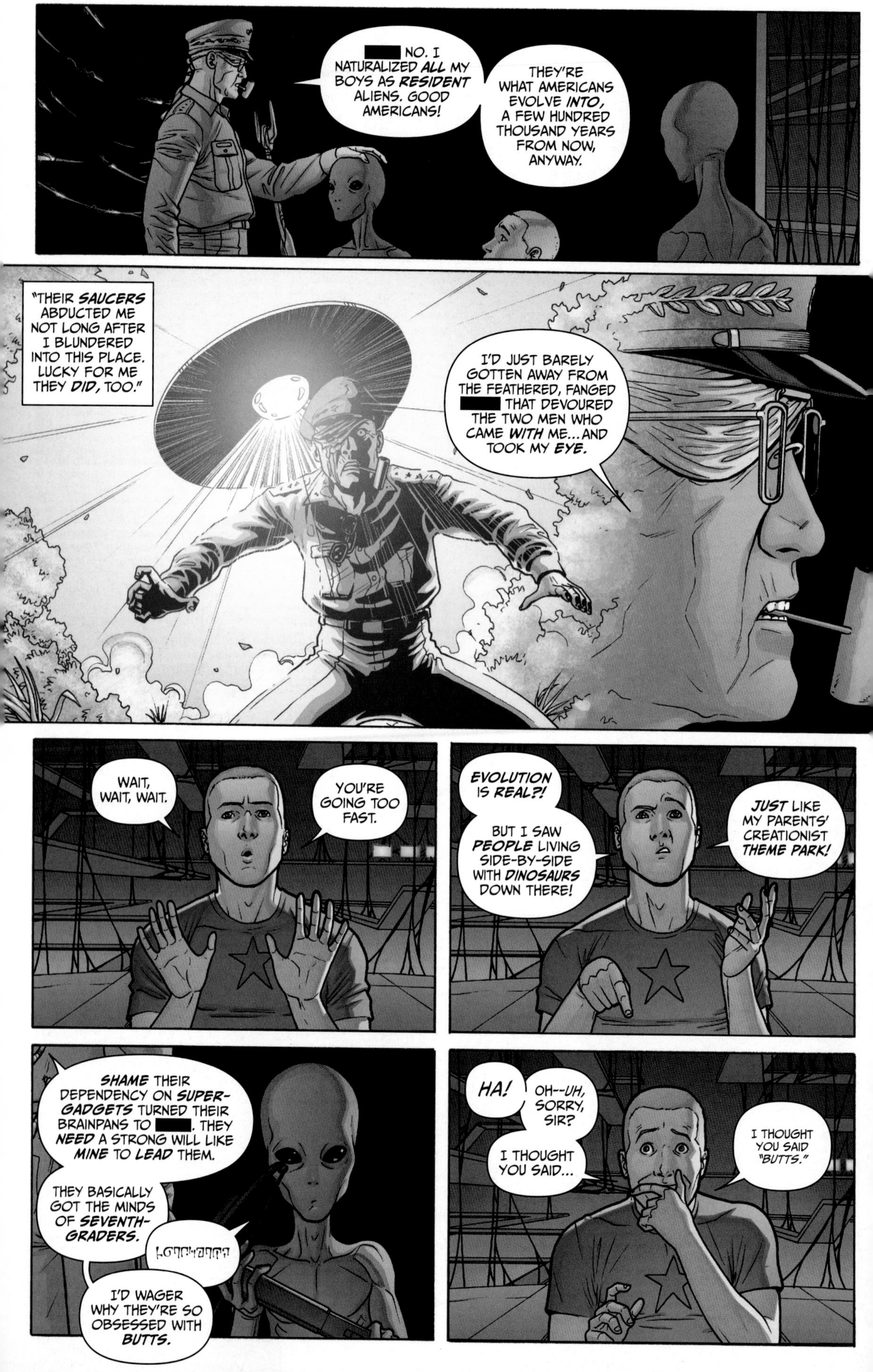
[redacted] NO. I NATURALIZED ALL MY BOYS AS RESIDENT ALIENS. GOOD AMERICANS!
THEY'RE WHAT AMERICANS EVOLVE INTO, A FEW HUNDRED THOUSAND YEARS FROM NOW, ANYWAY.
"THEIR SAUCERS ABDUCTED ME NOT LONG AFTER I BLUNDERED INTO THIS PLACE. LUCKY FOR ME THEY DID, TOO."
I'D JUST BARELY GOTTEN AWAY FROM THE FEATHERED, FANGED [redacted] THAT DEVOURED THE TWO MEN WHO CAME WITH ME... AND TOOK MY EYE.
WAIT, WAIT, WAIT.
YOU'RE GOING TOO FAST.
EVOLUTION IS REAL?!
BUT I SAW PEOPLE LIVING SIDE-BY-SIDE WITH DINOSAURS DOWN THERE!
JUST LIKE MY PARENTS' CREATIONIST THEME PARK!
SHAME THEIR DEPENDENCY ON SUPER-GADGETS TURNED THEIR BRAINPANS TO [redacted]. THEY NEED A STRONG WILL LIKE MINE TO LEAD THEM.
THEY BASICALLY GOT THE MINDS OF SEVENTH-GRADERS.
I'D WAGER WHY THEY'RE SO OBSESSED WITH BUTTS.
HA!
OH--UH, SORRY, SIR?
I THOUGHT YOU SAID...
I THOUGHT YOU SAID "BUTTS."

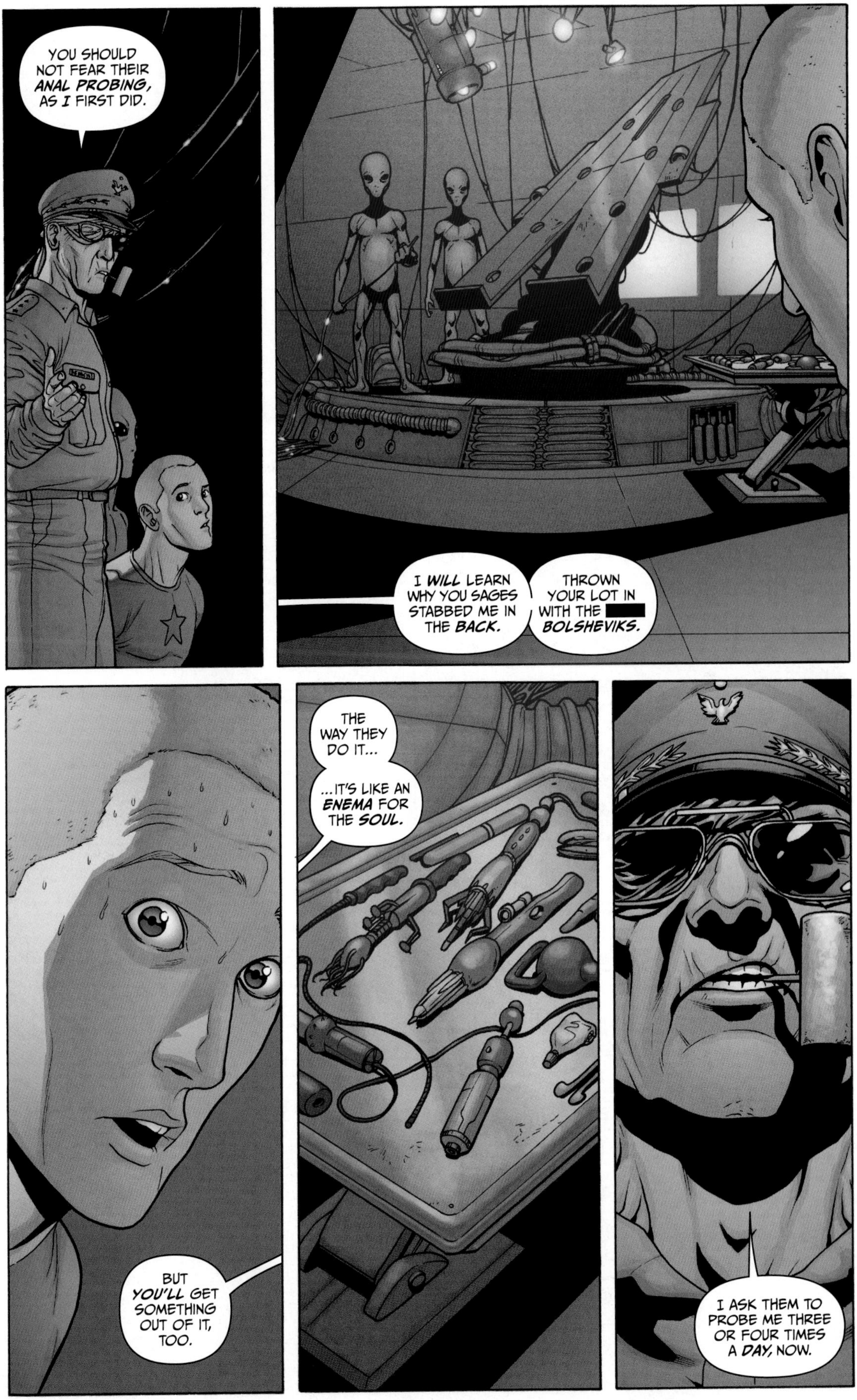
YOU SHOULD NOT FEAR THEIR ANAL PROBING, AS I FIRST DID.
I WILL LEARN WHY YOU SAGES STABBED ME IN THE BACK.
THROWN YOUR LOT IN WITH THE [redacted] BOLSHEVIKS.
BUT YOU'LL GET SOMETHING OUT OF IT, TOO.
THE WAY THEY DO IT...
...IT'S LIKE AN ENEMA FOR THE SOUL.
I ASK THEM TO PROBE ME THREE OR FOUR TIMES A DAY, NOW.

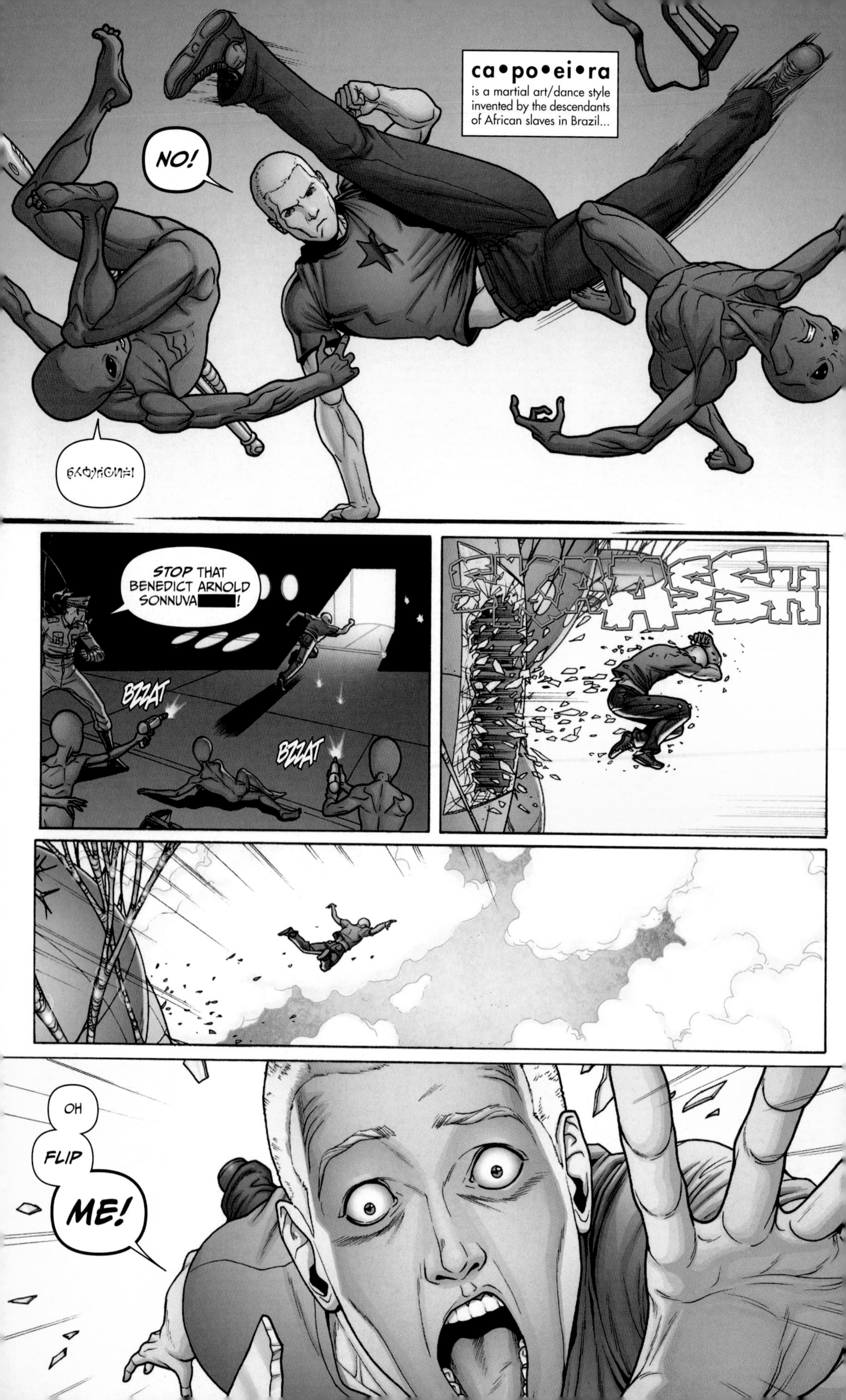
ca•po•ei•ra
is a martial art/dance style invented by the descendants of African slaves in Brazil...
NO!
STOP THAT BENEDICT ARNOLD SONNUVA[redacted]!
BZZAT
BZZAT
OH
FLIP
ME!

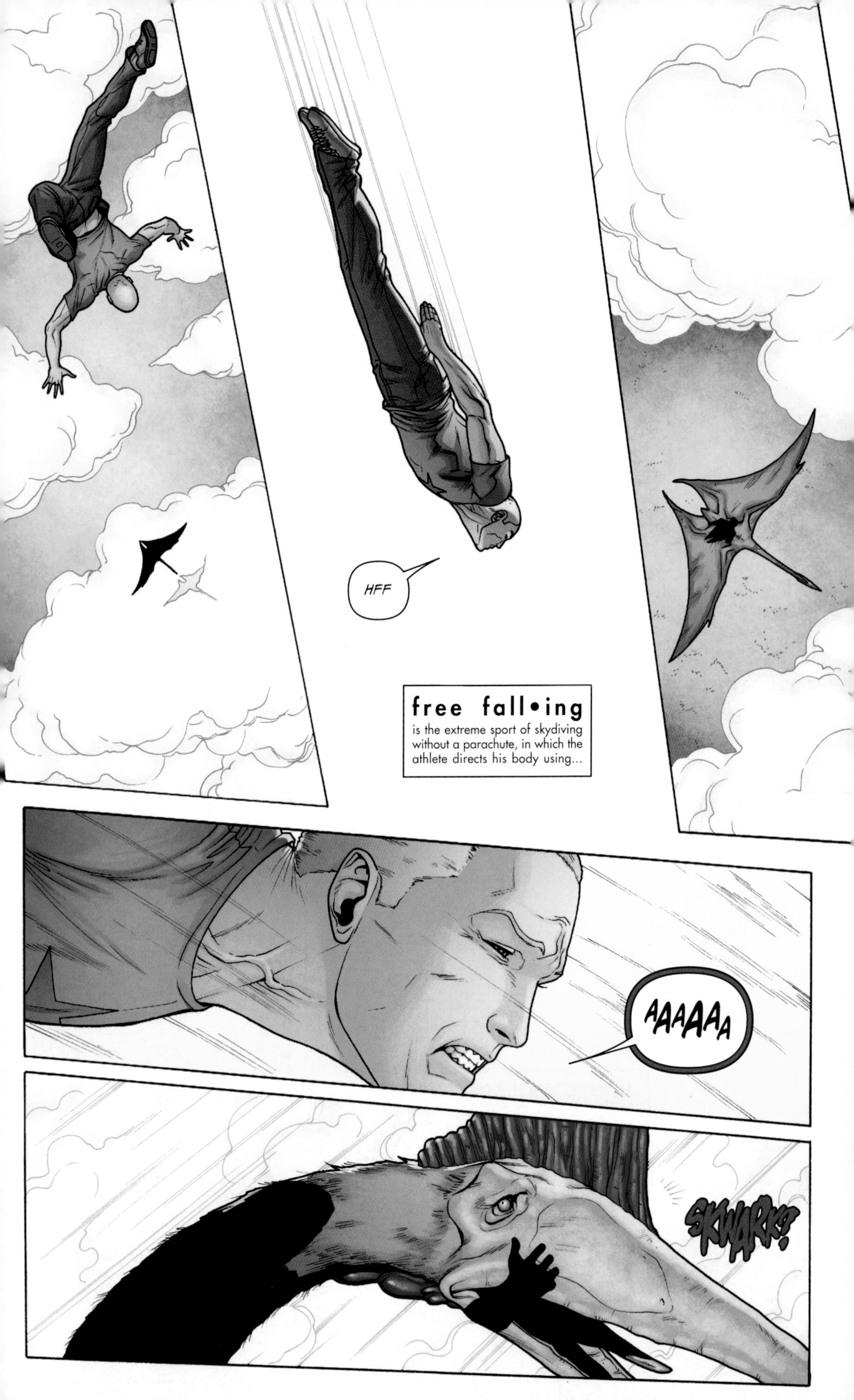
HFF
free fall•ing
is the extreme sport of skydiving without a parachute, in which the athlete directs his body using...
AAAAAA
SKWARK?!

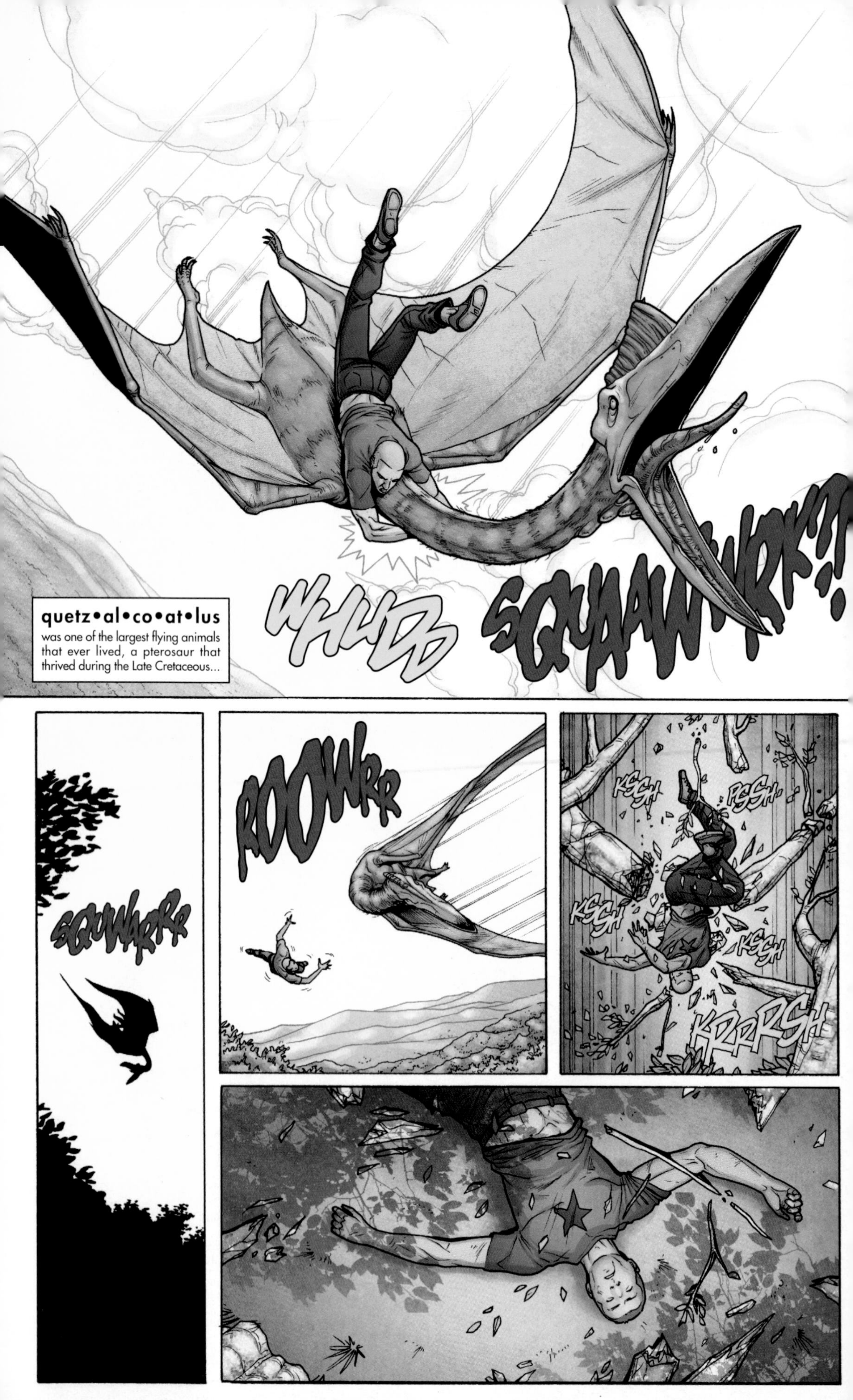

quetz•al•co•at•lus
was one of the largest flying animals that ever lived, a pterosaur that thrived during the Late Cretaceous...
WHUDD
SQUAAWWRK?!
SQUWARRR
ROOWRR
KSSH
PSSSH
KSSH
KSSH
KRRRSH

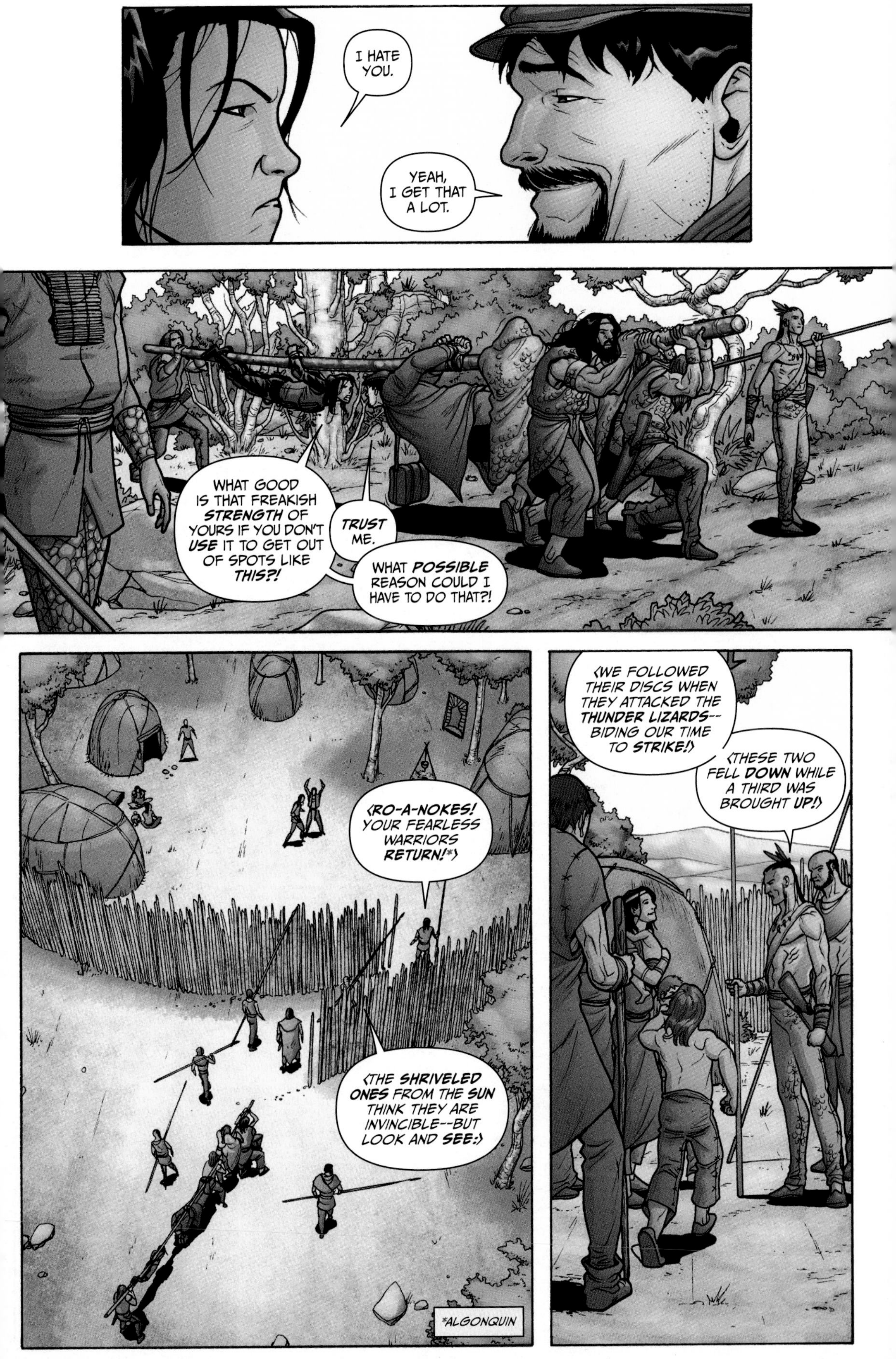
I HATE YOU.
YEAH, I GET THAT A LOT.
WHAT GOOD IS THAT FREAKISH STRENGTH OF YOURS IF YOU DON'T USE IT TO GET OUT OF SPOTS LIKE THIS?!
TRUST ME.
WHAT POSSIBLE REASON COULD I HAVE TO DO THAT?!
‹RO-A-NOKES! YOUR FEARLESS WARRIORS RETURN!*›
‹THE SHRIVELED ONES FROM THE SUN THINK THEY ARE INVINCIBLE--BUT LOOK AND SEE:›
*ALGONQUIN
‹WE FOLLOWED THEIR DISCS WHEN THEY ATTACKED THE THUNDER LIZARDS--BIDING OUR TIME TO STRIKE!›
‹THESE TWO FELL DOWN WHILE A THIRD WAS BROUGHT UP!›

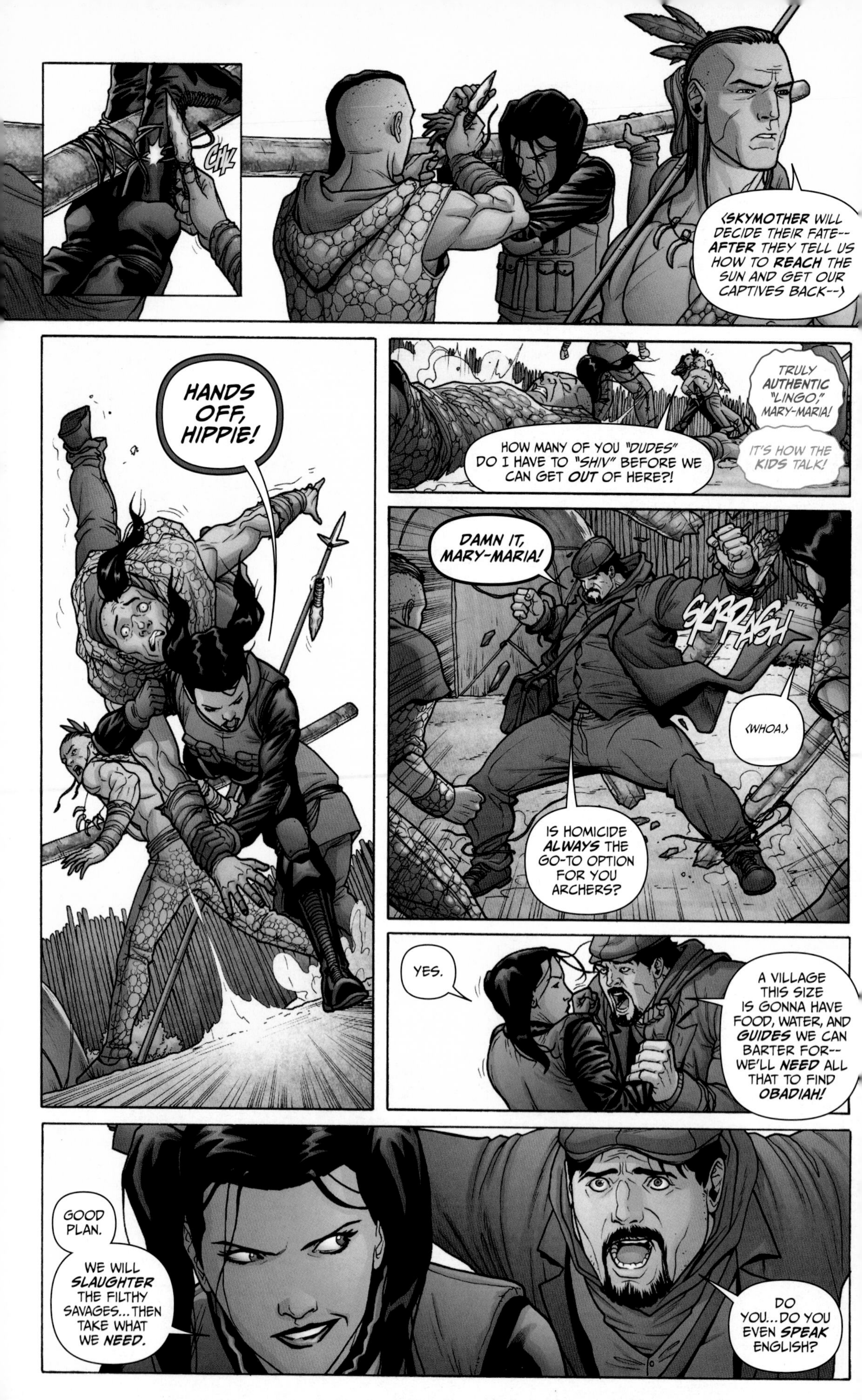
CHK
‹SKYMOTHER WILL DECIDE THEIR FATE-- AFTER THEY TELL US HOW TO REACH THE SUN AND GET OUR CAPTIVES BACK--›
HANDS OFF, HIPPIE!
HOW MANY OF YOU "DUDES" DO I HAVE TO "SHIV" BEFORE WE CAN GET OUT OF HERE?!
TRULY AUTHENTIC "LINGO," MARY-MARIA!
IT'S HOW THE KIDS TALK!
DAMN IT, MARY-MARIA!
SKRASH
‹WHOA.›
IS HOMICIDE ALWAYS THE GO-TO OPTION FOR YOU ARCHERS?
YES.
A VILLAGE THIS SIZE IS GONNA HAVE FOOD, WATER, AND GUIDES WE CAN BARTER FOR-- WE'LL NEED ALL THAT TO FIND OBADIAH!
GOOD PLAN.
WE WILL SLAUGHTER THE FILTHY SAVAGES...THEN TAKE WHAT WE NEED.
DO YOU...DO YOU EVEN SPEAK ENGLISH?

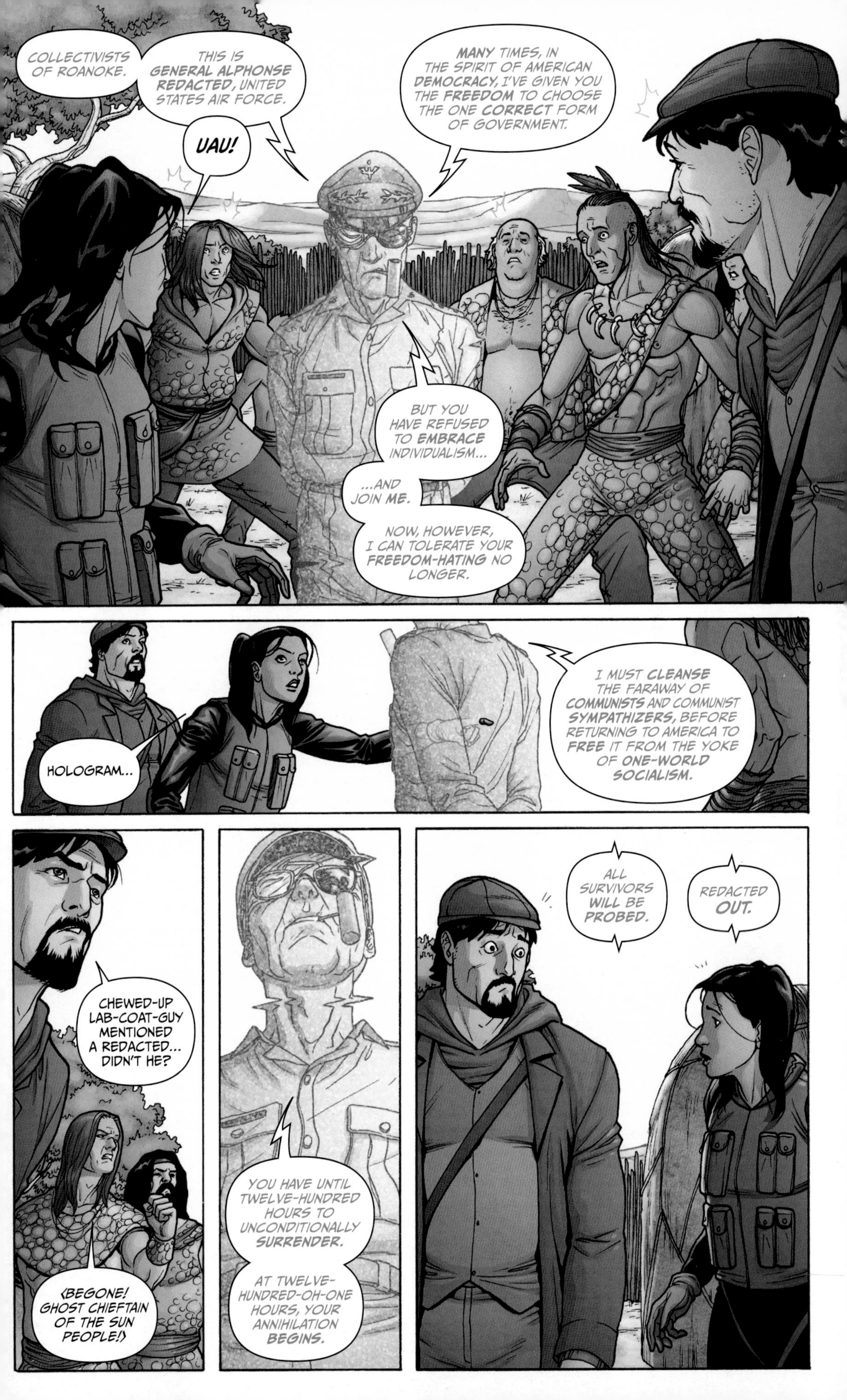
COLLECTIVISTS OF ROANOKE.
THIS IS GENERAL ALPHONSE REDACTED, UNITED STATES AIR FORCE.
UAU!
MANY TIMES, IN THE SPIRIT OF AMERICAN DEMOCRACY, I'VE GIVEN YOU THE FREEDOM TO CHOOSE THE ONE CORRECT FORM OF GOVERNMENT.
BUT YOU HAVE REFUSED TO EMBRACE INDIVIDUALISM...
...AND JOIN ME.
NOW, HOWEVER, I CAN TOLERATE YOUR FREEDOM-HATING NO LONGER.
HOLOGRAM...
I MUST CLEANSE THE FARAWAY OF COMMUNISTS AND COMMUNIST SYMPATHIZERS, BEFORE RETURNING TO AMERICA TO FREE IT FROM THE YOKE OF ONE-WORLD SOCIALISM.
CHEWED-UP LAB-COAT-GUY MENTIONED A REDACTED... DIDN'T HE?
<BEGONE! GHOST CHIEFTAIN OF THE SUN PEOPLE!>
YOU HAVE UNTIL TWELVE-HUNDRED HOURS TO UNCONDITIONALLY SURRENDER.
AT TWELVE-HUNDRED-OH-ONE HOURS, YOUR ANNIHILATION BEGINS.
ALL SURVIVORS WILL BE PROBED.
REDACTED OUT.

NNNNFF...

UHHHH...

HEY!

LCK LCK LCK

LCK LCK

EASY, LAD. MOVE SLOWLY.

THE GROUND GREETED YOU RATHER *ROUGHLY* WHEN YOU MADE ITS ACQUAINTANCE.

HEARST HERE HEARD YOU LAND A GOOD HALF-MILE AWAY.

GRAWK?

ARE YOU FRIEND OR FOE, SIR?

FRIENDSHIP. NOUN.

"A SHIP BIG ENOUGH TO CARRY *TWO* IN FAIR WEATHER, BUT ONLY ONE IN *FOUL*."

BUT AT THE MOMENT THE SEA IS *CALM* AND THE SKY IS *BLUE*.

SO, UH... *FRIEND?*

FRIEND. *AMBROSE BIERCE*, AT YOUR SERVICE.

THANK YOU, SIR. MY NAME IS OBADIAH ARCHER. I APPRECIATE YOU RESCUING ME. BUT NOTHING SEEMS *BROKEN*, SO I SHOULD SET ABOUT FINDING THE PEOPLE I CAME HERE WITH.

AND... WHERE *DID* YOU FIND YOUR WAY TO OUR FAIR FARAWAY, IF YOU DON'T MIND ME ASKING?

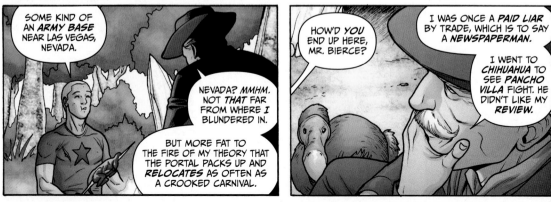

SOME KIND OF AN *ARMY BASE* NEAR LAS VEGAS, NEVADA.

NEVADA? MMHM. NOT *THAT* FAR FROM WHERE *I* BLUNDERED IN.

BUT MORE FAT TO THE FIRE OF MY THEORY THAT THE PORTAL PACKS UP AND *RELOCATES* AS OFTEN AS A CROOKED CARNIVAL.

HOW'D *YOU* END UP HERE, MR. BIERCE?

I WAS ONCE A *PAID LIAR* BY TRADE, WHICH IS TO SAY A *NEWSPAPERMAN*.

I WENT TO *CHIHUAHUA* TO SEE *PANCHO VILLA* FIGHT. HE DIDN'T LIKE MY *REVIEW*.

"THESE PAMPERED *CELEBRITIES* JUST CAN'T TAKE *CONSTRUCTIVE CRITICISM.*

"HE WROTE THE *BANDITO* VERSION OF A LETTER TO THE EDITOR.

"I FLED INTO *EL CAÑON DEL COBRE* TO KEEP HIM FROM *DELIVERING* IT.

BANG BANG

"I TRIED TO *HIDE* IN WHAT I TOOK TO BE AN ABANDONED *MINE.*

AAOOOAAAOOOOooo

"I WAS *MISTAKEN.*"

THAT WAS NEW YEAR'S DAY, NINETEEN-HUNDRED AND *FOURTEEN.*

AND I'VE BEEN HERE EVER *SINCE.*

WOW! THAT'S-- A HUNDRED YEARS AGO!

A LOT LESS TIME THAN THESE *BIG LIZARDS* HAVE BEEN HERE, I CAN GUARANTEE THAT.

WHAT'S A *YEAR,* BUT A PERIOD OF THREE HUNDRED AND SIXTY-FIVE *DISAPPOINTMENTS?*

YOU REMIND ME OF A FRIEND OF MINE.

TCH. AND HERE I THOUGHT I WAS ONE OF A KIND.

I CAN'T HELP YOU *OUT* OF HERE, BUT I KNOW WHERE YOU MAY BE ABLE TO FIND YOUR FRIENDS.

COME ALONG, HEARST!

GWARRRK

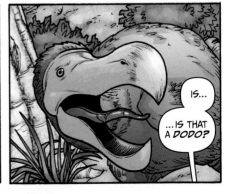

IS...

...IS THAT A *DODO?*

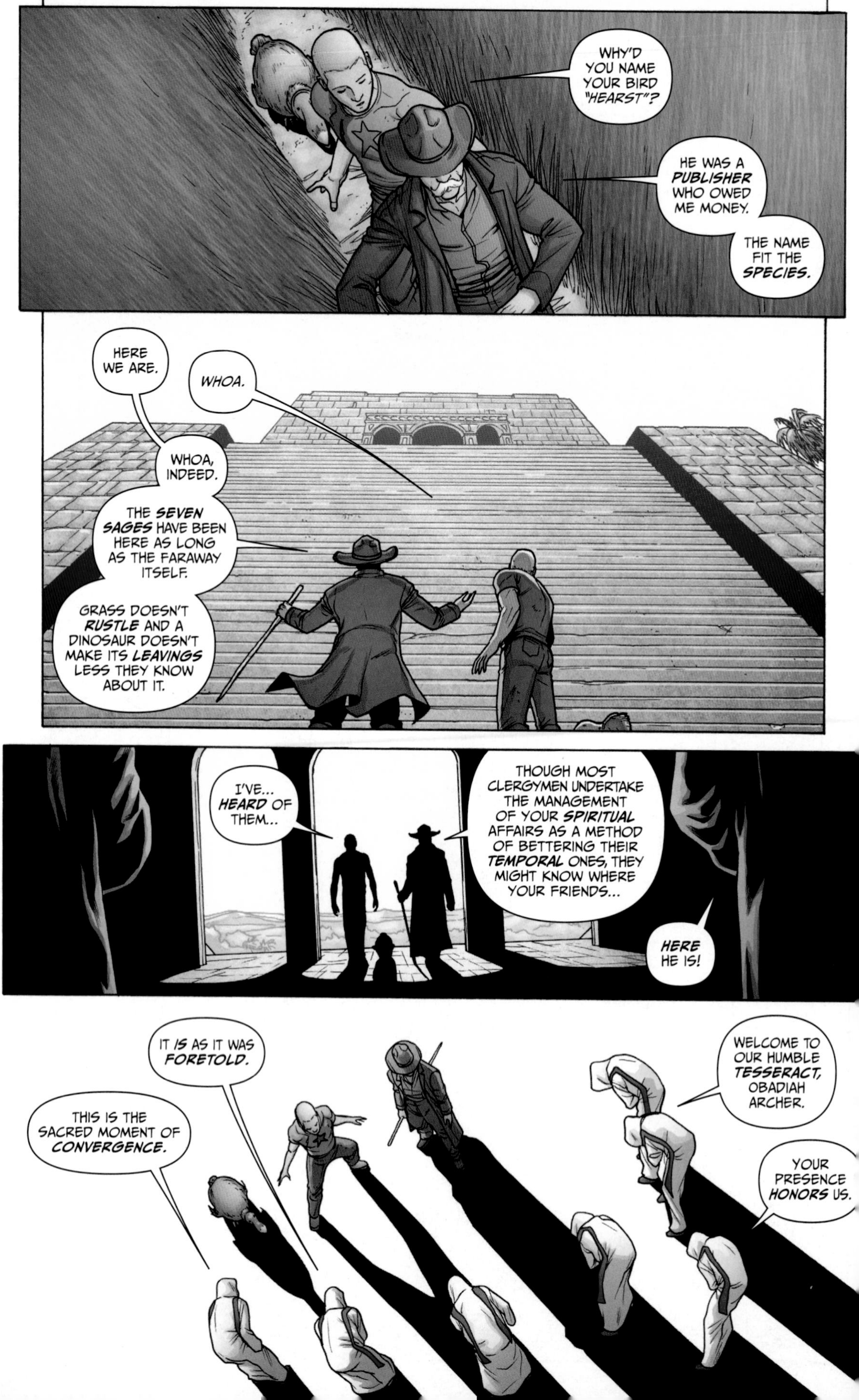
WHY'D YOU NAME YOUR BIRD "HEARST"?
HE WAS A PUBLISHER WHO OWED ME MONEY.
THE NAME FIT THE SPECIES.
HERE WE ARE.
WHOA.
WHOA, INDEED.
THE SEVEN SAGES HAVE BEEN HERE AS LONG AS THE FARAWAY ITSELF.
GRASS DOESN'T RUSTLE AND A DINOSAUR DOESN'T MAKE ITS LEAVINGS LESS THEY KNOW ABOUT IT.
I'VE... HEARD OF THEM...
THOUGH MOST CLERGYMEN UNDERTAKE THE MANAGEMENT OF YOUR SPIRITUAL AFFAIRS AS A METHOD OF BETTERING THEIR TEMPORAL ONES, THEY MIGHT KNOW WHERE YOUR FRIENDS...
HERE HE IS!
THIS IS THE SACRED MOMENT OF CONVERGENCE.
IT IS AS IT WAS FORETOLD.
WELCOME TO OUR HUMBLE TESSERACT, OBADIAH ARCHER.
YOUR PRESENCE HONORS US.

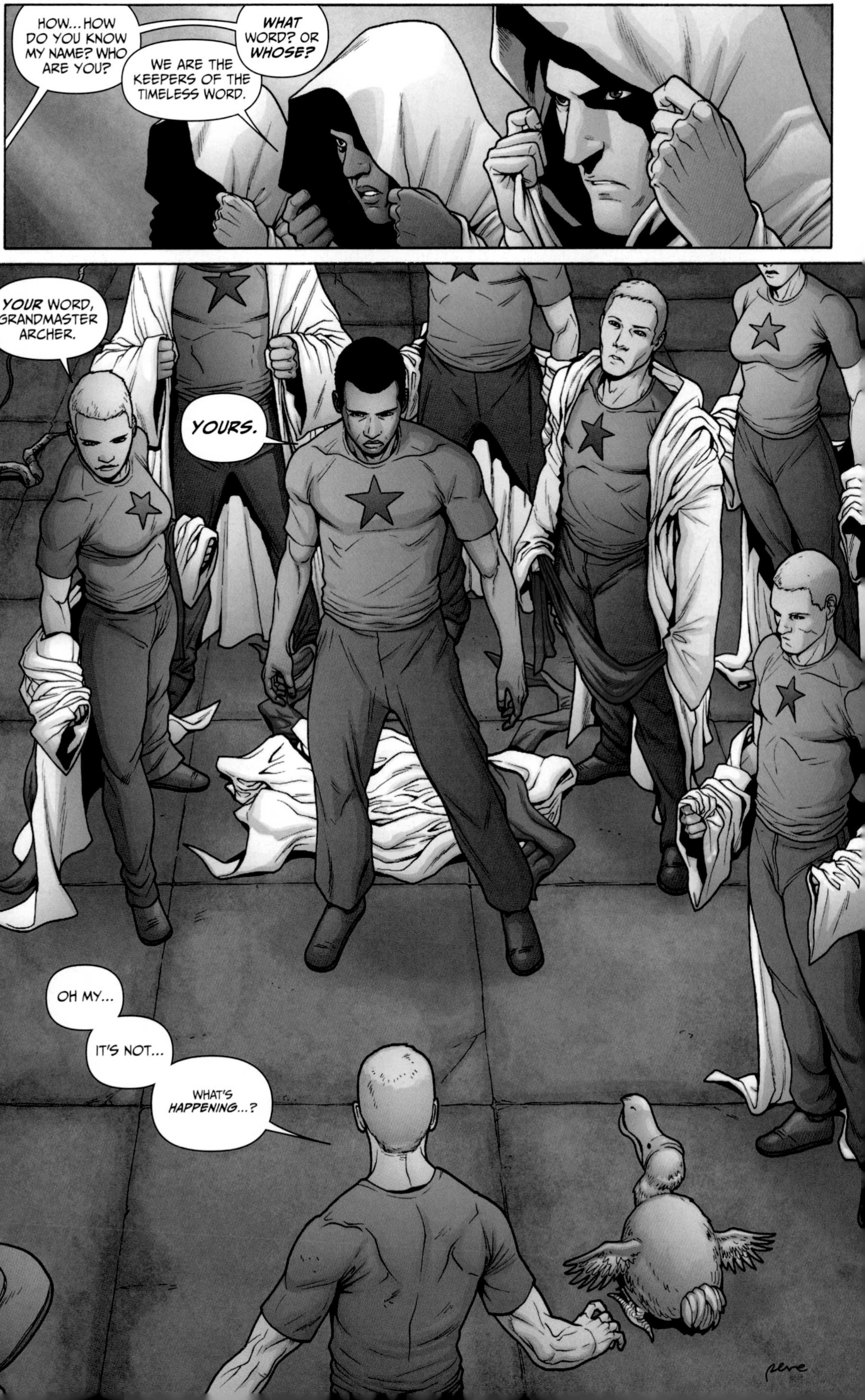
HOW... HOW DO YOU KNOW MY NAME? WHO ARE YOU?
WE ARE THE KEEPERS OF THE TIMELESS WORD.
WHAT WORD? OR WHOSE?
YOUR WORD, GRANDMASTER ARCHER.
YOURS.
OH MY...
IT'S NOT...
WHAT'S HAPPENING...?

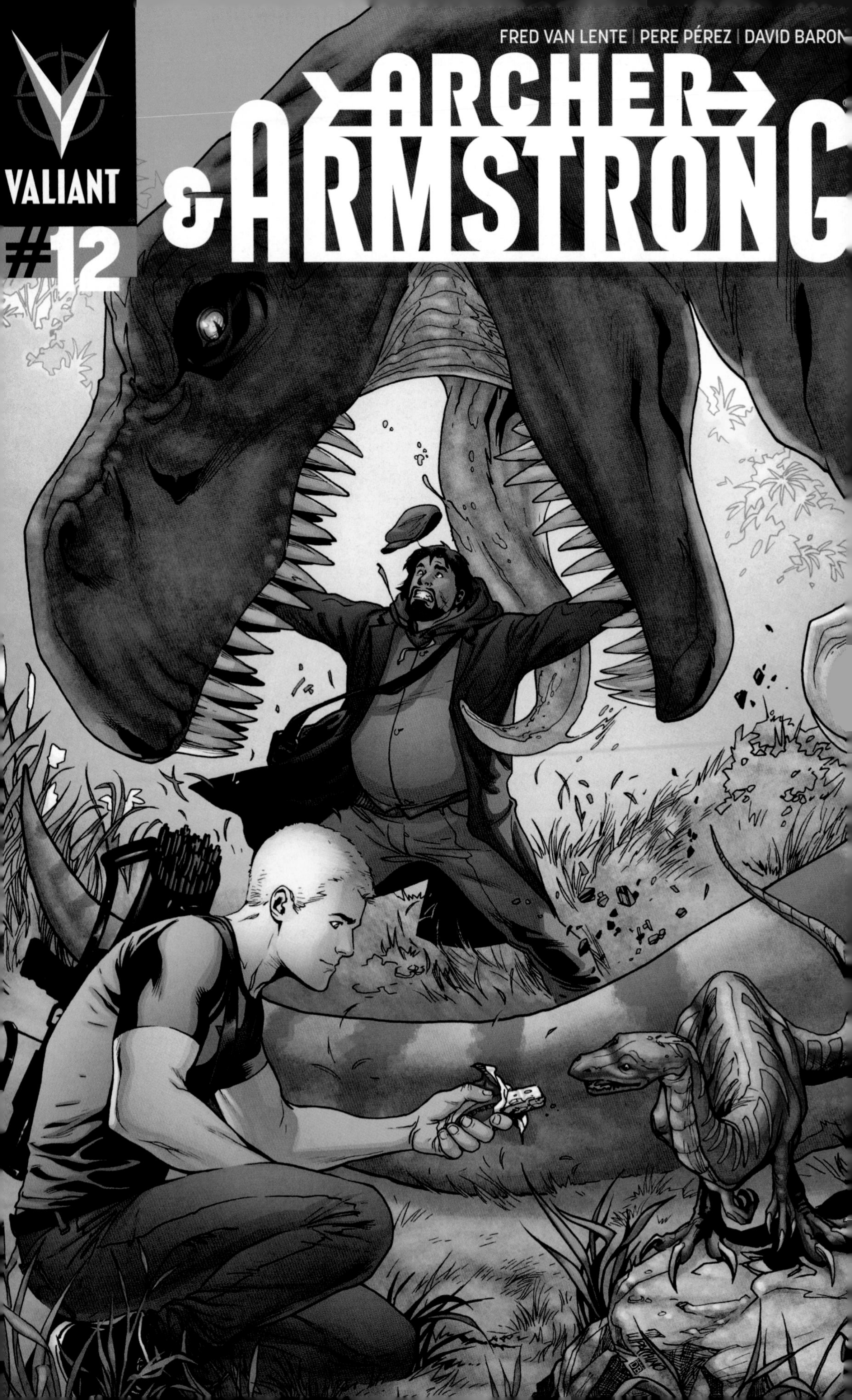

FRED VAN LENTE | PERE PÉREZ | DAVID BARON
VALIANT
#12
ARCHER & ARMSTRONG

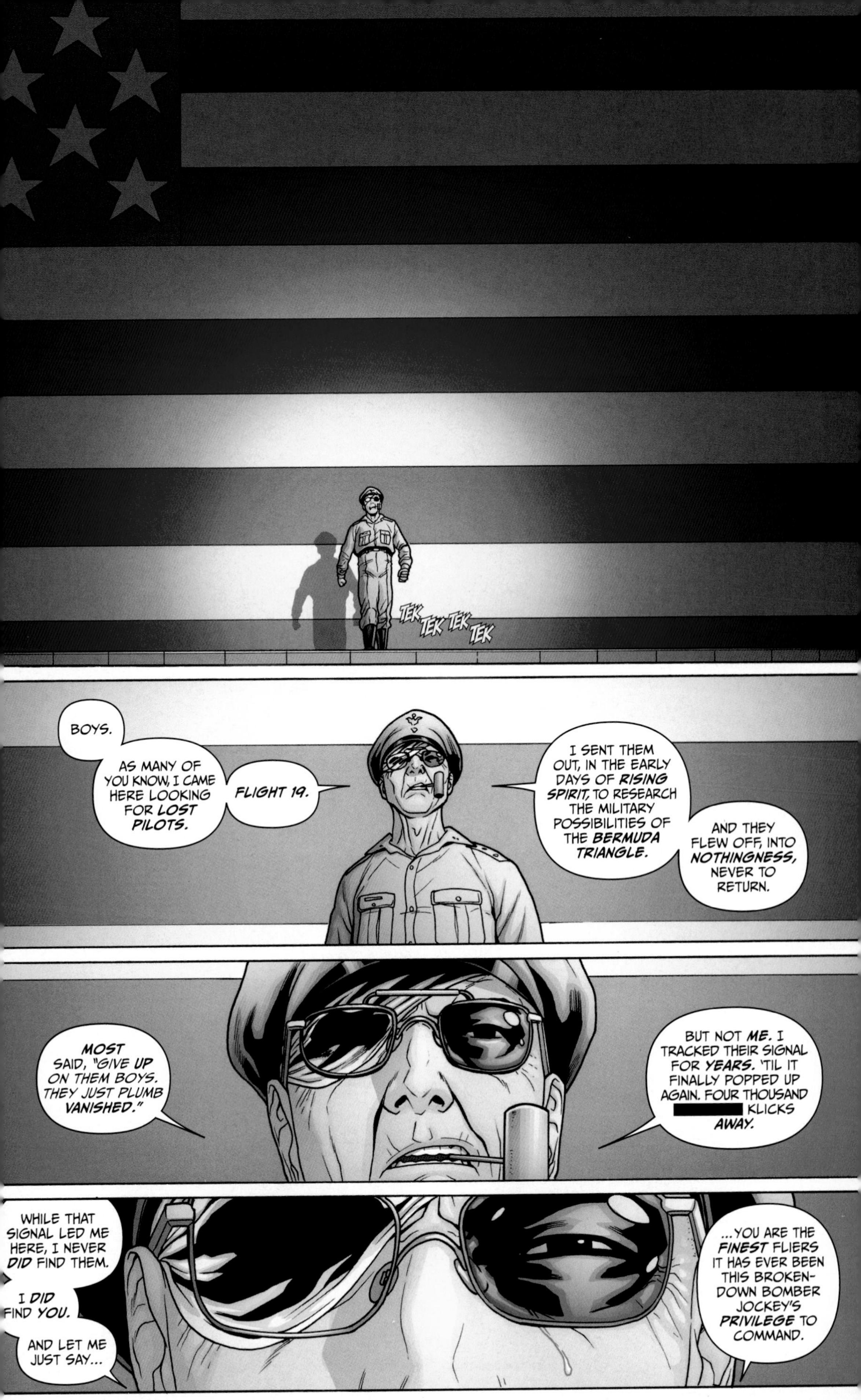
TEK TEK TEK TEK
BOYS.
AS MANY OF YOU KNOW, I CAME HERE LOOKING FOR LOST PILOTS.
FLIGHT 19.
I SENT THEM OUT, IN THE EARLY DAYS OF RISING SPIRIT, TO RESEARCH THE MILITARY POSSIBILITIES OF THE BERMUDA TRIANGLE.
AND THEY FLEW OFF, INTO NOTHINGNESS, NEVER TO RETURN.
MOST SAID, "GIVE UP ON THEM BOYS. THEY JUST PLUMB VANISHED."
BUT NOT ME. I TRACKED THEIR SIGNAL FOR YEARS. 'TIL IT FINALLY POPPED UP AGAIN. FOUR THOUSAND [redacted] KLICKS AWAY.
WHILE THAT SIGNAL LED ME HERE, I NEVER DID FIND THEM.
I DID FIND YOU.
AND LET ME JUST SAY...
...YOU ARE THE FINEST FLIERS IT HAS EVER BEEN THIS BROKEN-DOWN BOMBER JOCKEY'S PRIVILEGE TO COMMAND.

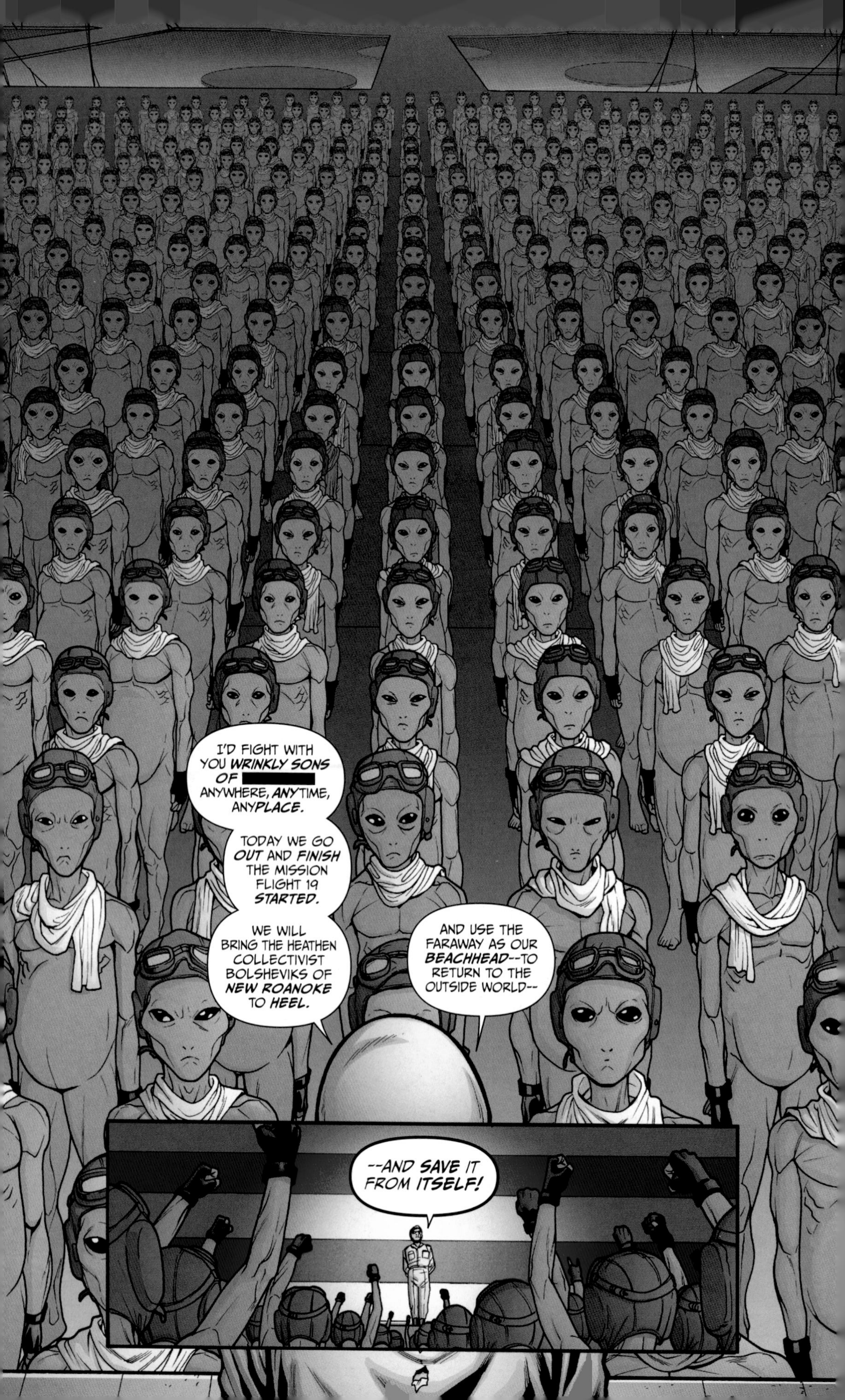
I'D FIGHT WITH YOU **WRINKLY SONS OF** [redacted] ANYWHERE, **ANY**TIME, ANY**PLACE.**
TODAY WE GO **OUT** AND **FINISH** THE MISSION FLIGHT 19 **STARTED.**
WE WILL BRING THE HEATHEN COLLECTIVIST BOLSHEVIKS OF **NEW ROANOKE** TO **HEEL.**
AND USE THE FARAWAY AS OUR **BEACHHEAD**--TO RETURN TO THE OUTSIDE WORLD--
--AND **SAVE** IT FROM **ITSELF!**

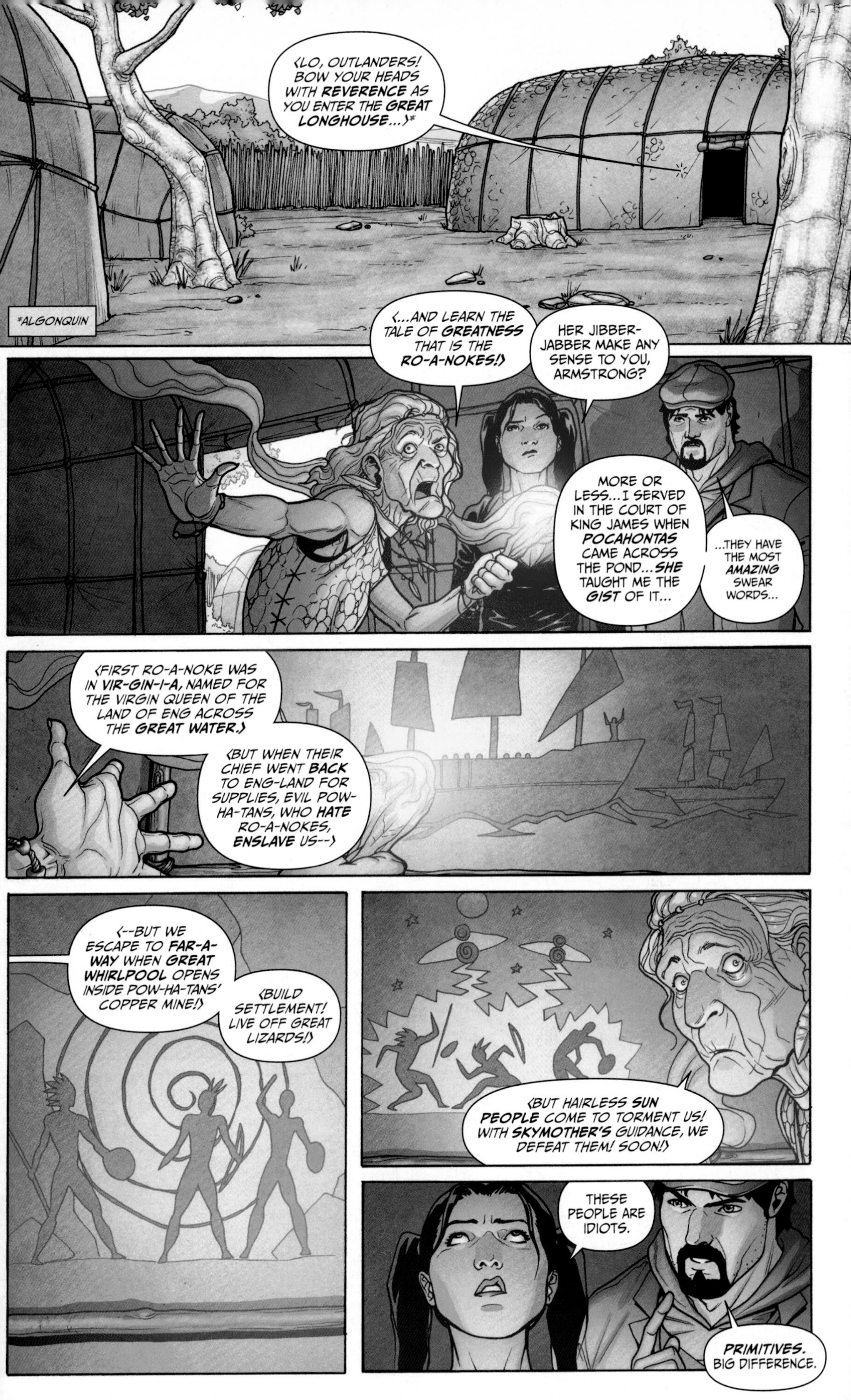

‹LO, OUTLANDERS! BOW YOUR HEADS WITH REVERENCE AS YOU ENTER THE GREAT LONGHOUSE...›*
*ALGONQUIN
‹...AND LEARN THE TALE OF GREATNESS THAT IS THE RO-A-NOKES!›
HER JIBBER-JABBER MAKE ANY SENSE TO YOU, ARMSTRONG?
MORE OR LESS... I SERVED IN THE COURT OF KING JAMES WHEN POCAHONTAS CAME ACROSS THE POND... SHE TAUGHT ME THE GIST OF IT...
...THEY HAVE THE MOST AMAZING SWEAR WORDS...
‹FIRST RO-A-NOKE WAS IN VIR-GIN-I-A, NAMED FOR THE VIRGIN QUEEN OF THE LAND OF ENG ACROSS THE GREAT WATER.›
‹BUT WHEN THEIR CHIEF WENT BACK TO ENG-LAND FOR SUPPLIES, EVIL POW-HA-TANS, WHO HATE RO-A-NOKES, ENSLAVE US--›
‹--BUT WE ESCAPE TO FAR-A-WAY WHEN GREAT WHIRLPOOL OPENS INSIDE POW-HA-TANS' COPPER MINE!›
‹BUILD SETTLEMENT! LIVE OFF GREAT LIZARDS!›
‹BUT HAIRLESS SUN PEOPLE COME TO TORMENT US! WITH SKYMOTHER'S GUIDANCE, WE DEFEAT THEM! SOON!›
THESE PEOPLE ARE IDIOTS.
PRIMITIVES. BIG DIFFERENCE.

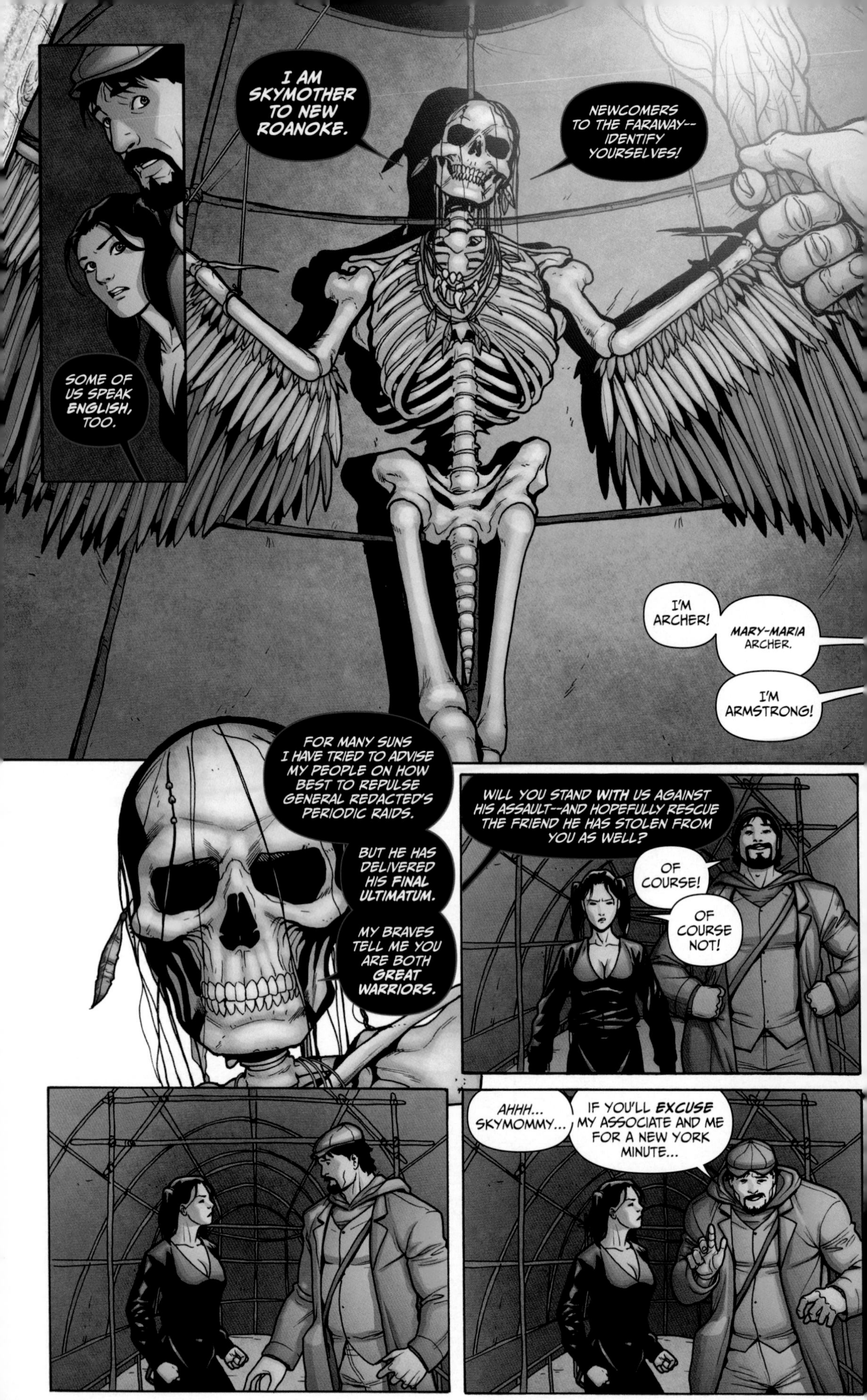

I AM SKYMOTHER TO NEW ROANOKE.
NEWCOMERS TO THE FARAWAY-- IDENTIFY YOURSELVES!
SOME OF US SPEAK ENGLISH, TOO.
I'M ARCHER!
MARY-MARIA ARCHER.
I'M ARMSTRONG!
FOR MANY SUNS I HAVE TRIED TO ADVISE MY PEOPLE ON HOW BEST TO REPULSE GENERAL REDACTED'S PERIODIC RAIDS.
BUT HE HAS DELIVERED HIS FINAL ULTIMATUM.
MY BRAVES TELL ME YOU ARE BOTH GREAT WARRIORS.
WILL YOU STAND WITH US AGAINST HIS ASSAULT--AND HOPEFULLY RESCUE THE FRIEND HE HAS STOLEN FROM YOU AS WELL?
OF COURSE!
OF COURSE NOT!
AHHH... SKYMOMMY...
IF YOU'LL EXCUSE MY ASSOCIATE AND ME FOR A NEW YORK MINUTE...

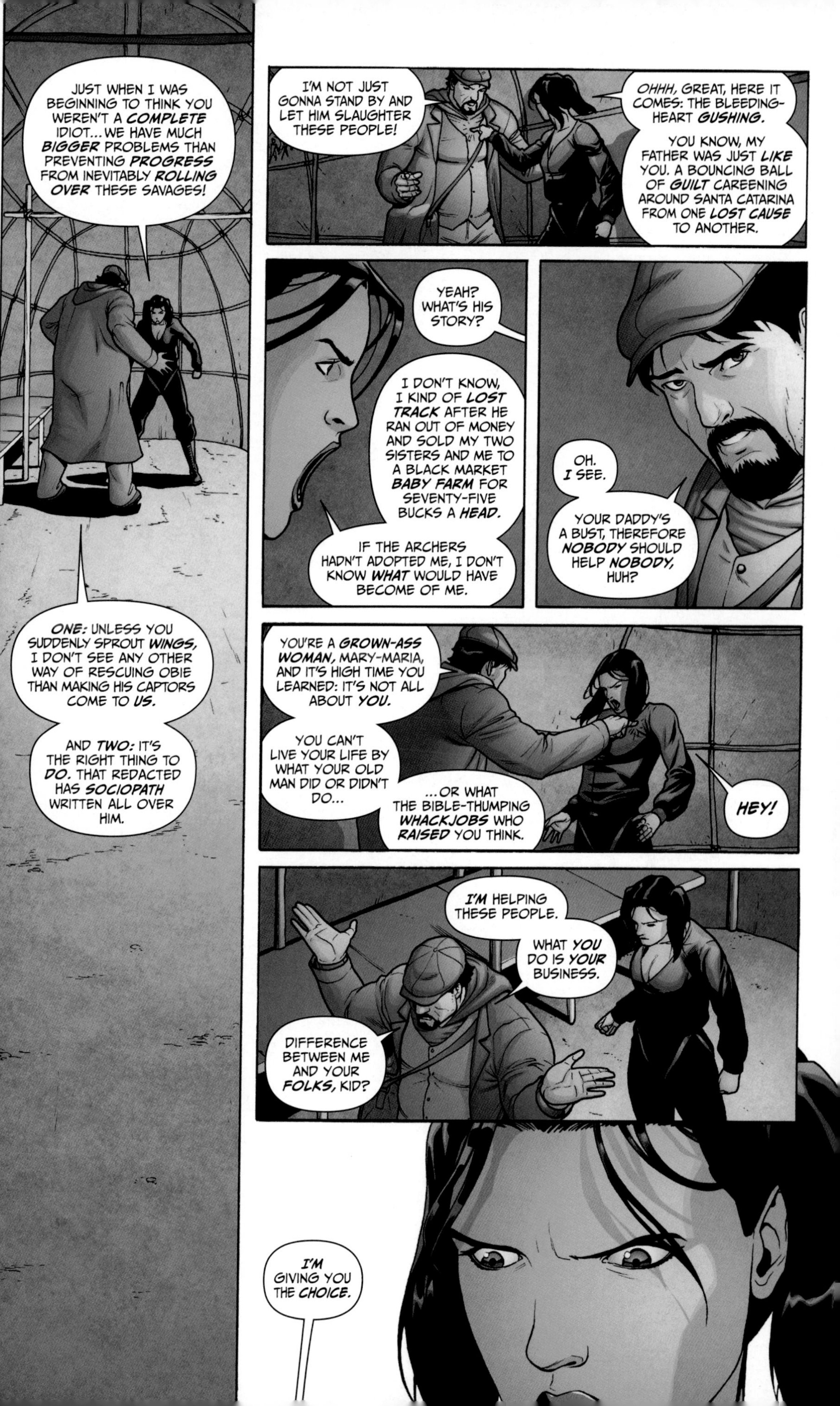

JUST WHEN I WAS BEGINNING TO THINK YOU WEREN'T A COMPLETE IDIOT... WE HAVE MUCH BIGGER PROBLEMS THAN PREVENTING PROGRESS FROM INEVITABLY ROLLING OVER THESE SAVAGES!
ONE: UNLESS YOU SUDDENLY SPROUT WINGS, I DON'T SEE ANY OTHER WAY OF RESCUING OBIE THAN MAKING HIS CAPTORS COME TO US.
AND TWO: IT'S THE RIGHT THING TO DO. THAT REDACTED HAS SOCIOPATH WRITTEN ALL OVER HIM.
I'M NOT JUST GONNA STAND BY AND LET HIM SLAUGHTER THESE PEOPLE!
OHHH, GREAT, HERE IT COMES: THE BLEEDING-HEART GUSHING.
YOU KNOW, MY FATHER WAS JUST LIKE YOU. A BOUNCING BALL OF GUILT CAREENING AROUND SANTA CATARINA FROM ONE LOST CAUSE TO ANOTHER.
YEAH? WHAT'S HIS STORY?
I DON'T KNOW, I KIND OF LOST TRACK AFTER HE RAN OUT OF MONEY AND SOLD MY TWO SISTERS AND ME TO A BLACK MARKET BABY FARM FOR SEVENTY-FIVE BUCKS A HEAD.
IF THE ARCHERS HADN'T ADOPTED ME, I DON'T KNOW WHAT WOULD HAVE BECOME OF ME.
OH. I SEE.
YOUR DADDY'S A BUST, THEREFORE NOBODY SHOULD HELP NOBODY, HUH?
YOU'RE A GROWN-ASS WOMAN, MARY-MARIA, AND IT'S HIGH TIME YOU LEARNED: IT'S NOT ALL ABOUT YOU.
YOU CAN'T LIVE YOUR LIFE BY WHAT YOUR OLD MAN DID OR DIDN'T DO...
...OR WHAT THE BIBLE-THUMPING WHACKJOBS WHO RAISED YOU THINK.
HEY!
I'M HELPING THESE PEOPLE.
WHAT YOU DO IS YOUR BUSINESS.
DIFFERENCE BETWEEN ME AND YOUR FOLKS, KID?
I'M GIVING YOU THE CHOICE.

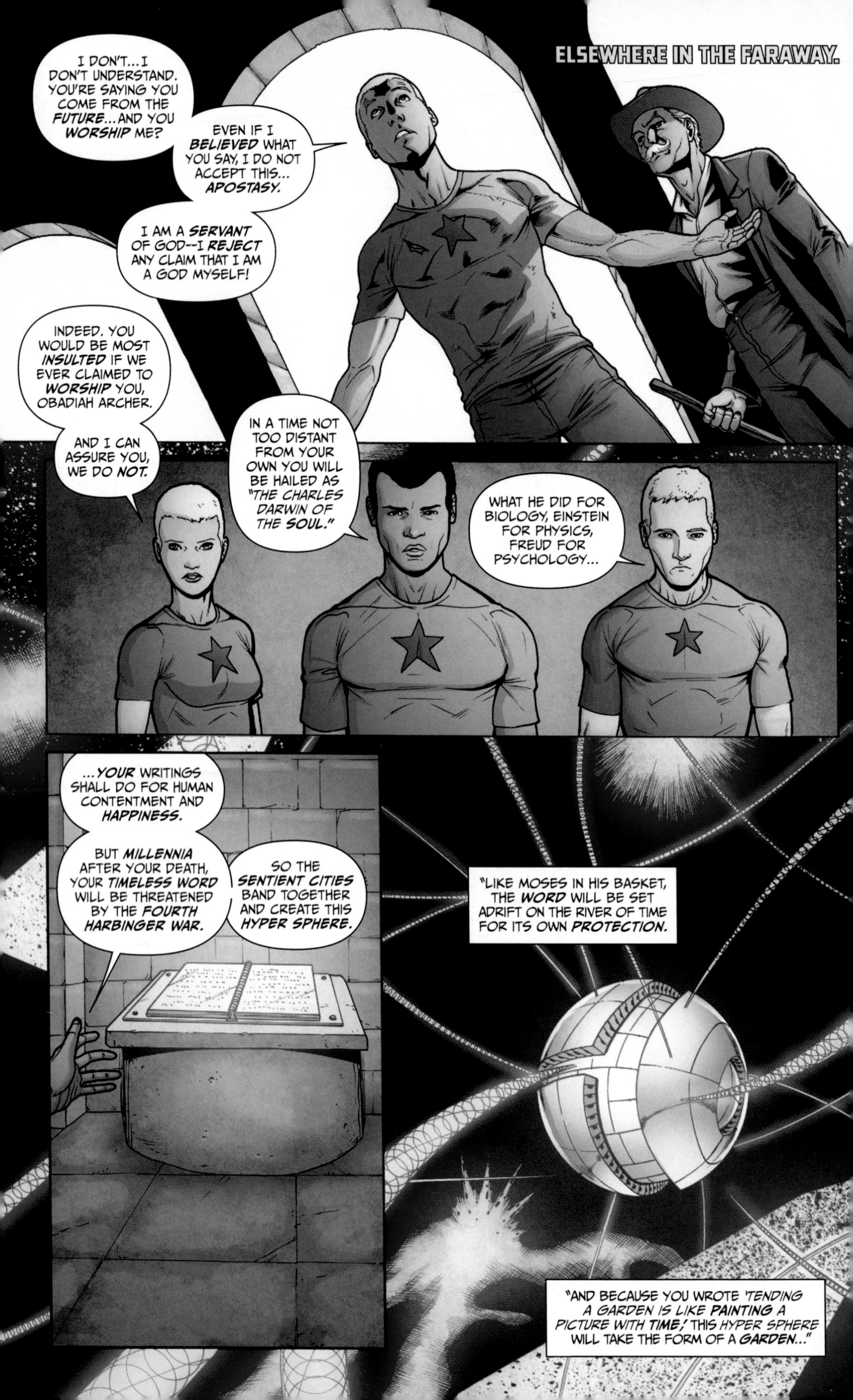
ELSEWHERE IN THE FARAWAY.
I DON'T...I DON'T UNDERSTAND. YOU'RE SAYING YOU COME FROM THE FUTURE...AND YOU WORSHIP ME?
EVEN IF I BELIEVED WHAT YOU SAY, I DO NOT ACCEPT THIS... APOSTASY.
I AM A SERVANT OF GOD--I REJECT ANY CLAIM THAT I AM A GOD MYSELF!
INDEED. YOU WOULD BE MOST INSULTED IF WE EVER CLAIMED TO WORSHIP YOU, OBADIAH ARCHER.
AND I CAN ASSURE YOU, WE DO NOT.
IN A TIME NOT TOO DISTANT FROM YOUR OWN YOU WILL BE HAILED AS "THE CHARLES DARWIN OF THE SOUL."
WHAT HE DID FOR BIOLOGY, EINSTEIN FOR PHYSICS, FREUD FOR PSYCHOLOGY...
...YOUR WRITINGS SHALL DO FOR HUMAN CONTENTMENT AND HAPPINESS.
BUT MILLENNIA AFTER YOUR DEATH, YOUR TIMELESS WORD WILL BE THREATENED BY THE FOURTH HARBINGER WAR.
SO THE SENTIENT CITIES BAND TOGETHER AND CREATE THIS HYPER SPHERE.
"LIKE MOSES IN HIS BASKET, THE WORD WILL BE SET ADRIFT ON THE RIVER OF TIME FOR ITS OWN PROTECTION.
"AND BECAUSE YOU WROTE 'TENDING A GARDEN IS LIKE PAINTING A PICTURE WITH TIME,' THIS HYPER SPHERE WILL TAKE THE FORM OF A GARDEN..."

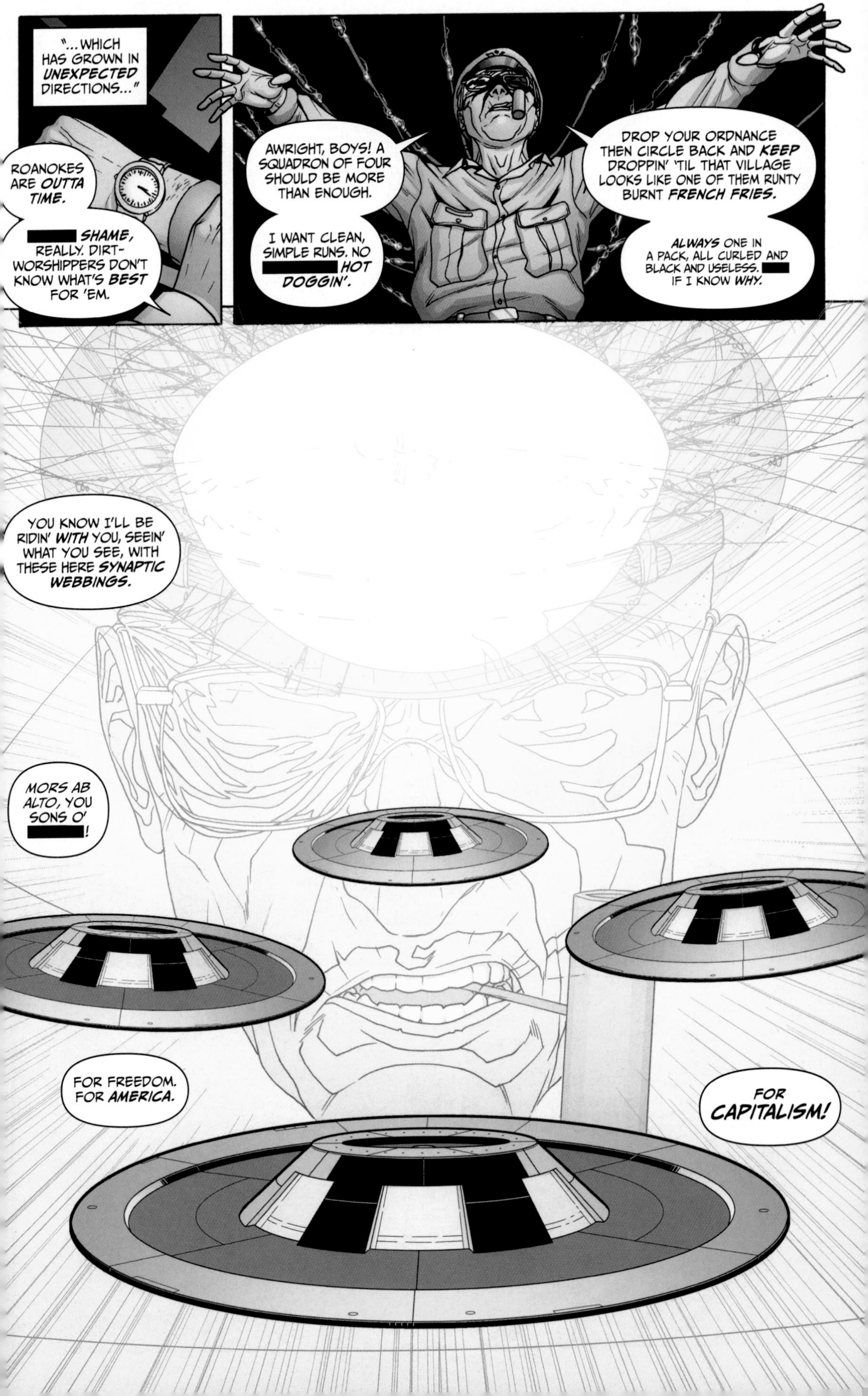
"...WHICH HAS GROWN IN *UNEXPECTED* DIRECTIONS..."
ROANOKES ARE *OUTTA TIME.*
[redacted] *SHAME,* REALLY. DIRT-WORSHIPPERS DON'T KNOW WHAT'S *BEST* FOR 'EM.
AWRIGHT, BOYS! A SQUADRON OF FOUR SHOULD BE MORE THAN ENOUGH.
I WANT CLEAN, SIMPLE RUNS. NO [redacted] *HOT DOGGIN'.*
DROP YOUR ORDNANCE THEN CIRCLE BACK AND *KEEP* DROPPIN' 'TIL THAT VILLAGE LOOKS LIKE ONE OF THEM RUNTY BURNT *FRENCH FRIES.*
ALWAYS ONE IN A PACK, ALL CURLED AND BLACK AND USELESS. [redacted] IF I KNOW *WHY.*
YOU KNOW I'LL BE RIDIN' *WITH* YOU, SEEIN' WHAT YOU SEE, WITH THESE HERE *SYNAPTIC WEBBINGS.*
MORS AB ALTO, YOU SONS O' [redacted]!
FOR FREEDOM. FOR *AMERICA.*
FOR CAPITALISM!

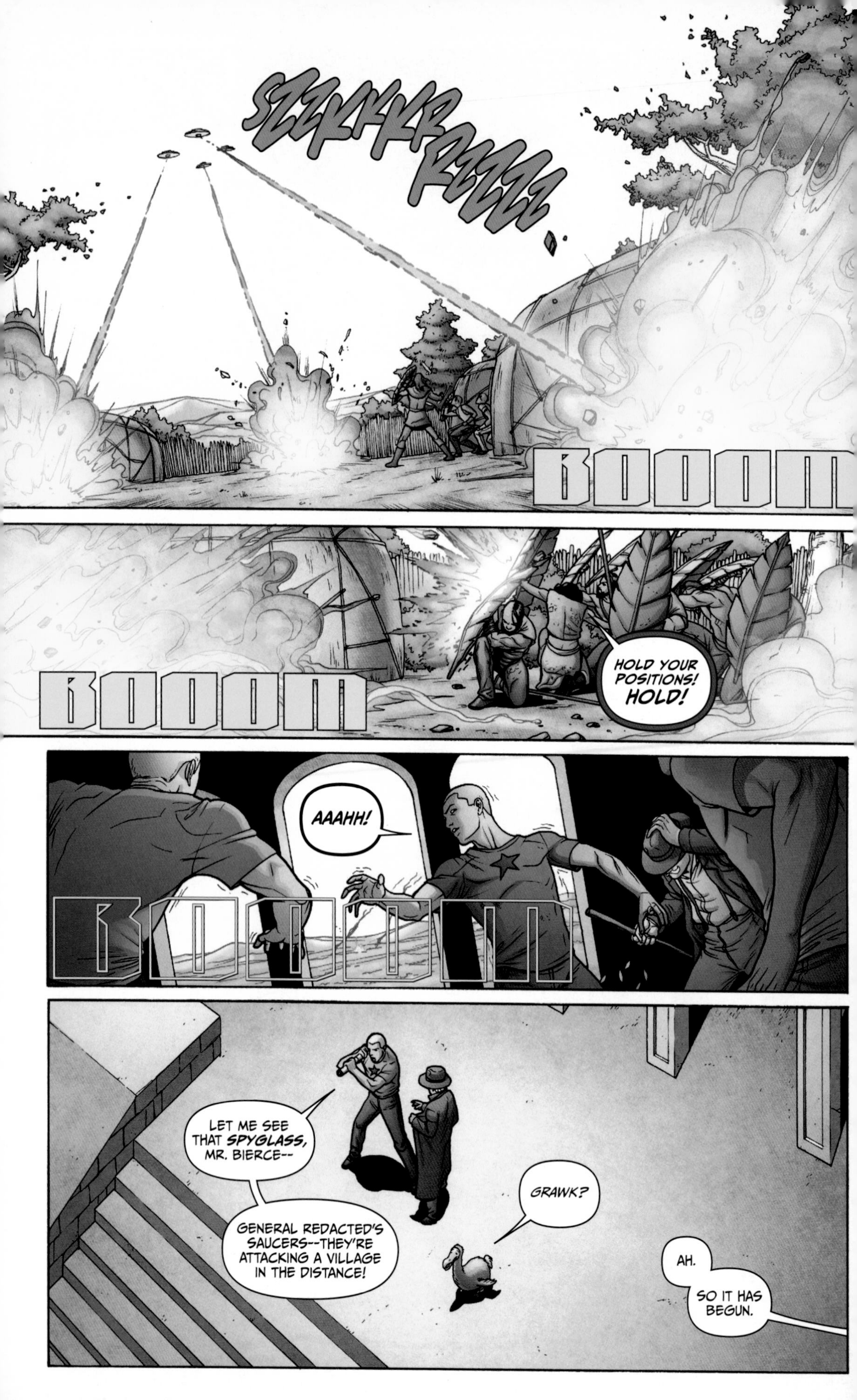

SZZKKKR
RZZZZZ
BOOOM
BOOOM
HOLD YOUR POSITIONS! HOLD!
AAAHH!
BOOOM
LET ME SEE THAT SPYGLASS, MR. BIERCE--
GENERAL REDACTED'S SAUCERS--THEY'RE ATTACKING A VILLAGE IN THE DISTANCE!
GRAWK?
AH.
SO IT HAS BEGUN.

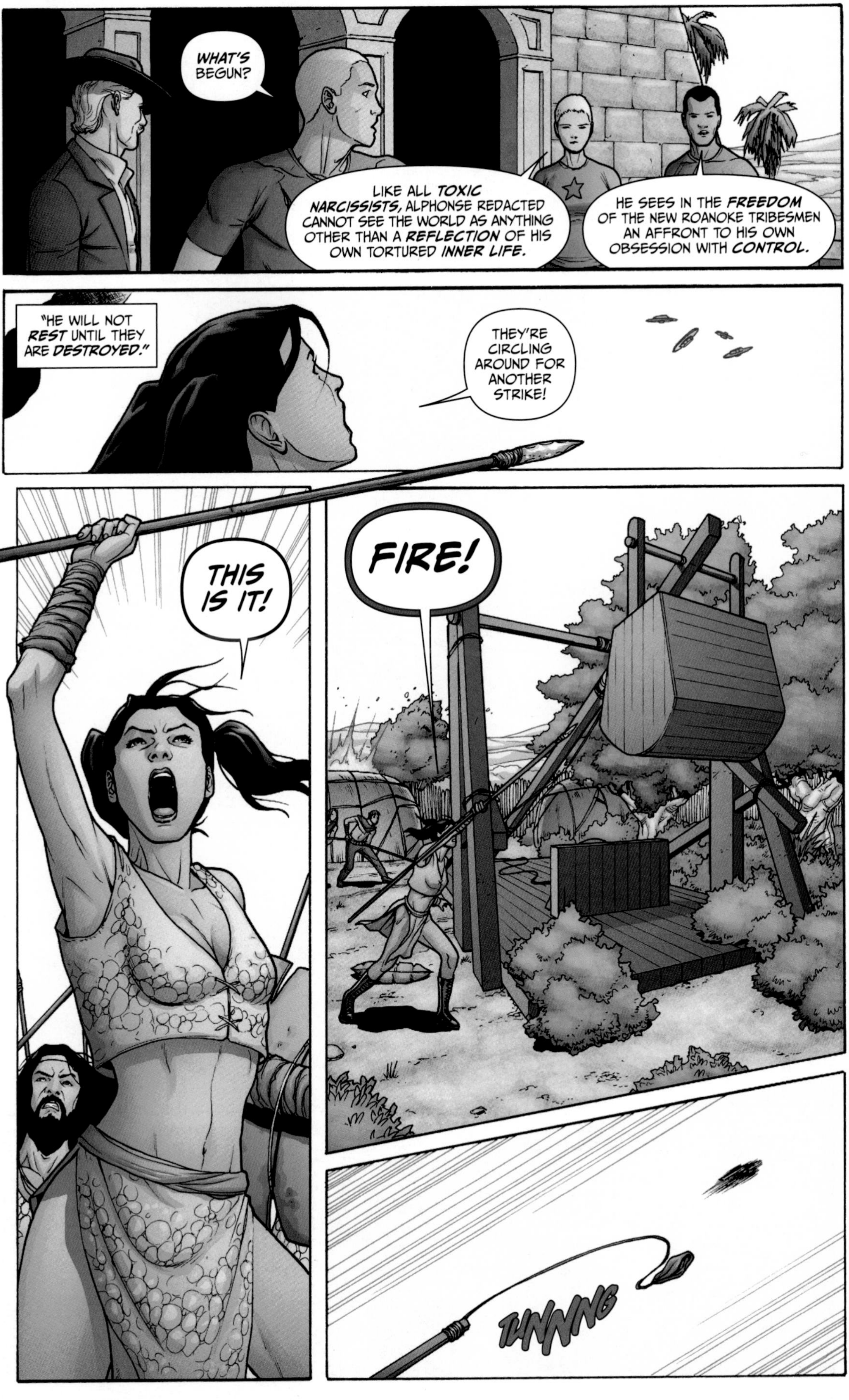

WHAT'S BEGUN?
LIKE ALL TOXIC NARCISSISTS, ALPHONSE REDACTED CANNOT SEE THE WORLD AS ANYTHING OTHER THAN A REFLECTION OF HIS OWN TORTURED INNER LIFE.
HE SEES IN THE FREEDOM OF THE NEW ROANOKE TRIBESMEN AN AFFRONT TO HIS OWN OBSESSION WITH CONTROL.
"HE WILL NOT REST UNTIL THEY ARE DESTROYED."
THEY'RE CIRCLING AROUND FOR ANOTHER STRIKE!
THIS IS IT!
FIRE!
TWNNG

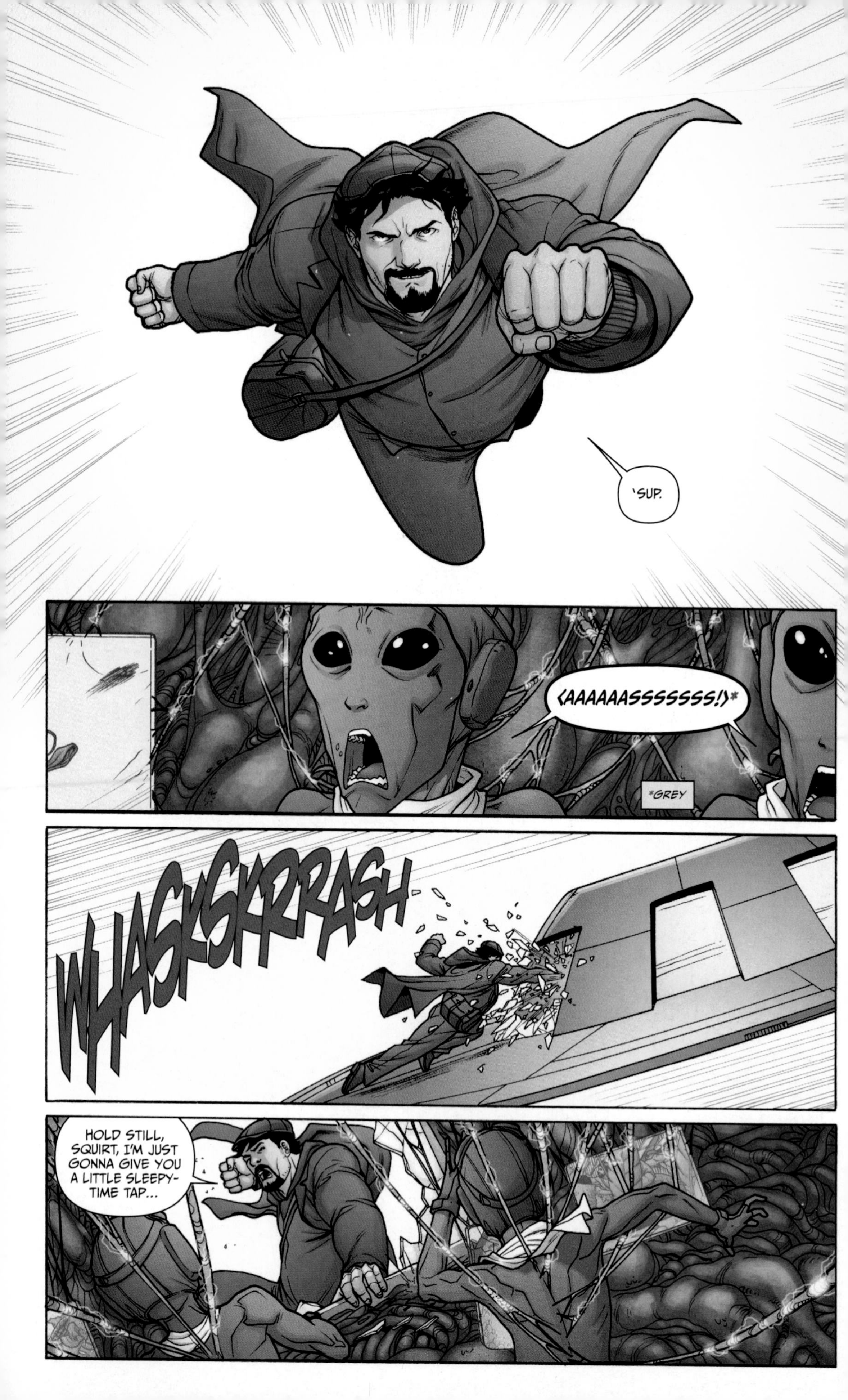
'SUP.
<AAAAAASSSSSSS!>*
*GREY
WHASKSKRRASH
HOLD STILL, SQUIRT, I'M JUST GONNA GIVE YOU A LITTLE SLEEPY-TIME TAP...

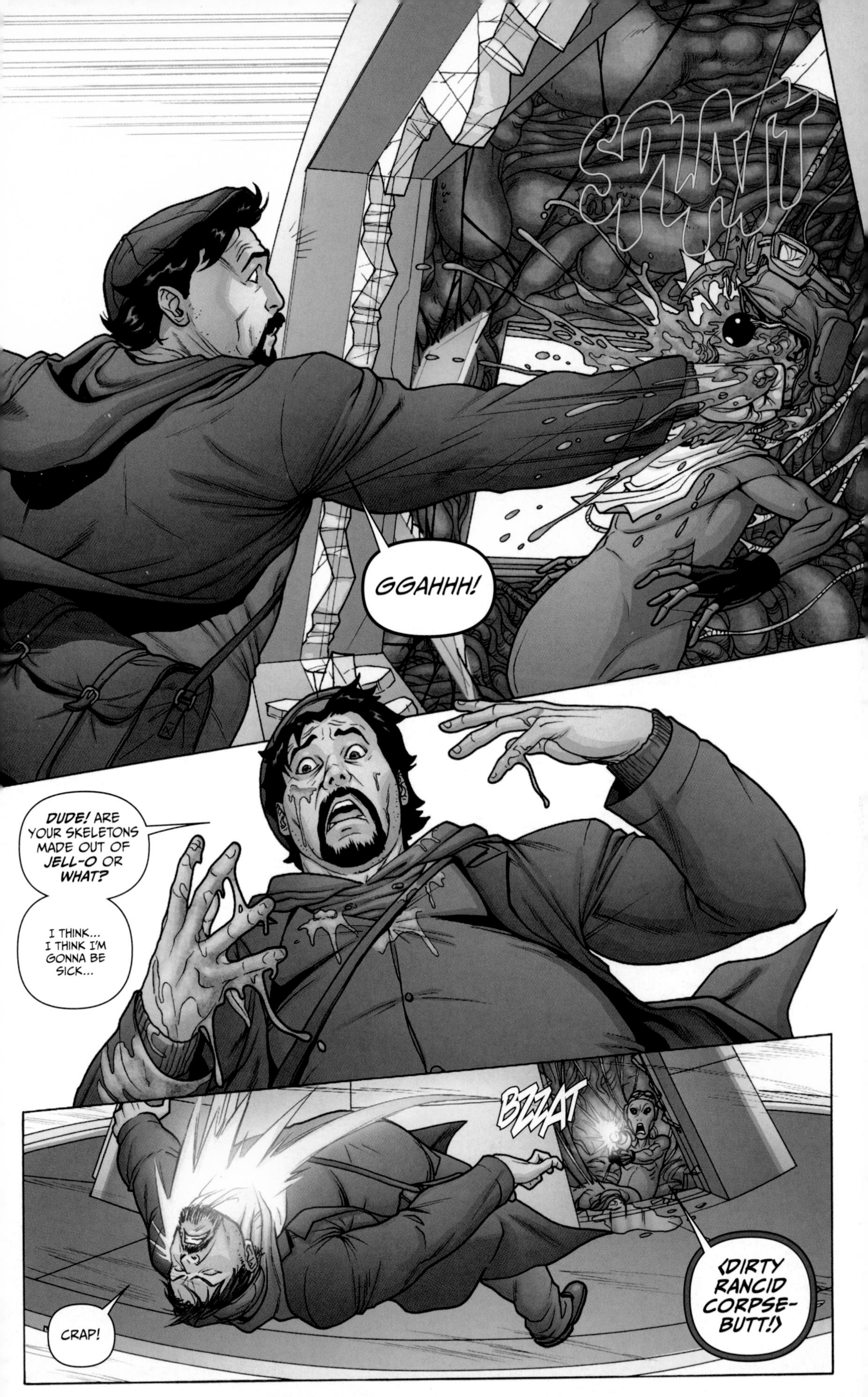
SQUIT
GGAHHH!
DUDE! ARE YOUR SKELETONS MADE OUT OF JELL-O OR WHAT?
I THINK... I THINK I'M GONNA BE SICK...
BZZAT
<DIRTY RANCID CORPSE-BUTT!>
CRAP!

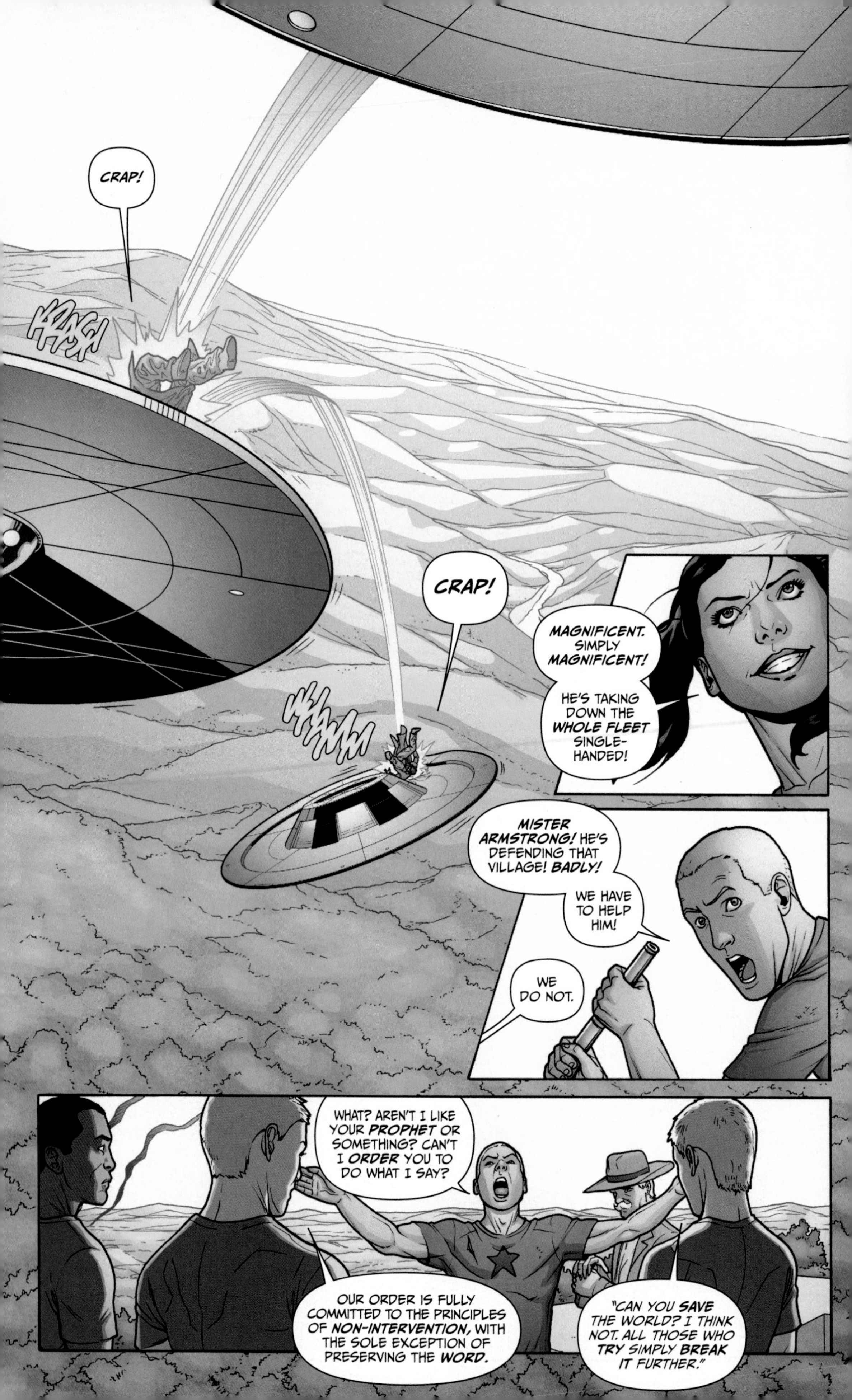
CRAP!
CRAP!
MAGNIFICENT. SIMPLY MAGNIFICENT!
HE'S TAKING DOWN THE WHOLE FLEET SINGLE-HANDED!
MISTER ARMSTRONG! HE'S DEFENDING THAT VILLAGE! BADLY!
WE HAVE TO HELP HIM!
WE DO NOT.
WHAT? AREN'T I LIKE YOUR PROPHET OR SOMETHING? CAN'T I ORDER YOU TO DO WHAT I SAY?
OUR ORDER IS FULLY COMMITTED TO THE PRINCIPLES OF NON-INTERVENTION, WITH THE SOLE EXCEPTION OF PRESERVING THE WORD.
"CAN YOU SAVE THE WORLD? I THINK NOT. ALL THOSE WHO TRY SIMPLY BREAK IT FURTHER."

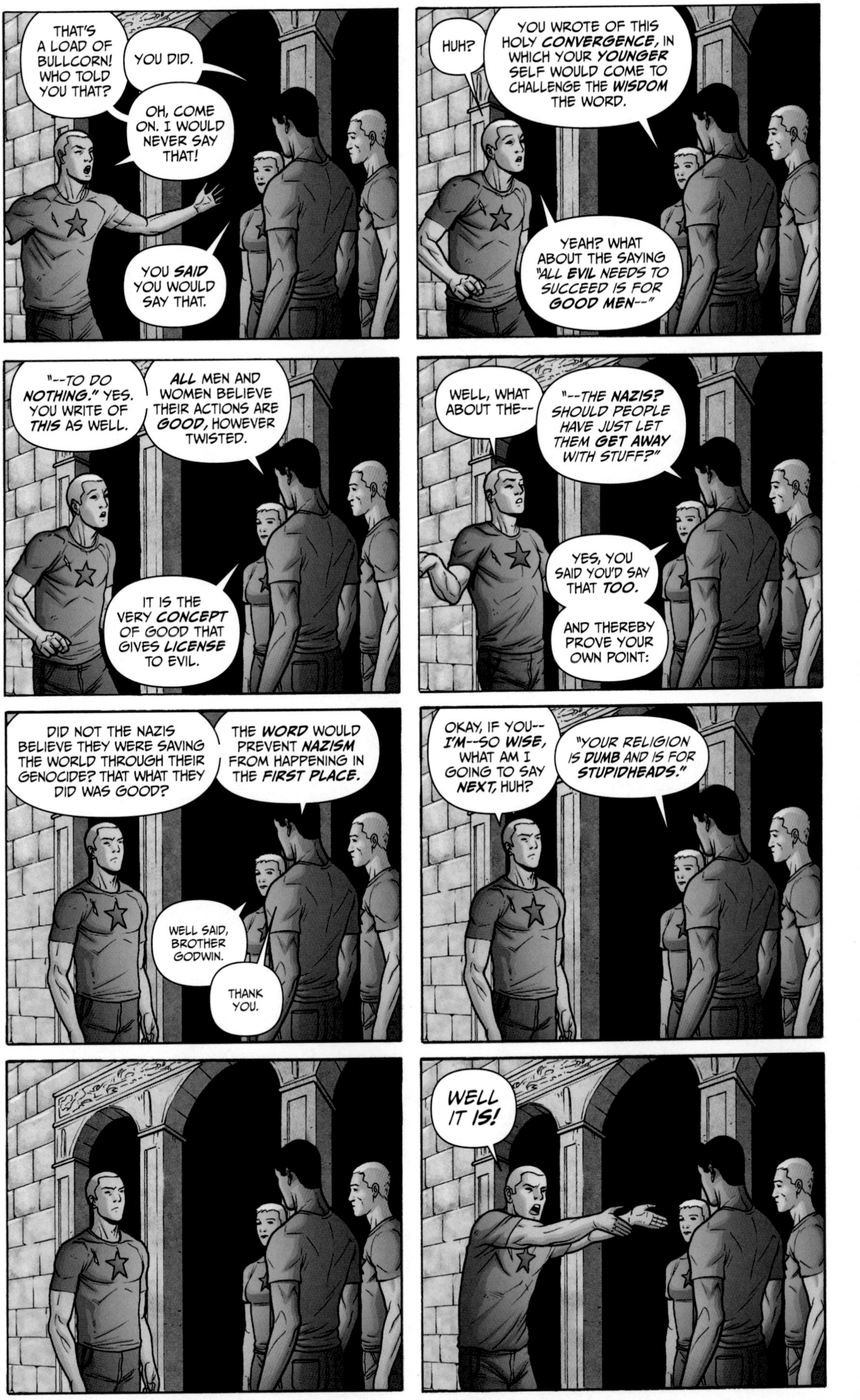
THAT'S A LOAD OF BULLCORN! WHO TOLD YOU THAT?
YOU DID.
OH, COME ON. I WOULD NEVER SAY THAT!
YOU SAID YOU WOULD SAY THAT.
HUH?
YOU WROTE OF THIS HOLY CONVERGENCE, IN WHICH YOUR YOUNGER SELF WOULD COME TO CHALLENGE THE WISDOM THE WORD.
YEAH? WHAT ABOUT THE SAYING "ALL EVIL NEEDS TO SUCCEED IS FOR GOOD MEN--"
"--TO DO NOTHING." YES. YOU WRITE OF THIS AS WELL.
ALL MEN AND WOMEN BELIEVE THEIR ACTIONS ARE GOOD, HOWEVER TWISTED.
IT IS THE VERY CONCEPT OF GOOD THAT GIVES LICENSE TO EVIL.
WELL, WHAT ABOUT THE--
"--THE NAZIS? SHOULD PEOPLE HAVE JUST LET THEM GET AWAY WITH STUFF?"
YES, YOU SAID YOU'D SAY THAT TOO.
AND THEREBY PROVE YOUR OWN POINT:
DID NOT THE NAZIS BELIEVE THEY WERE SAVING THE WORLD THROUGH THEIR GENOCIDE? THAT WHAT THEY DID WAS GOOD?
THE WORD WOULD PREVENT NAZISM FROM HAPPENING IN THE FIRST PLACE.
WELL SAID, BROTHER GODWIN.
THANK YOU.
OKAY, IF YOU-- I'M--SO WISE, WHAT AM I GOING TO SAY NEXT, HUH?
"YOUR RELIGION IS DUMB AND IS FOR STUPIDHEADS."
WELL IT IS!

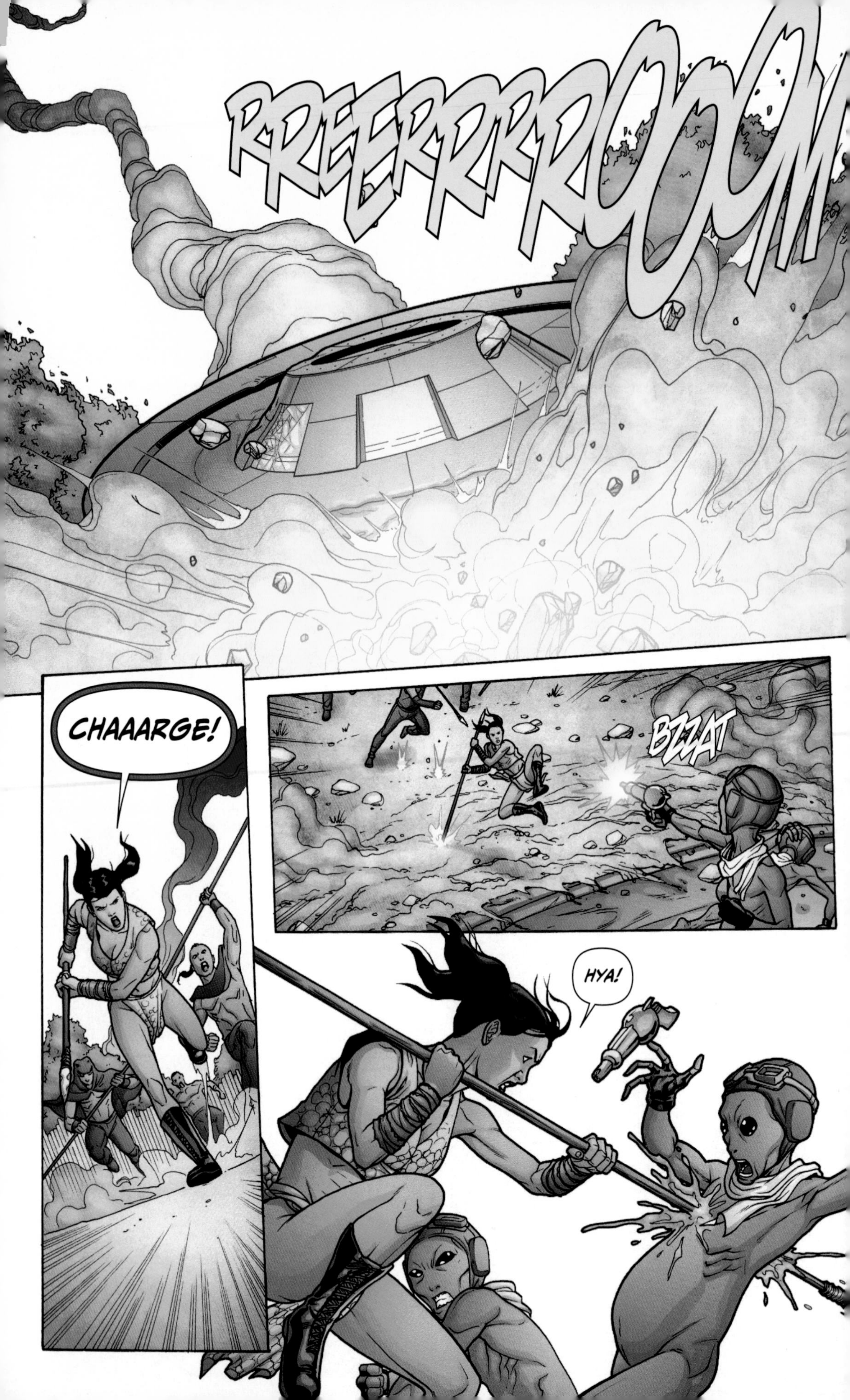
RREERRRROOOM
CHAAARGE!
BZZAT
HYA!

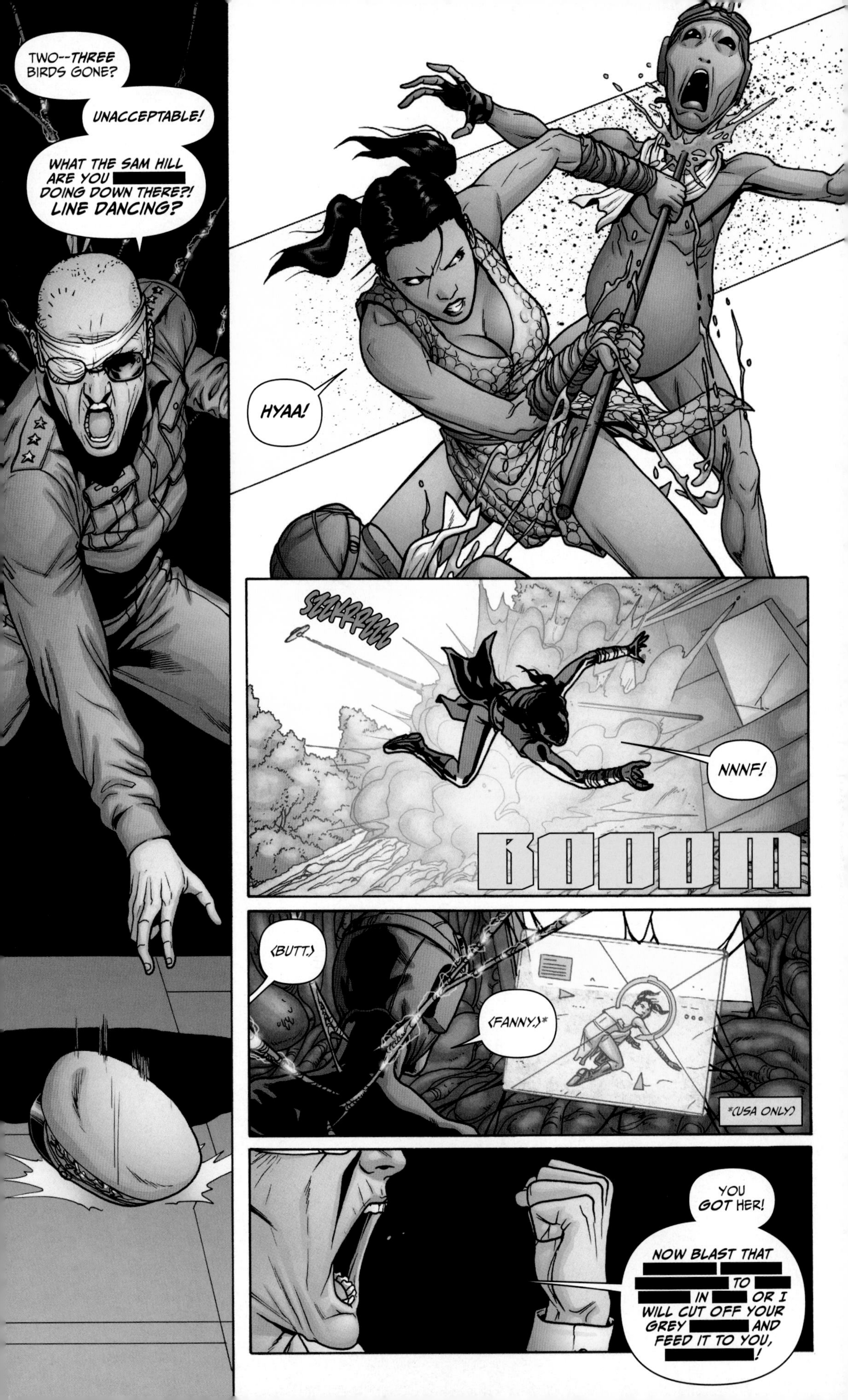

TWO--THREE BIRDS GONE?
UNACCEPTABLE!
WHAT THE SAM HILL ARE YOU [redacted] DOING DOWN THERE?! LINE DANCING?
HYAA!
NNNF!
BOOOM
‹BUTT.›
‹FANNY.›*
*(USA ONLY)
YOU GOT HER!
NOW BLAST THAT [redacted] TO [redacted] IN [redacted] OR I WILL CUT OFF YOUR GREY [redacted] AND FEED IT TO YOU, [redacted]!

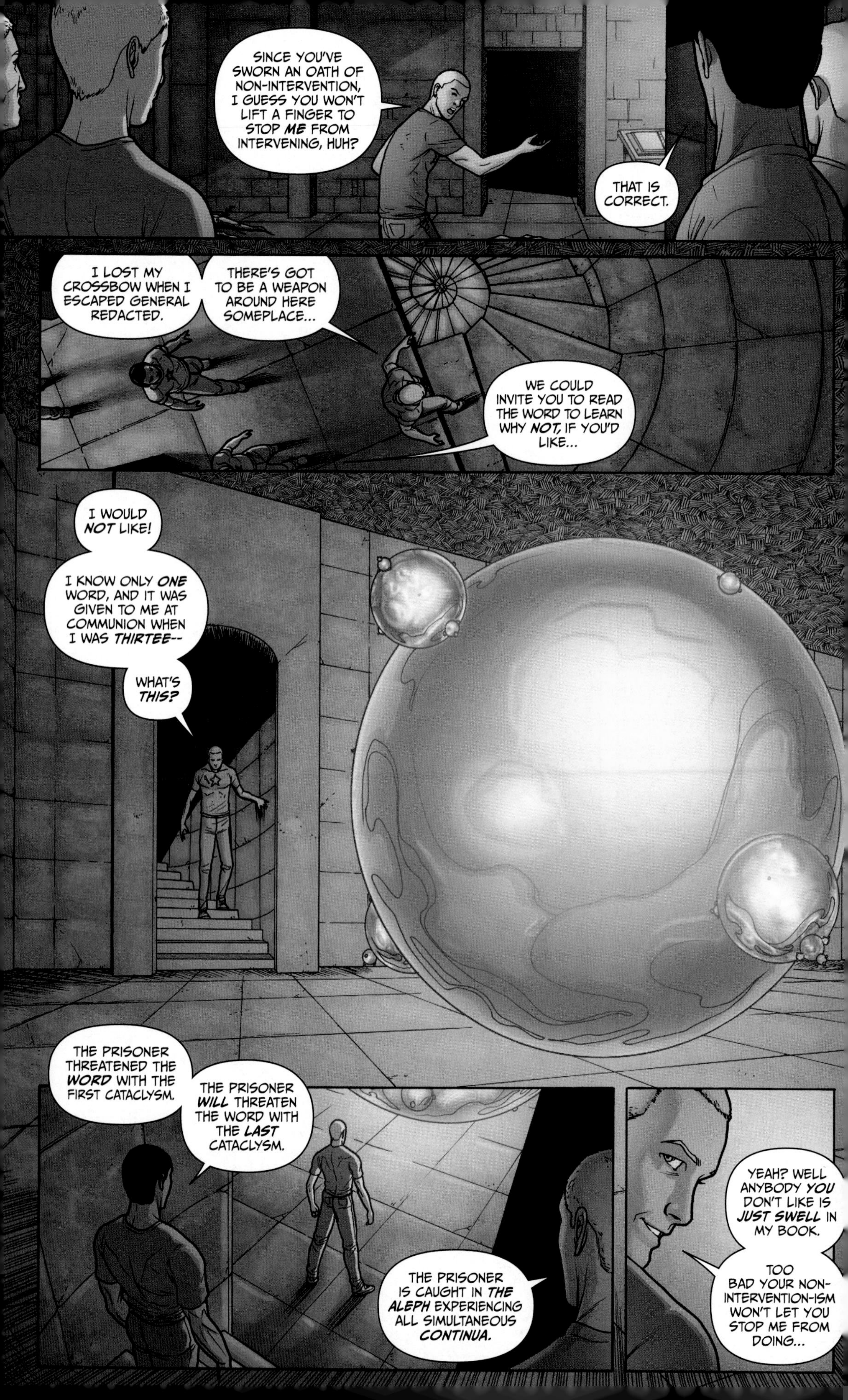

SINCE YOU'VE SWORN AN OATH OF NON-INTERVENTION, I GUESS YOU WON'T LIFT A FINGER TO STOP ME FROM INTERVENING, HUH?
THAT IS CORRECT.
I LOST MY CROSSBOW WHEN I ESCAPED GENERAL REDACTED.
THERE'S GOT TO BE A WEAPON AROUND HERE SOMEPLACE...
WE COULD INVITE YOU TO READ THE WORD TO LEARN WHY NOT, IF YOU'D LIKE...
I WOULD NOT LIKE!
I KNOW ONLY ONE WORD, AND IT WAS GIVEN TO ME AT COMMUNION WHEN I WAS THIRTEE--
WHAT'S THIS?
THE PRISONER THREATENED THE WORD WITH THE FIRST CATACLYSM.
THE PRISONER WILL THREATEN THE WORD WITH THE LAST CATACLYSM.
THE PRISONER IS CAUGHT IN THE ALEPH EXPERIENCING ALL SIMULTANEOUS CONTINUA.
YEAH? WELL ANYBODY YOU DON'T LIKE IS JUST SWELL IN MY BOOK.
TOO BAD YOUR NON-INTERVENTION-ISM WON'T LET YOU STOP ME FROM DOING...

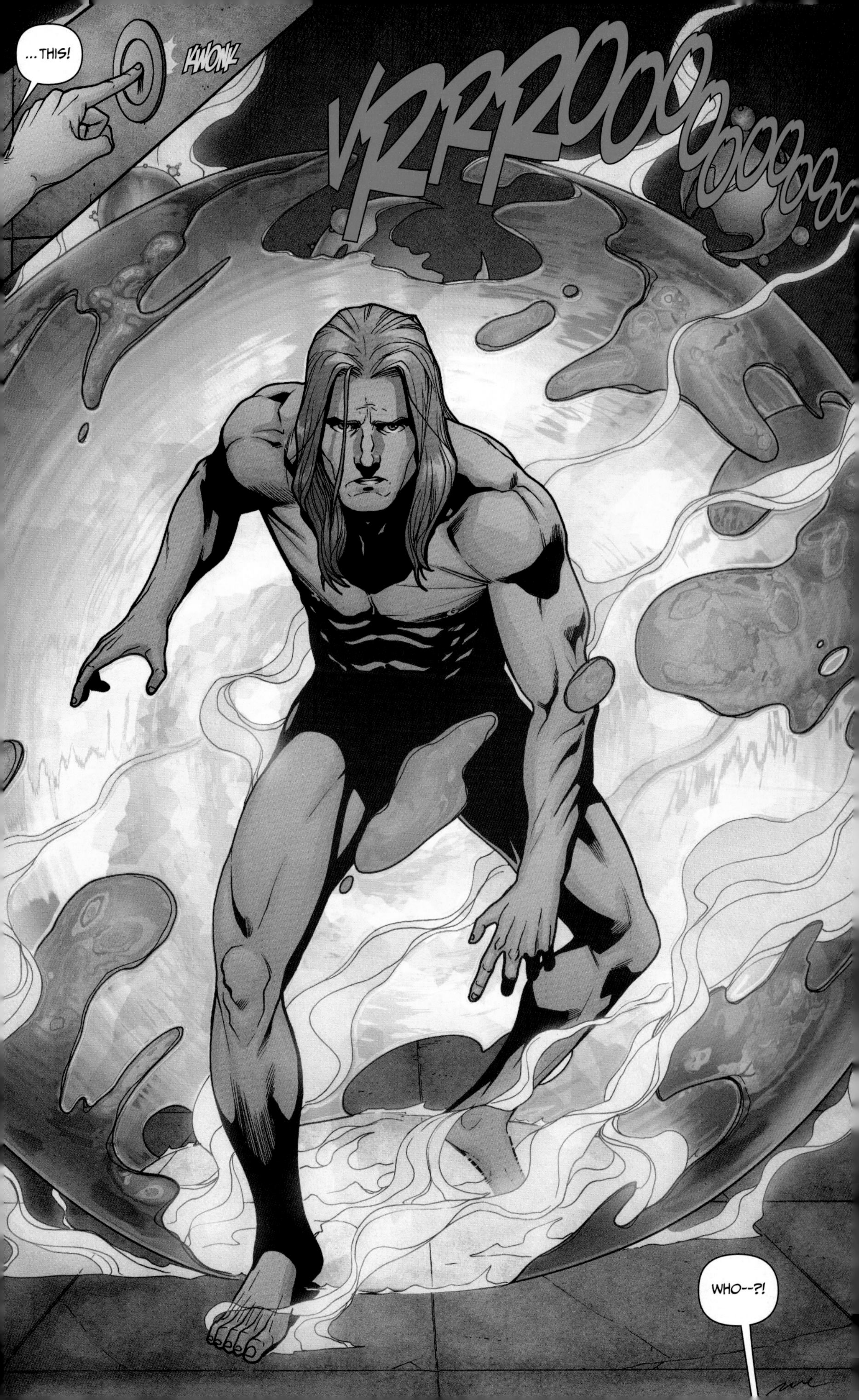
...THIS!
KWONK
VRRROOOOOOOOOOO
WHO--?!

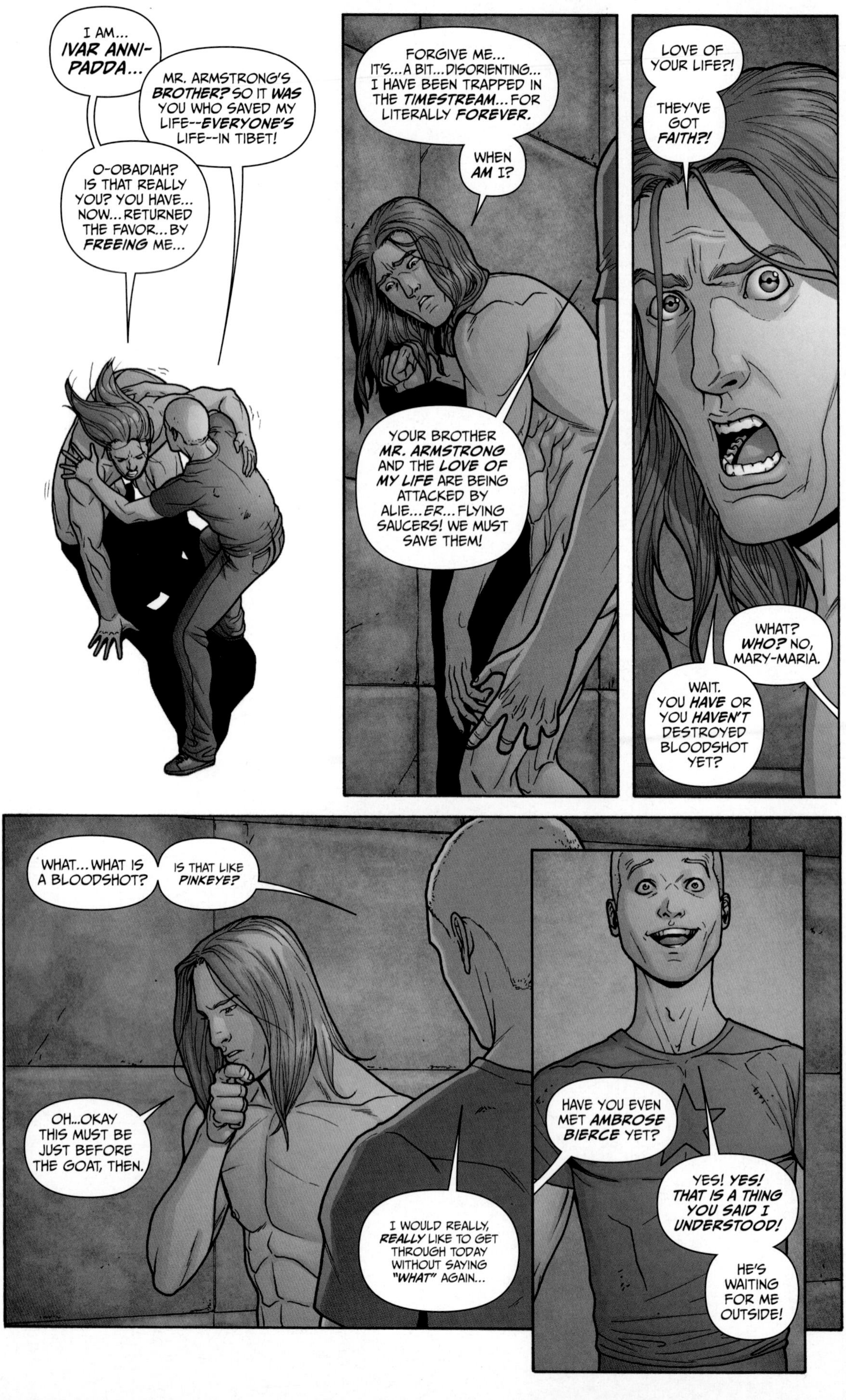
I AM... IVAR ANNI-PADDA...
MR. ARMSTRONG'S BROTHER? SO IT WAS YOU WHO SAVED MY LIFE--EVERYONE'S LIFE--IN TIBET!
O-OBADIAH? IS THAT REALLY YOU? YOU HAVE... NOW... RETURNED THE FAVOR... BY FREEING ME...
FORGIVE ME... IT'S... A BIT... DISORIENTING... I HAVE BEEN TRAPPED IN THE TIMESTREAM... FOR LITERALLY FOREVER.
WHEN AM I?
YOUR BROTHER MR. ARMSTRONG AND THE LOVE OF MY LIFE ARE BEING ATTACKED BY ALIE... ER... FLYING SAUCERS! WE MUST SAVE THEM!
LOVE OF YOUR LIFE?!
THEY'VE GOT FAITH?!
WHAT? WHO? NO, MARY-MARIA.
WAIT. YOU HAVE OR YOU HAVEN'T DESTROYED BLOODSHOT YET?
WHAT... WHAT IS A BLOODSHOT?
IS THAT LIKE PINKEYE?
OH...OKAY THIS MUST BE JUST BEFORE THE GOAT, THEN.
I WOULD REALLY, REALLY LIKE TO GET THROUGH TODAY WITHOUT SAYING "WHAT" AGAIN...
HAVE YOU EVEN MET AMBROSE BIERCE YET?
YES! YES! THAT IS A THING YOU SAID I UNDERSTOOD!
HE'S WAITING FOR ME OUTSIDE!

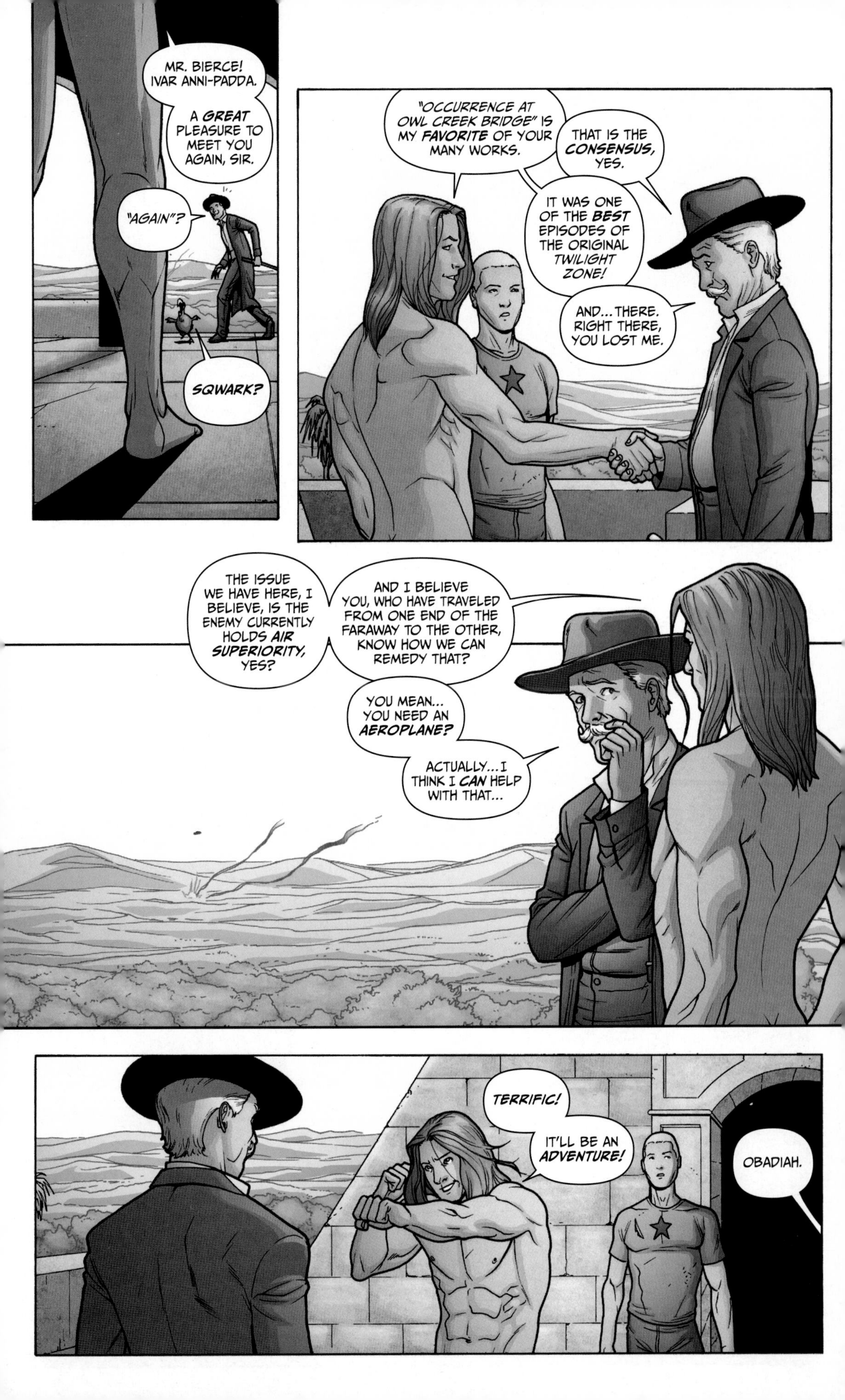
MR. BIERCE! IVAR ANNI-PADDA.
A GREAT PLEASURE TO MEET YOU AGAIN, SIR.
"AGAIN"?
SQWARK?
"OCCURRENCE AT OWL CREEK BRIDGE" IS MY FAVORITE OF YOUR MANY WORKS.
THAT IS THE CONSENSUS, YES.
IT WAS ONE OF THE BEST EPISODES OF THE ORIGINAL TWILIGHT ZONE!
AND... THERE. RIGHT THERE, YOU LOST ME.
THE ISSUE WE HAVE HERE, I BELIEVE, IS THE ENEMY CURRENTLY HOLDS AIR SUPERIORITY, YES?
AND I BELIEVE YOU, WHO HAVE TRAVELED FROM ONE END OF THE FARAWAY TO THE OTHER, KNOW HOW WE CAN REMEDY THAT?
YOU MEAN... YOU NEED AN AEROPLANE?
ACTUALLY... I THINK I CAN HELP WITH THAT...
TERRIFIC!
IT'LL BE AN ADVENTURE!
OBADIAH.

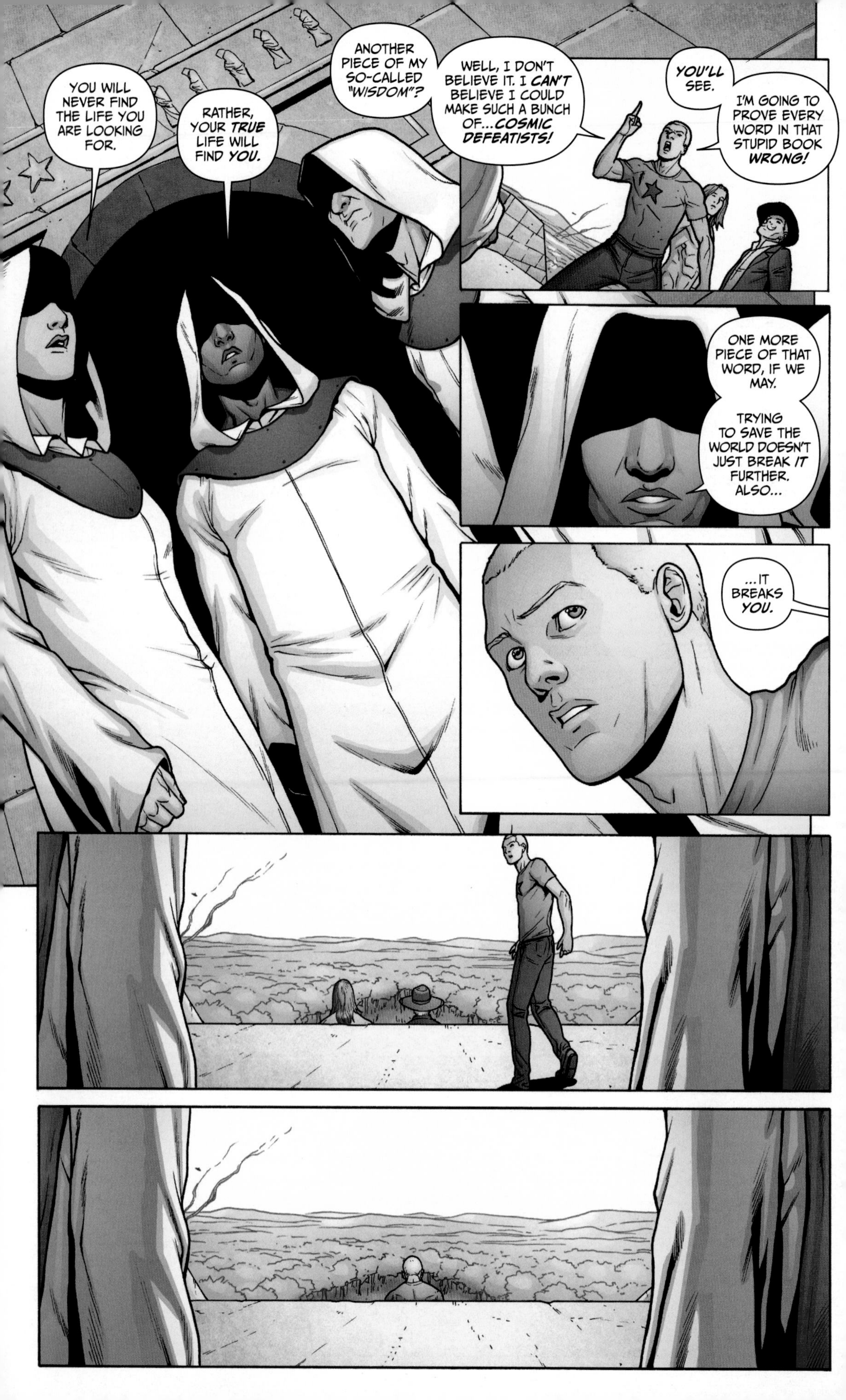
YOU WILL NEVER FIND THE LIFE YOU ARE LOOKING FOR.
RATHER, YOUR TRUE LIFE WILL FIND YOU.
ANOTHER PIECE OF MY SO-CALLED "WISDOM"?
WELL, I DON'T BELIEVE IT. I CAN'T BELIEVE I COULD MAKE SUCH A BUNCH OF...COSMIC DEFEATISTS!
YOU'LL SEE.
I'M GOING TO PROVE EVERY WORD IN THAT STUPID BOOK WRONG!
ONE MORE PIECE OF THAT WORD, IF WE MAY.
TRYING TO SAVE THE WORLD DOESN'T JUST BREAK IT FURTHER. ALSO...
...IT BREAKS YOU.

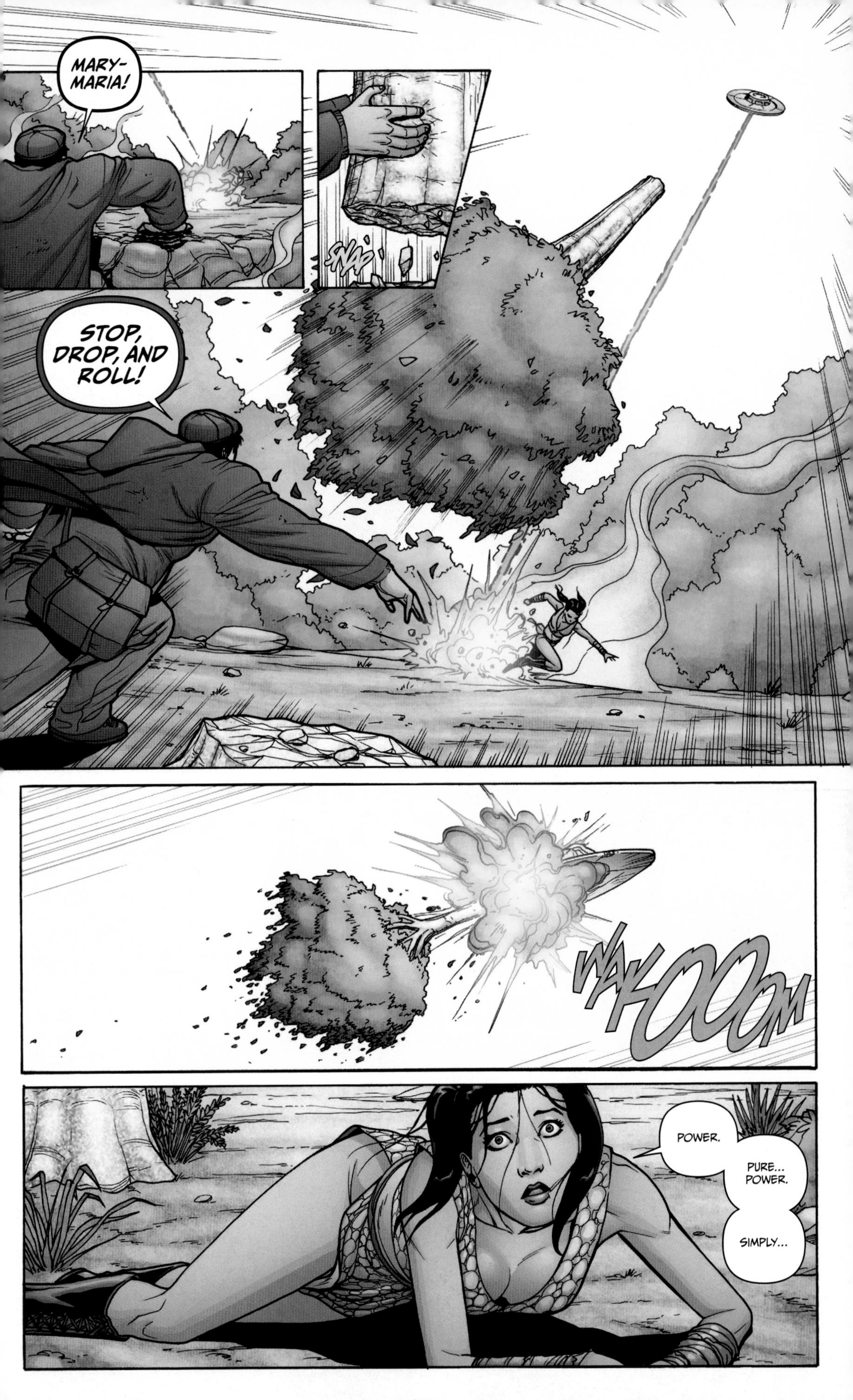
MARY-MARIA!
SNAP
STOP, DROP, AND ROLL!
WAKOOOM
POWER.
PURE... POWER.
SIMPLY...

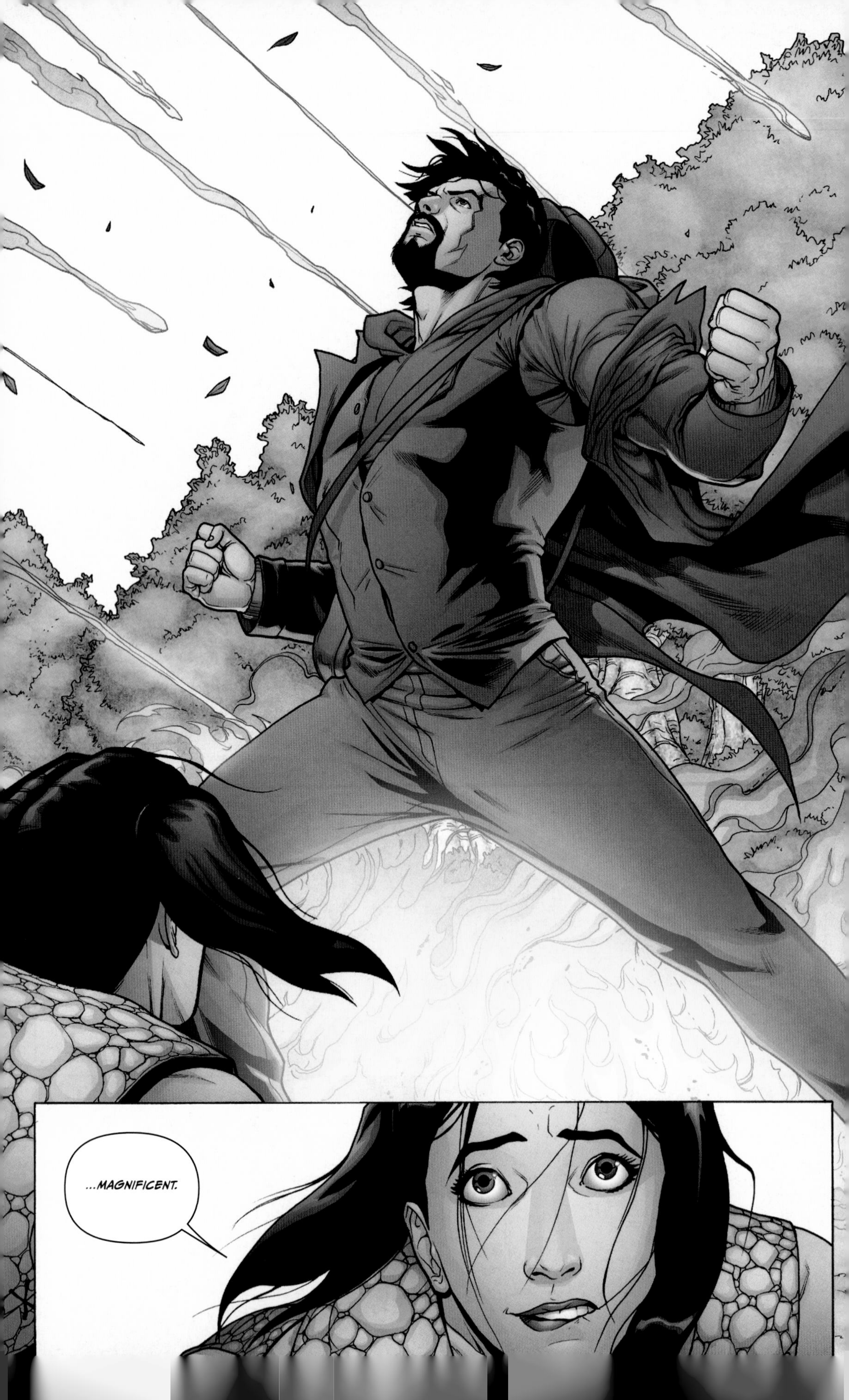
...MAGNIFICENT.

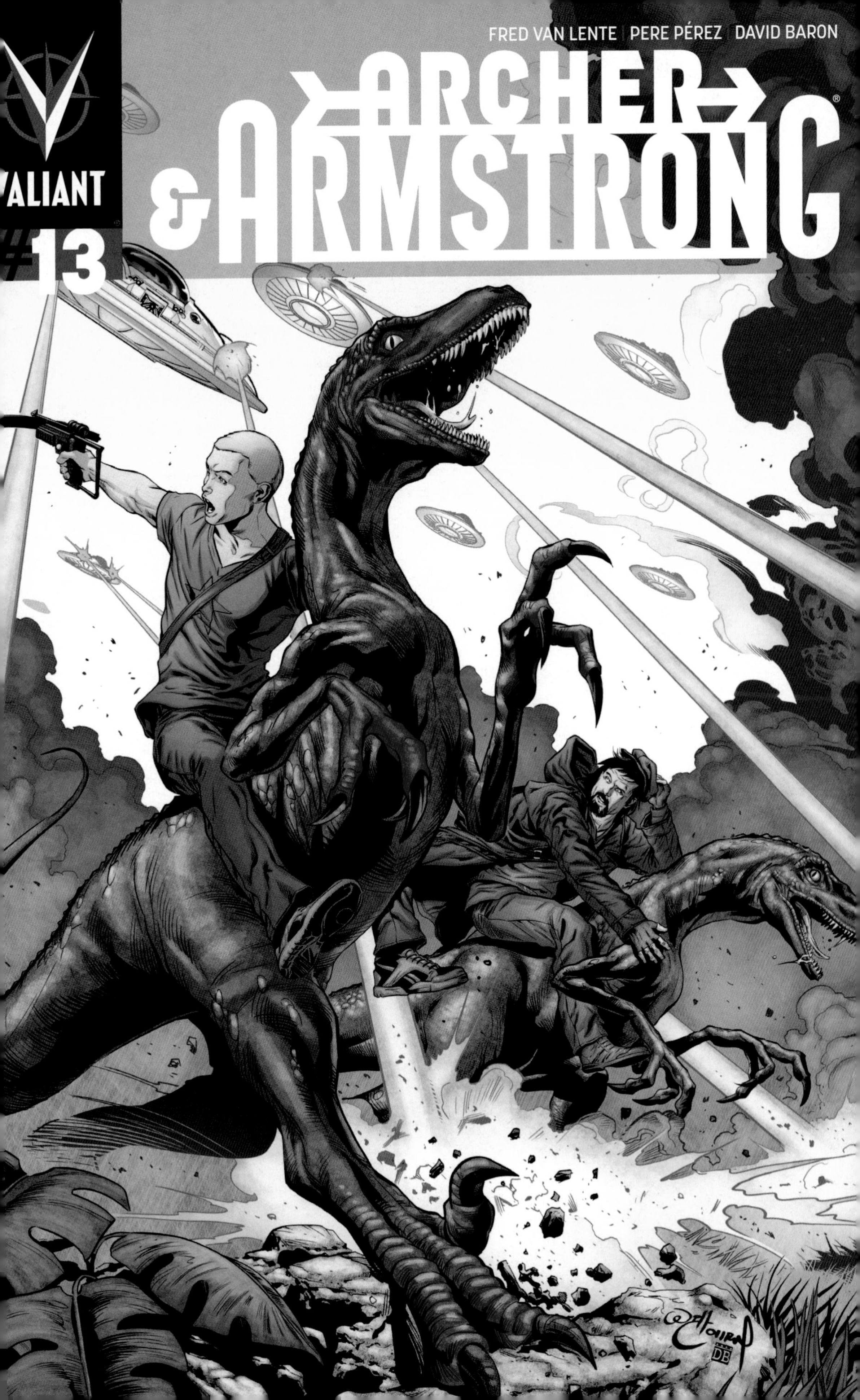
FRED VAN LENTE | PERE PÉREZ | DAVID BARON
VALIANT
ARCHER & ARMSTRONG
#13

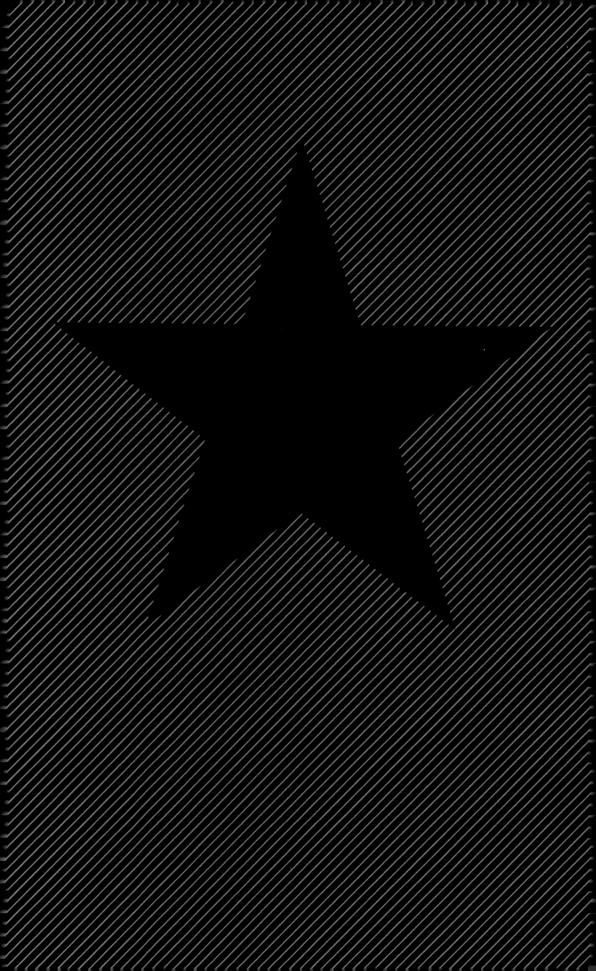

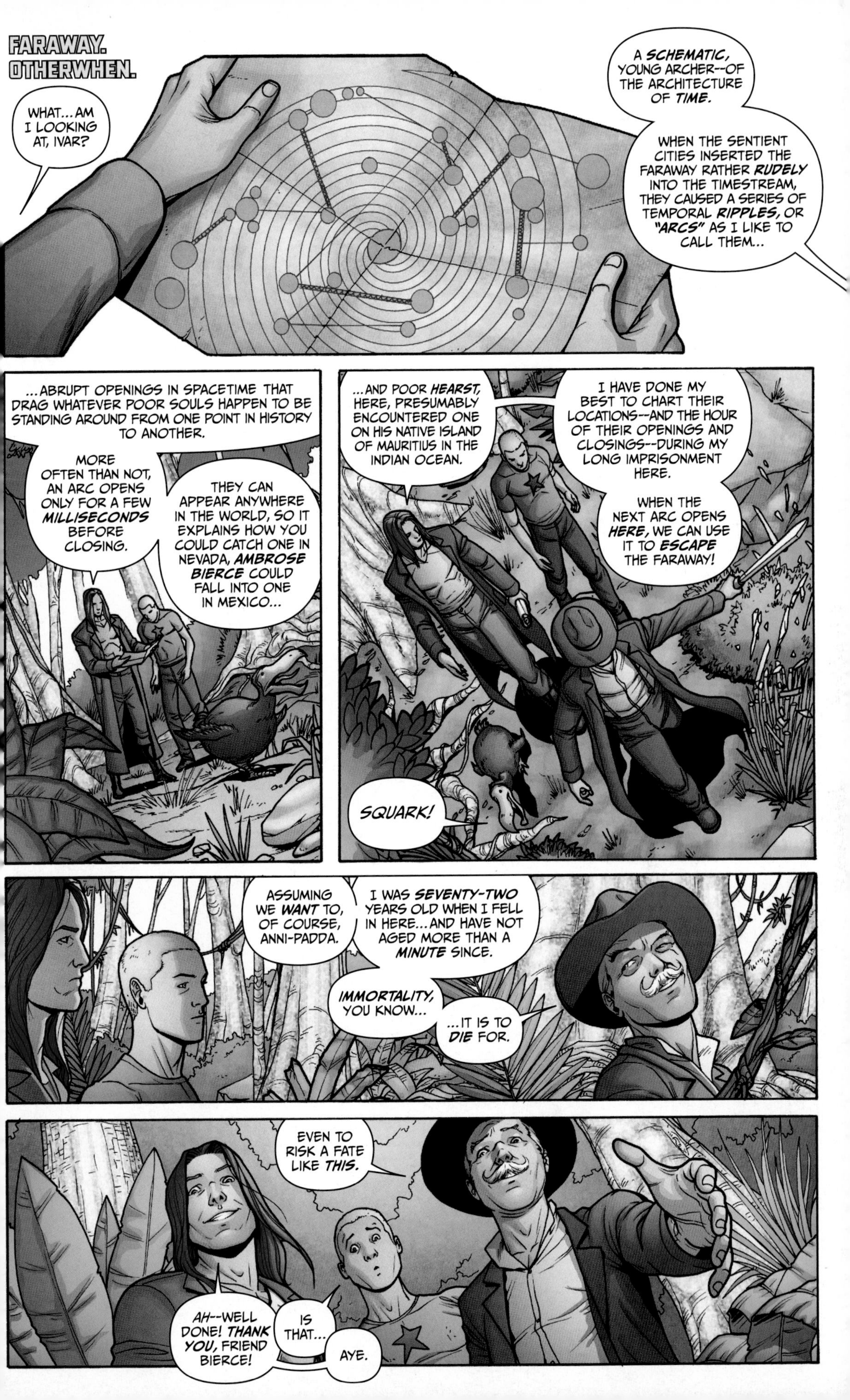
FARAWAY. OTHERWHEN.
WHAT... AM I LOOKING AT, IVAR?
A SCHEMATIC, YOUNG ARCHER--OF THE ARCHITECTURE OF TIME.
WHEN THE SENTIENT CITIES INSERTED THE FARAWAY RATHER RUDELY INTO THE TIMESTREAM, THEY CAUSED A SERIES OF TEMPORAL RIPPLES, OR "ARCS" AS I LIKE TO CALL THEM...
...ABRUPT OPENINGS IN SPACETIME THAT DRAG WHATEVER POOR SOULS HAPPEN TO BE STANDING AROUND FROM ONE POINT IN HISTORY TO ANOTHER.
MORE OFTEN THAN NOT, AN ARC OPENS ONLY FOR A FEW MILLISECONDS BEFORE CLOSING.
THEY CAN APPEAR ANYWHERE IN THE WORLD, SO IT EXPLAINS HOW YOU COULD CATCH ONE IN NEVADA, AMBROSE BIERCE COULD FALL INTO ONE IN MEXICO...
...AND POOR HEARST, HERE, PRESUMABLY ENCOUNTERED ONE ON HIS NATIVE ISLAND OF MAURITIUS IN THE INDIAN OCEAN.
I HAVE DONE MY BEST TO CHART THEIR LOCATIONS--AND THE HOUR OF THEIR OPENINGS AND CLOSINGS--DURING MY LONG IMPRISONMENT HERE.
WHEN THE NEXT ARC OPENS HERE, WE CAN USE IT TO ESCAPE THE FARAWAY!
SQUARK!
ASSUMING WE WANT TO, OF COURSE, ANNI-PADDA.
I WAS SEVENTY-TWO YEARS OLD WHEN I FELL IN HERE... AND HAVE NOT AGED MORE THAN A MINUTE SINCE.
IMMORTALITY, YOU KNOW...
...IT IS TO DIE FOR.
EVEN TO RISK A FATE LIKE THIS.
AH--WELL DONE! THANK YOU, FRIEND BIERCE!
IS THAT...
AYE.

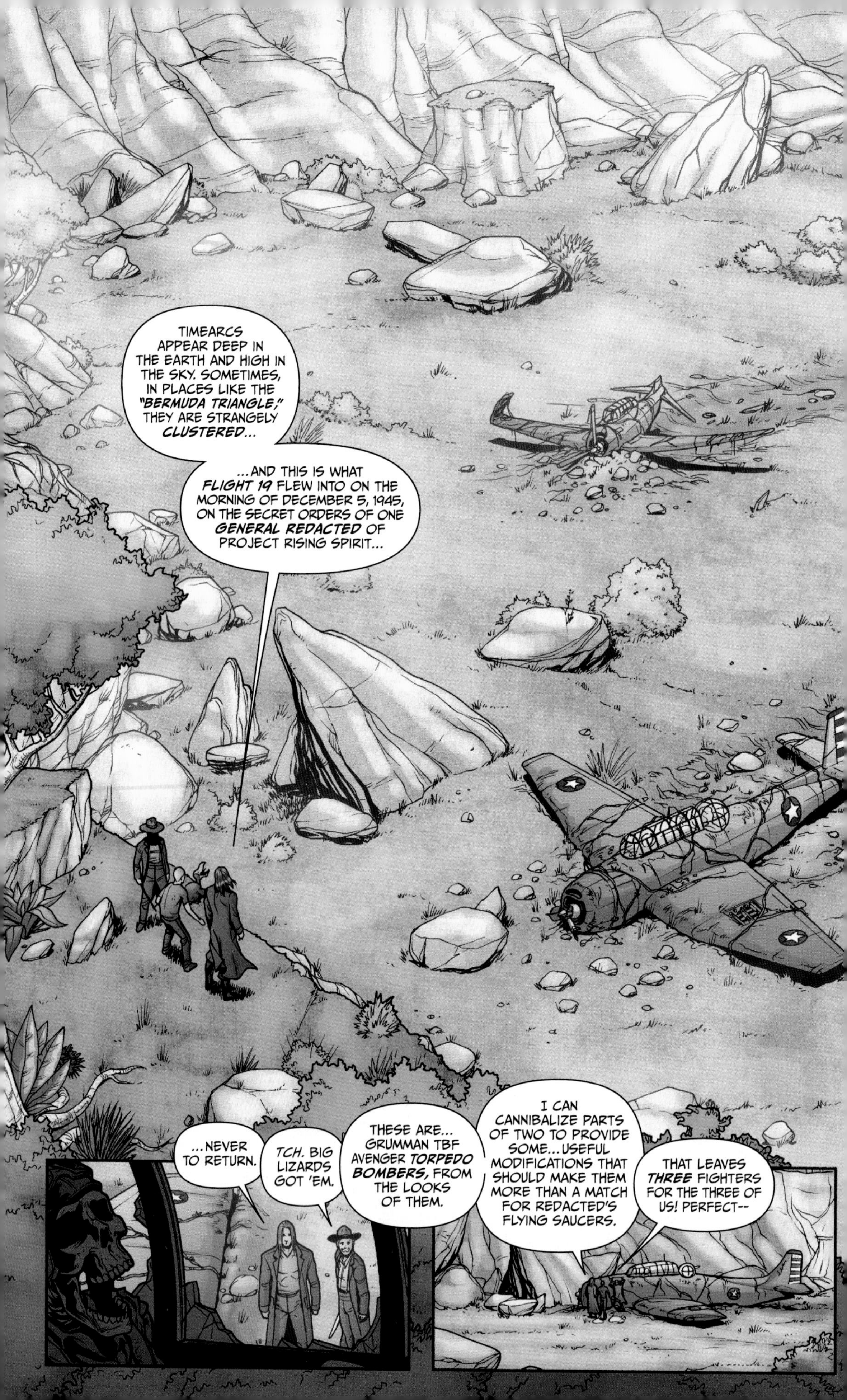
TIMEARCS APPEAR DEEP IN THE EARTH AND HIGH IN THE SKY. SOMETIMES, IN PLACES LIKE THE *"BERMUDA TRIANGLE,"* THEY ARE STRANGELY *CLUSTERED*...
...AND THIS IS WHAT *FLIGHT 19* FLEW INTO ON THE MORNING OF DECEMBER 5, 1945, ON THE SECRET ORDERS OF ONE *GENERAL REDACTED* OF PROJECT RISING SPIRIT...
...NEVER TO RETURN.
TCH. BIG LIZARDS GOT 'EM.
THESE ARE... GRUMMAN TBF AVENGER *TORPEDO BOMBERS,* FROM THE LOOKS OF THEM.
I CAN CANNIBALIZE PARTS OF TWO TO PROVIDE SOME...USEFUL MODIFICATIONS THAT SHOULD MAKE THEM MORE THAN A MATCH FOR REDACTED'S FLYING SAUCERS.
THAT LEAVES *THREE* FIGHTERS FOR THE THREE OF US! PERFECT--

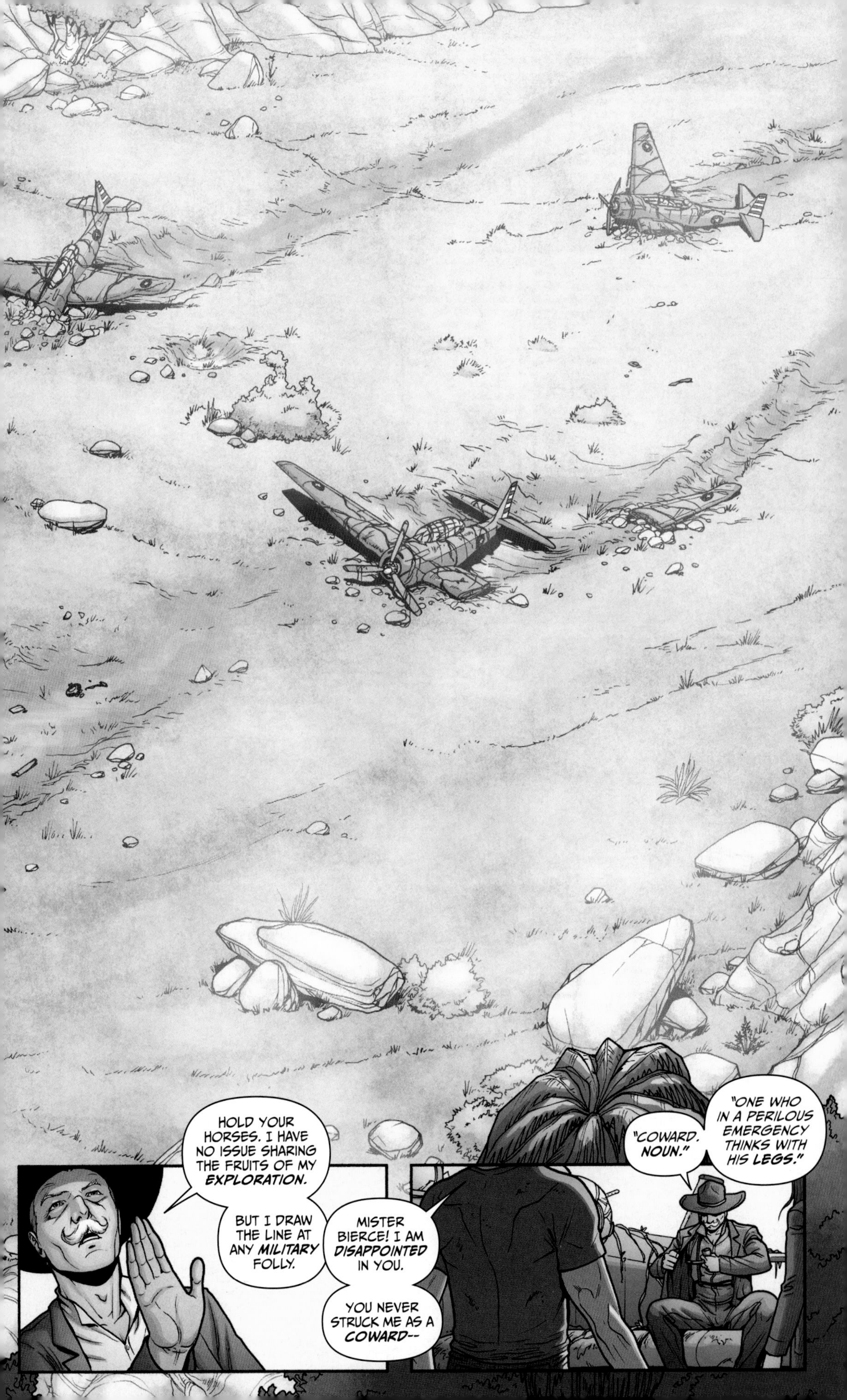
HOLD YOUR HORSES. I HAVE NO ISSUE SHARING THE FRUITS OF MY EXPLORATION.
BUT I DRAW THE LINE AT ANY MILITARY FOLLY.
MISTER BIERCE! I AM DISAPPOINTED IN YOU.
YOU NEVER STRUCK ME AS A COWARD--
"COWARD. NOUN."
"ONE WHO IN A PERILOUS EMERGENCY THINKS WITH HIS LEGS."

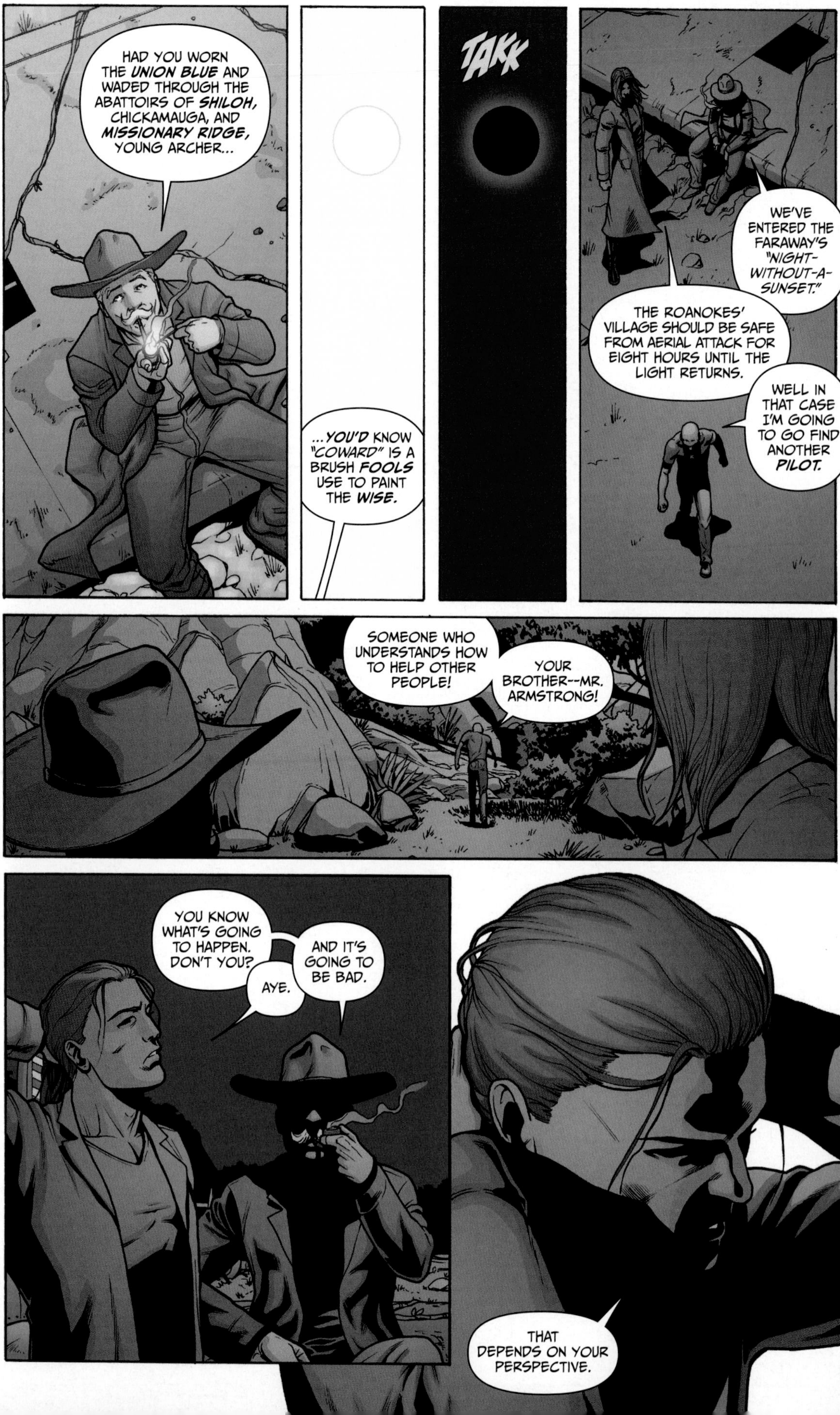
HAD YOU WORN THE UNION BLUE AND WADED THROUGH THE ABATTOIRS OF SHILOH, CHICKAMAUGA, AND MISSIONARY RIDGE, YOUNG ARCHER...
...YOU'D KNOW "COWARD" IS A BRUSH FOOLS USE TO PAINT THE WISE.
TAKK
WE'VE ENTERED THE FARAWAY'S "NIGHT-WITHOUT-A-SUNSET."
THE ROANOKES' VILLAGE SHOULD BE SAFE FROM AERIAL ATTACK FOR EIGHT HOURS UNTIL THE LIGHT RETURNS.
WELL IN THAT CASE I'M GOING TO GO FIND ANOTHER PILOT.
SOMEONE WHO UNDERSTANDS HOW TO HELP OTHER PEOPLE!
YOUR BROTHER--MR. ARMSTRONG!
YOU KNOW WHAT'S GOING TO HAPPEN. DON'T YOU?
AYE.
AND IT'S GOING TO BE BAD.
THAT DEPENDS ON YOUR PERSPECTIVE.

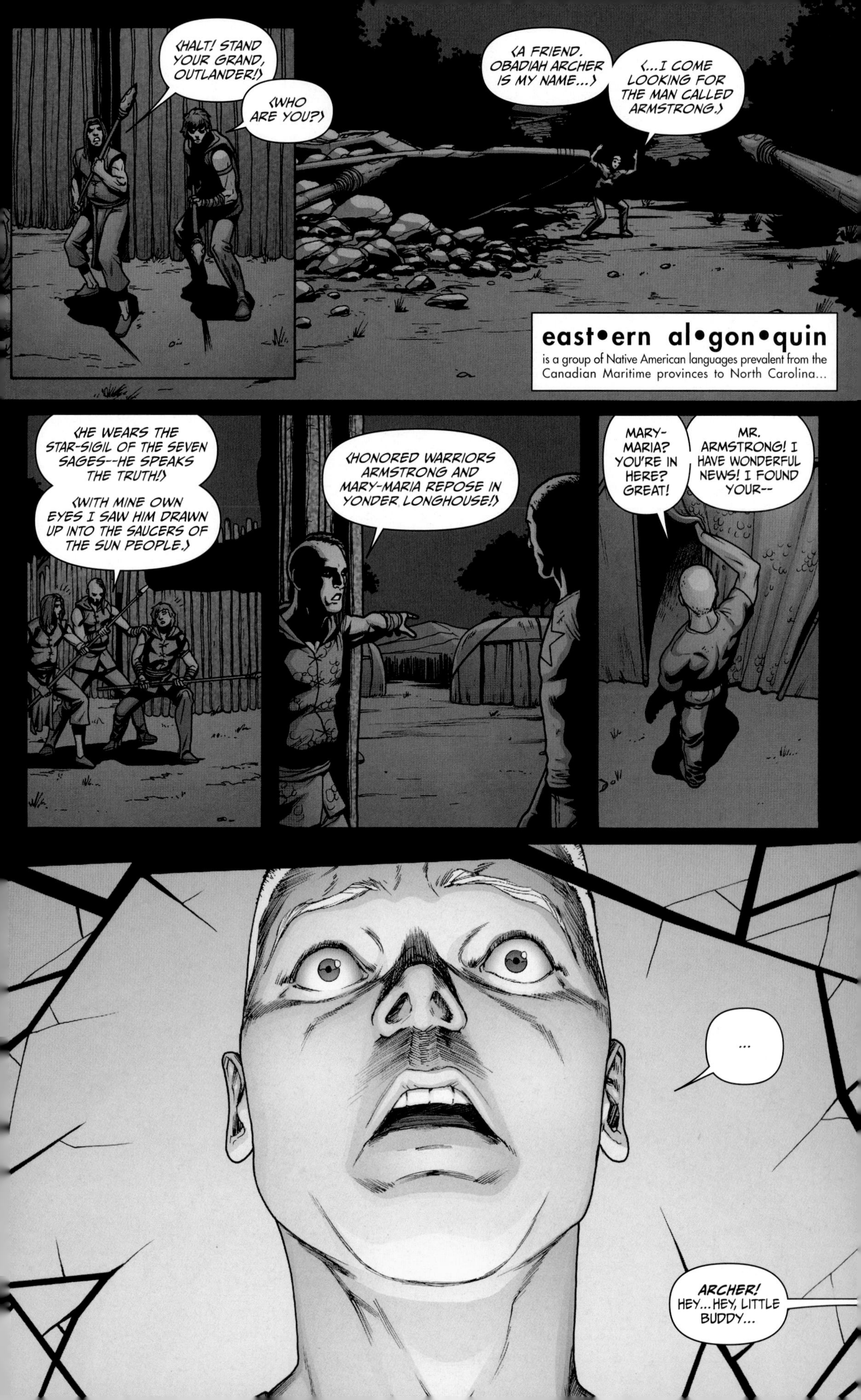

‹HALT! STAND YOUR GRAND, OUTLANDER!›
‹WHO ARE YOU?›
‹A FRIEND. OBADIAH ARCHER IS MY NAME...›
‹...I COME LOOKING FOR THE MAN CALLED ARMSTRONG.›
east•ern al•gon•quin
is a group of Native American languages prevalent from the Canadian Maritime provinces to North Carolina...
‹HE WEARS THE STAR-SIGIL OF THE SEVEN SAGES--HE SPEAKS THE TRUTH!›
‹WITH MINE OWN EYES I SAW HIM DRAWN UP INTO THE SAUCERS OF THE SUN PEOPLE.›
‹HONORED WARRIORS ARMSTRONG AND MARY-MARIA REPOSE IN YONDER LONGHOUSE!›
MR. ARMSTRONG! I HAVE WONDERFUL NEWS! I FOUND YOUR--
MARY-MARIA? YOU'RE IN HERE? GREAT!
...
ARCHER! HEY...HEY, LITTLE BUDDY...

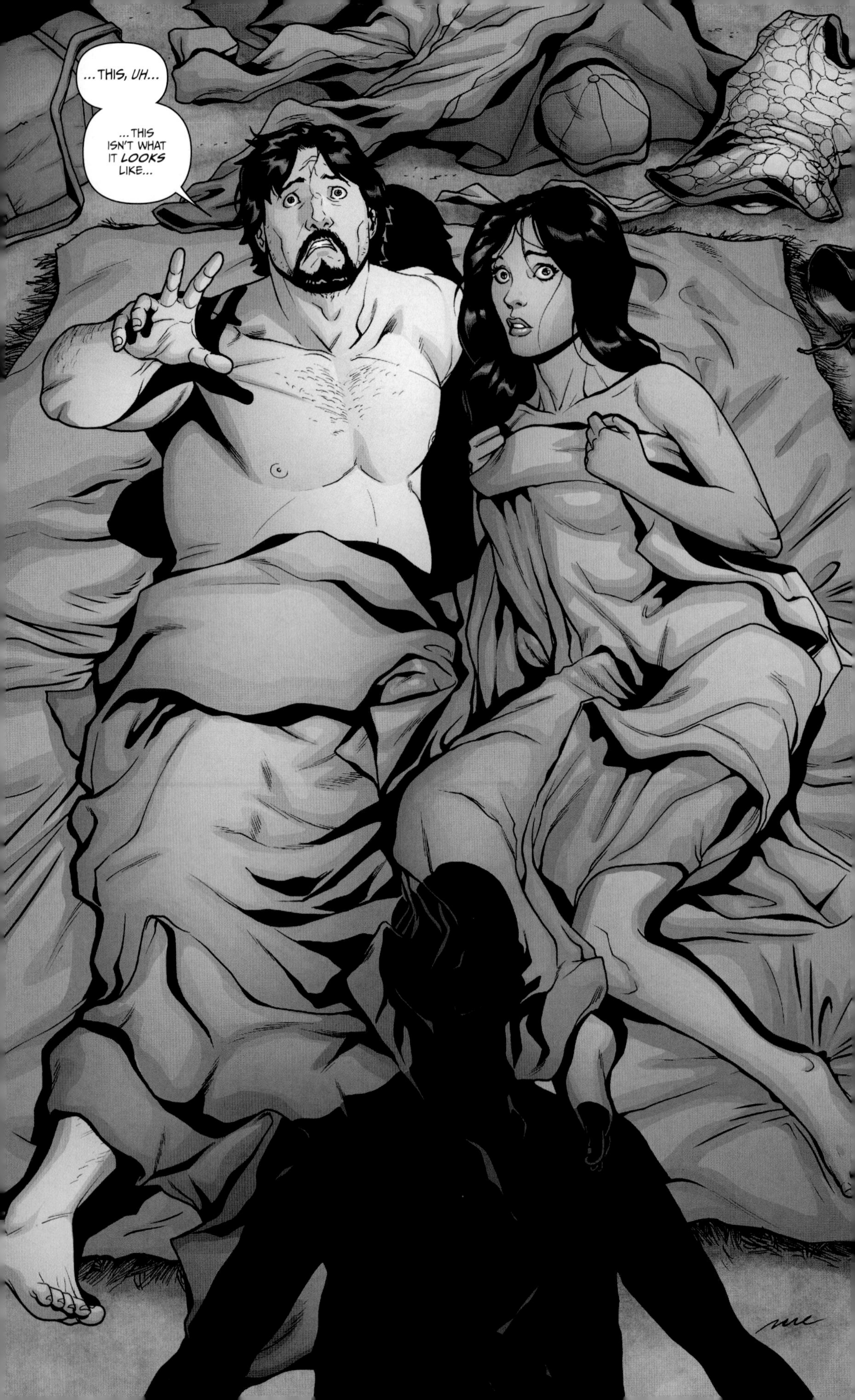
...THIS, UH...
...THIS ISN'T WHAT IT LOOKS LIKE...

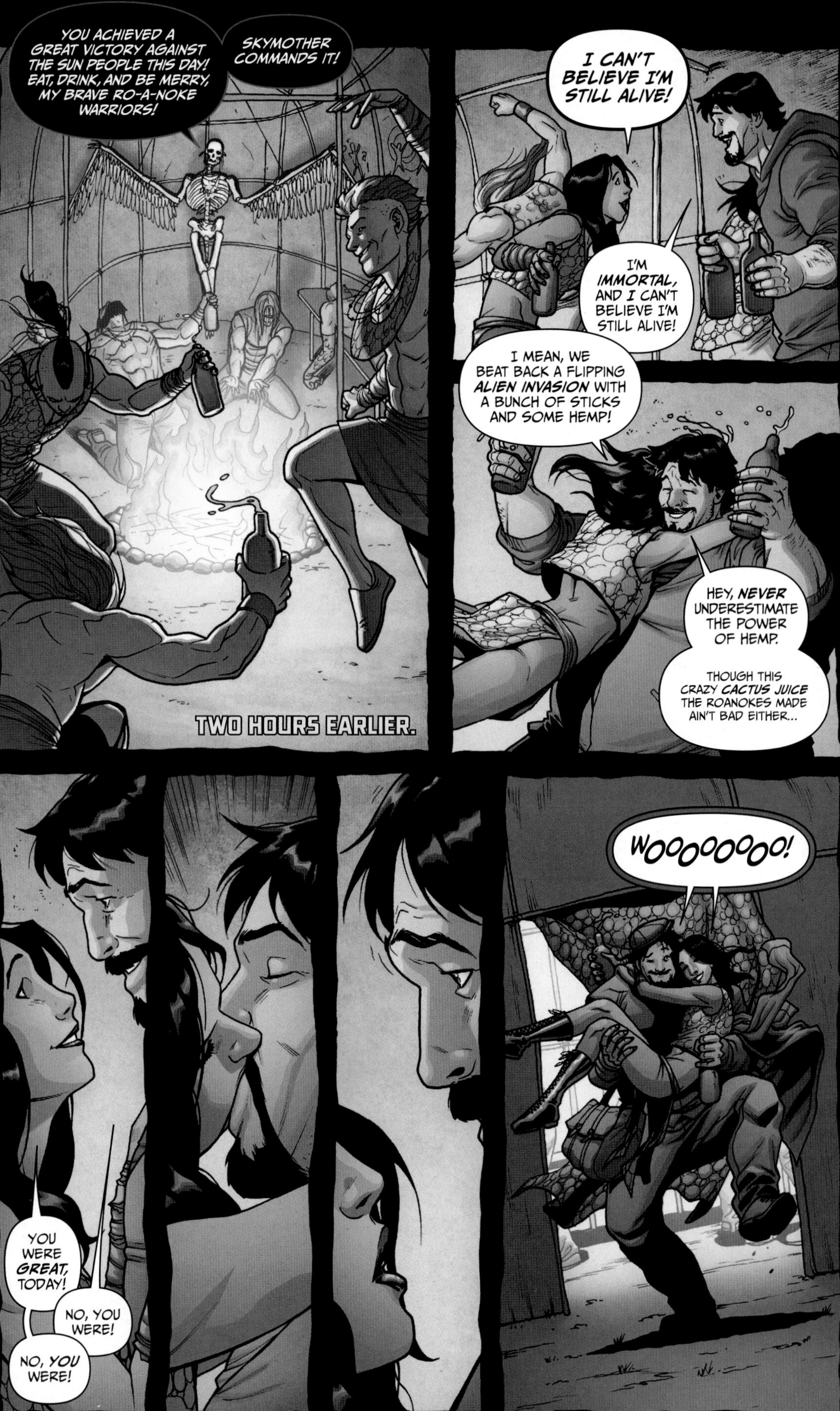

YOU ACHIEVED A GREAT VICTORY AGAINST THE SUN PEOPLE THIS DAY! EAT, DRINK, AND BE MERRY, MY BRAVE RO-A-NOKE WARRIORS!
SKYMOTHER COMMANDS IT!
TWO HOURS EARLIER.
I CAN'T BELIEVE I'M STILL ALIVE!
I'M IMMORTAL, AND I CAN'T BELIEVE I'M STILL ALIVE!
I MEAN, WE BEAT BACK A FLIPPING ALIEN INVASION WITH A BUNCH OF STICKS AND SOME HEMP!
HEY, NEVER UNDERESTIMATE THE POWER OF HEMP.
THOUGH THIS CRAZY CACTUS JUICE THE ROANOKES MADE AIN'T BAD EITHER...
YOU WERE GREAT, TODAY!
NO, YOU WERE!
NO, YOU WERE!
WOOOOOOOO!

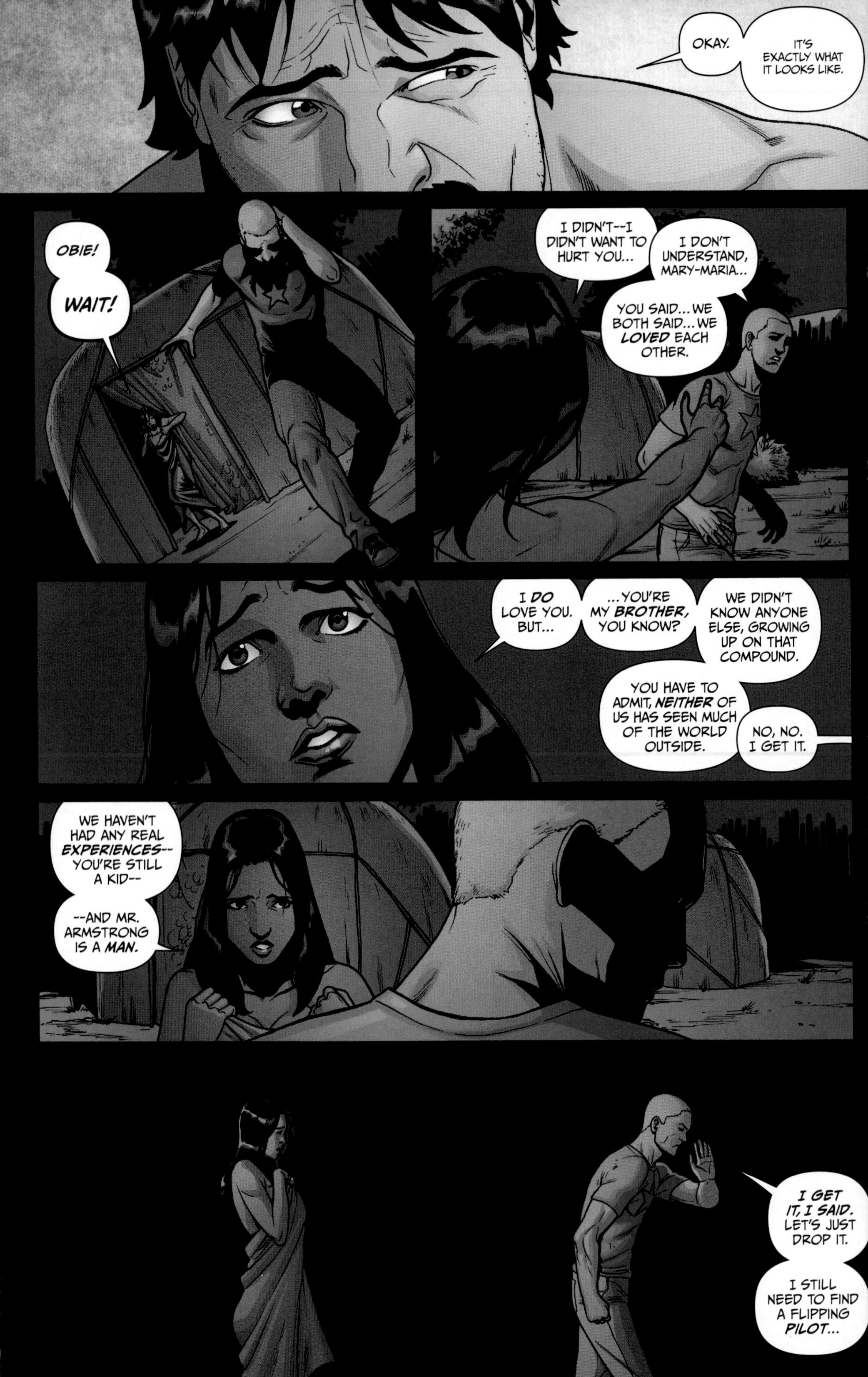
OKAY.
IT'S EXACTLY WHAT IT LOOKS LIKE.
OBIE!
WAIT!
I DIDN'T--I DIDN'T WANT TO HURT YOU...
I DON'T UNDERSTAND, MARY-MARIA...
YOU SAID... WE BOTH SAID... WE *LOVED* EACH OTHER.
I *DO* LOVE YOU. BUT...
...YOU'RE MY *BROTHER,* YOU KNOW?
WE DIDN'T KNOW ANYONE ELSE, GROWING UP ON THAT COMPOUND.
YOU HAVE TO ADMIT, *NEITHER* OF US HAS SEEN MUCH OF THE WORLD OUTSIDE.
NO, NO. I GET IT.
WE HAVEN'T HAD ANY REAL *EXPERIENCES*--YOU'RE STILL A KID--
--AND MR. ARMSTRONG IS A *MAN.*
I GET IT, I SAID. LET'S JUST DROP IT.
I STILL NEED TO FIND A FLIPPING *PILOT*...

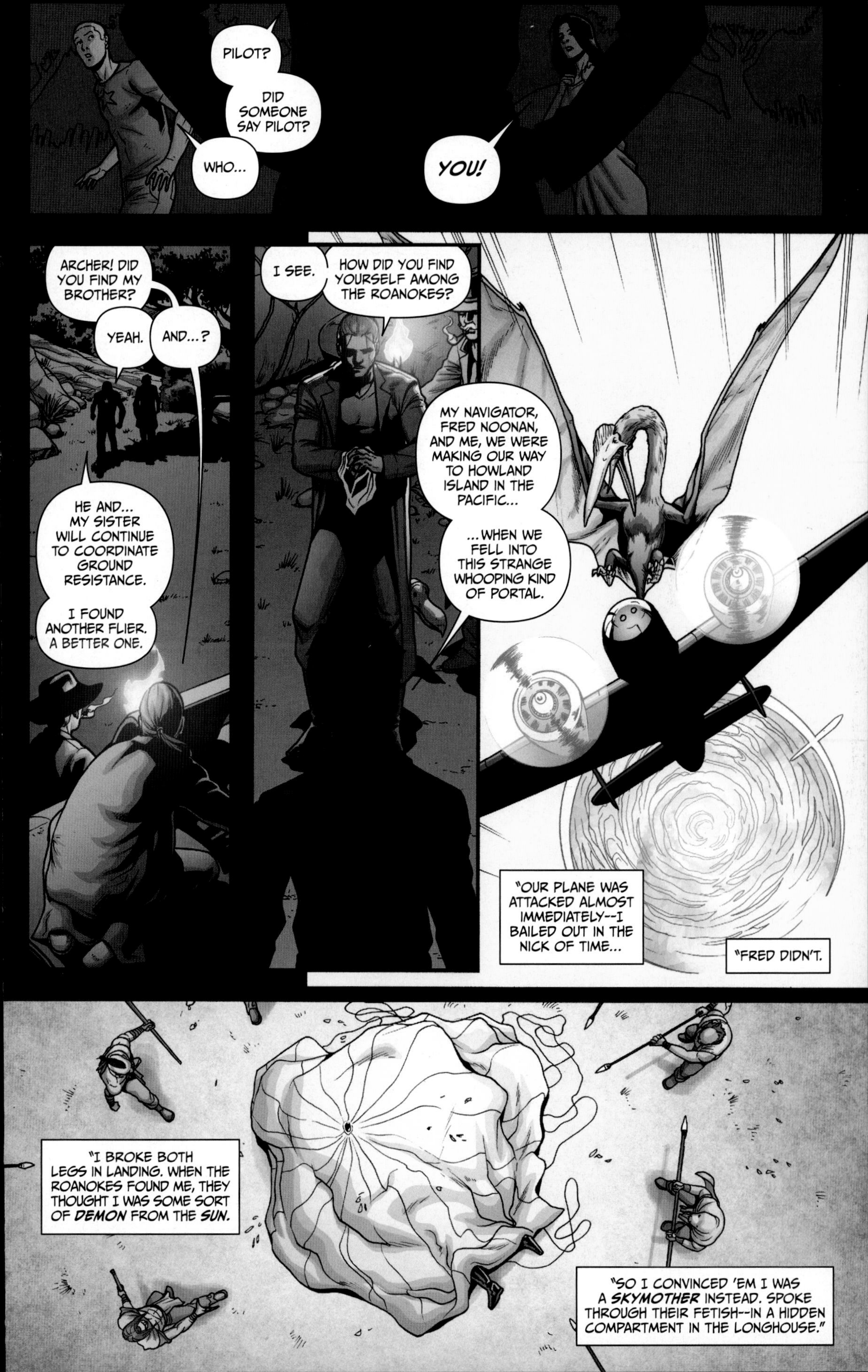
PILOT?
DID SOMEONE SAY PILOT?
WHO...
YOU!
ARCHER! DID YOU FIND MY BROTHER?
YEAH.
AND...?
HE AND... MY SISTER WILL CONTINUE TO COORDINATE GROUND RESISTANCE.
I FOUND ANOTHER FLIER. A BETTER ONE.
I SEE.
HOW DID YOU FIND YOURSELF AMONG THE ROANOKES?
MY NAVIGATOR, FRED NOONAN, AND ME, WE WERE MAKING OUR WAY TO HOWLAND ISLAND IN THE PACIFIC...
...WHEN WE FELL INTO THIS STRANGE WHOOPING KIND OF PORTAL.
"OUR PLANE WAS ATTACKED ALMOST IMMEDIATELY--I BAILED OUT IN THE NICK OF TIME...
"FRED DIDN'T.
"I BROKE BOTH LEGS IN LANDING. WHEN THE ROANOKES FOUND ME, THEY THOUGHT I WAS SOME SORT OF ***DEMON*** FROM THE ***SUN.***
"SO I CONVINCED 'EM I WAS A ***SKYMOTHER*** INSTEAD. SPOKE THROUGH THEIR FETISH--IN A HIDDEN COMPARTMENT IN THE LONGHOUSE."

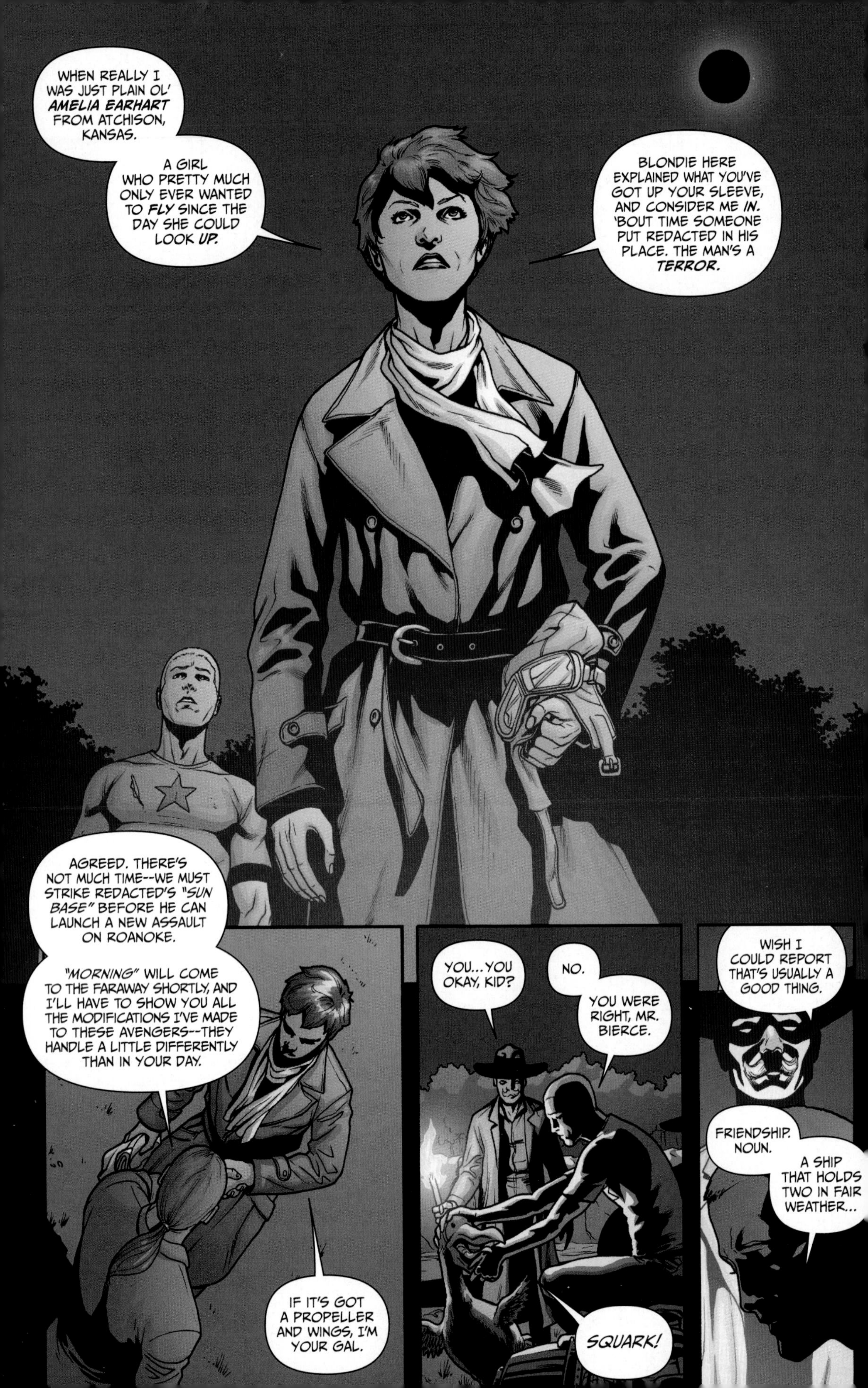
WHEN REALLY I WAS JUST PLAIN OL' *AMELIA EARHART* FROM ATCHISON, KANSAS.
A GIRL WHO PRETTY MUCH ONLY EVER WANTED TO *FLY* SINCE THE DAY SHE COULD LOOK *UP.*
BLONDIE HERE EXPLAINED WHAT YOU'VE GOT UP YOUR SLEEVE, AND CONSIDER ME *IN.* 'BOUT TIME SOMEONE PUT REDACTED IN HIS PLACE. THE MAN'S A *TERROR.*
AGREED. THERE'S NOT MUCH TIME--WE MUST STRIKE REDACTED'S *"SUN BASE"* BEFORE HE CAN LAUNCH A NEW ASSAULT ON ROANOKE.
"MORNING" WILL COME TO THE FARAWAY SHORTLY, AND I'LL HAVE TO SHOW YOU ALL THE MODIFICATIONS I'VE MADE TO THESE AVENGERS--THEY HANDLE A LITTLE DIFFERENTLY THAN IN YOUR DAY.
IF IT'S GOT A PROPELLER AND WINGS, I'M YOUR GAL.
YOU... YOU OKAY, KID?
NO.
YOU WERE RIGHT, MR. BIERCE.
SQUARK!
WISH I COULD REPORT THAT'S USUALLY A GOOD THING.
FRIENDSHIP. NOUN.
A SHIP THAT HOLDS TWO IN FAIR WEATHER...

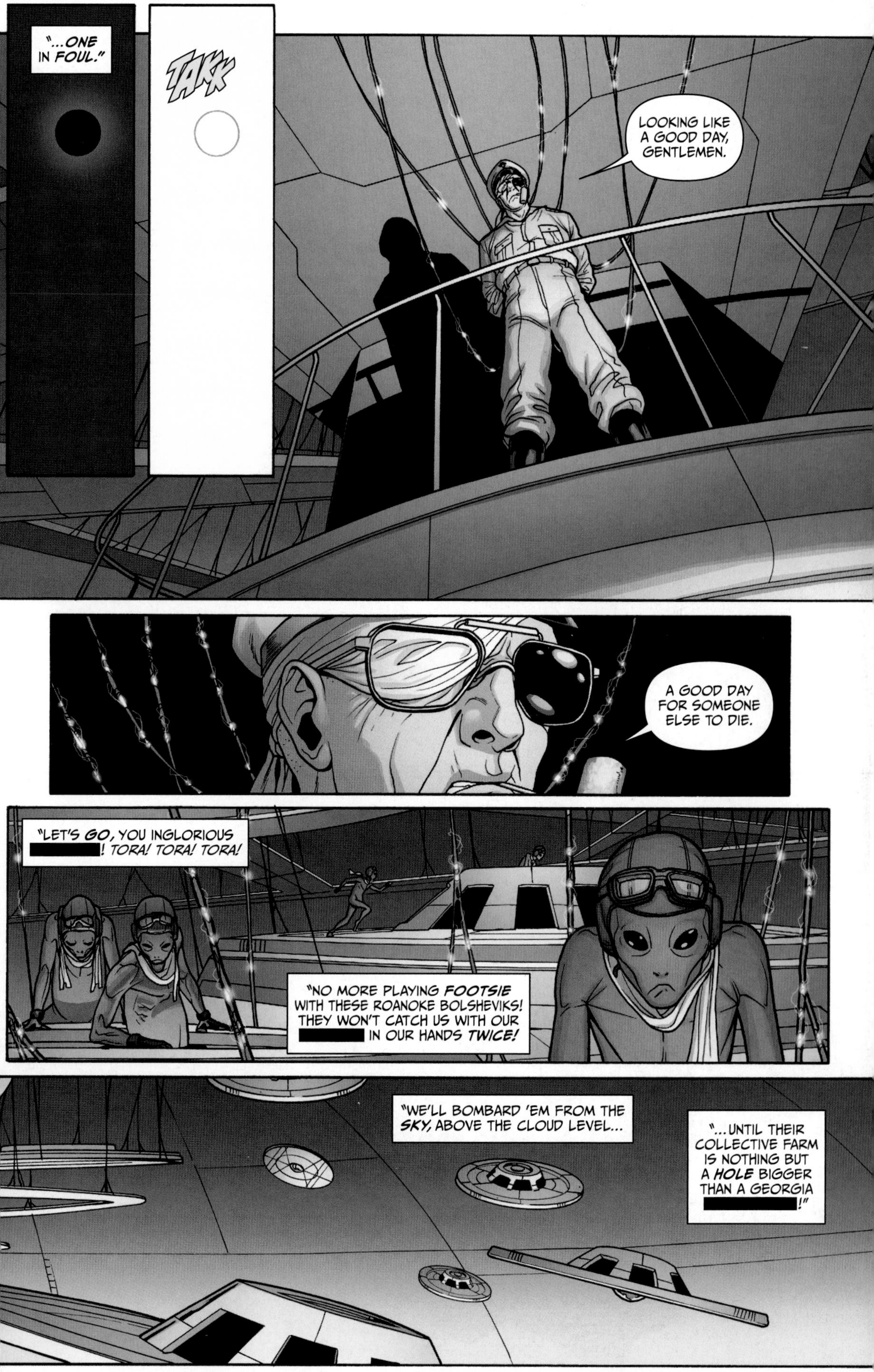
"...ONE IN *FOUL.*"
TAKK
LOOKING LIKE A GOOD DAY, GENTLEMEN.
A GOOD DAY FOR SOMEONE ELSE TO DIE.
"LET'S *GO,* YOU INGLORIOUS [redacted]! *TORA! TORA! TORA!*
"NO MORE PLAYING *FOOTSIE* WITH THESE ROANOKE BOLSHEVIKS! THEY WON'T CATCH US WITH OUR [redacted] IN OUR HANDS *TWICE!*
"WE'LL BOMBARD 'EM FROM THE *SKY,* ABOVE THE CLOUD LEVEL...
"...UNTIL THEIR COLLECTIVE FARM IS NOTHING BUT A *HOLE* BIGGER THAN A GEORGIA [redacted]!"

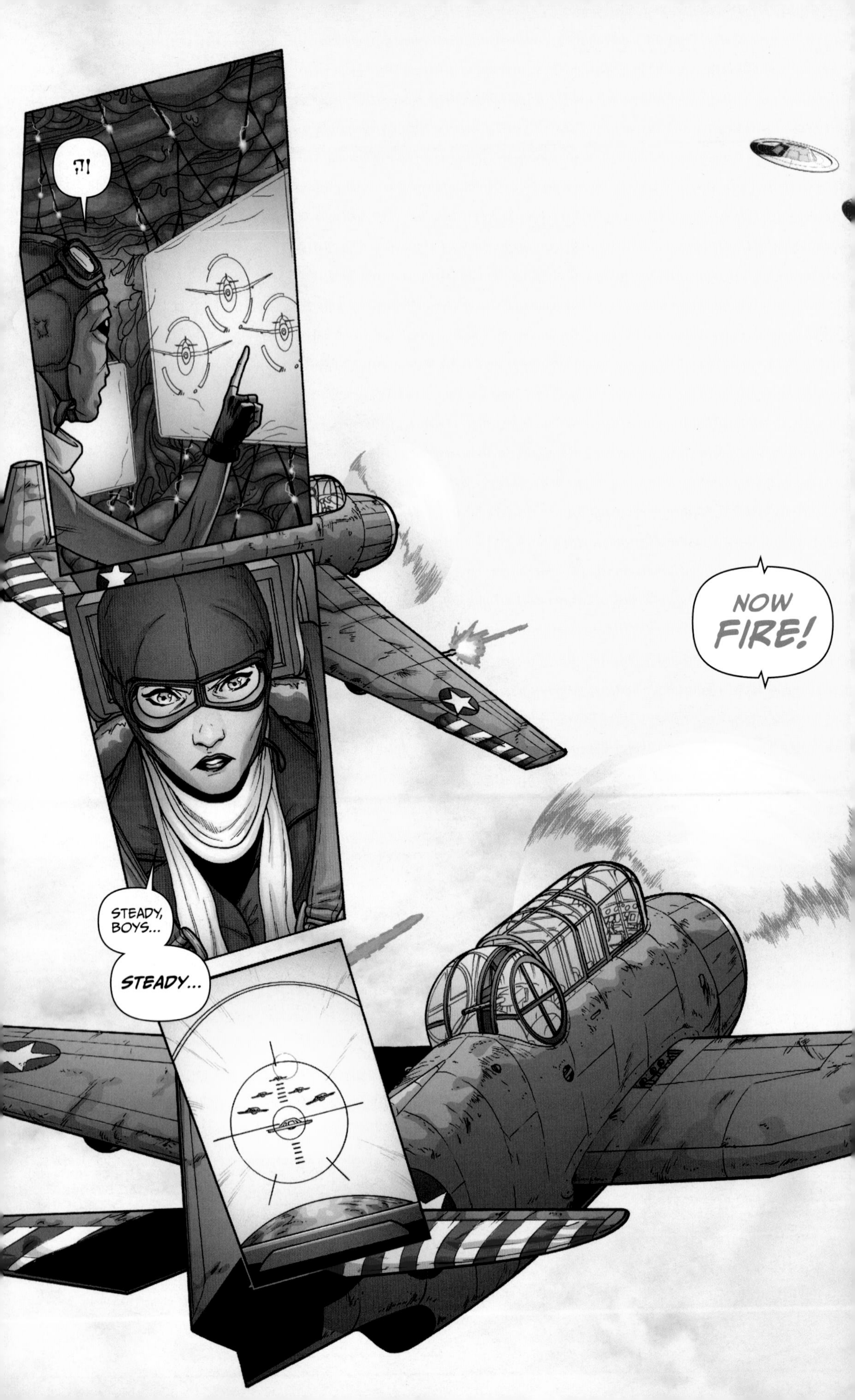
?!
STEADY, BOYS...
STEADY...
NOW FIRE!

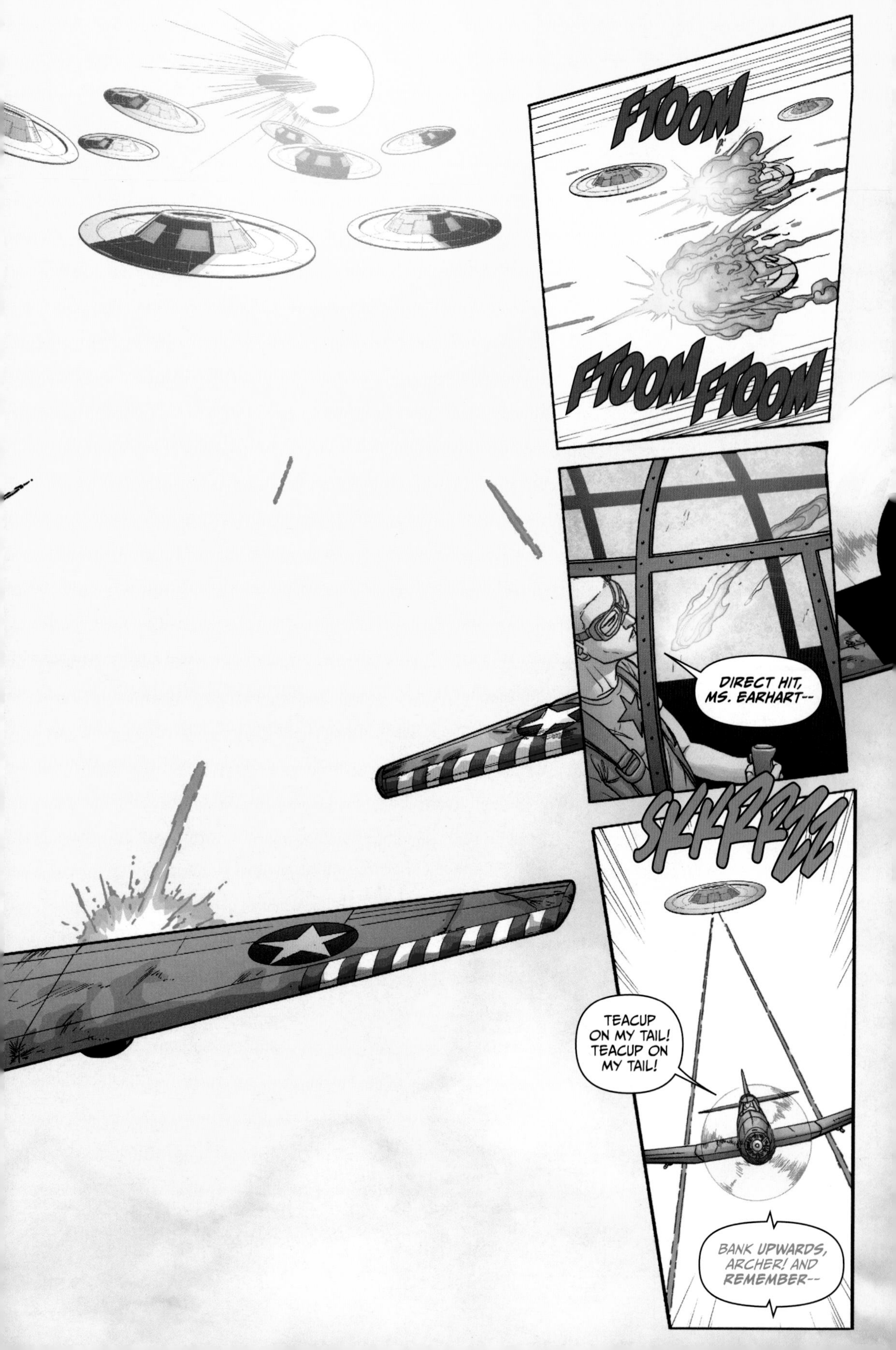
FTOOM
FTOOM FTOOM
DIRECT HIT, MS. EARHART--
SKRRRZZ
TEACUP ON MY TAIL! TEACUP ON MY TAIL!
BANK UPWARDS, ARCHER! AND REMEMBER--

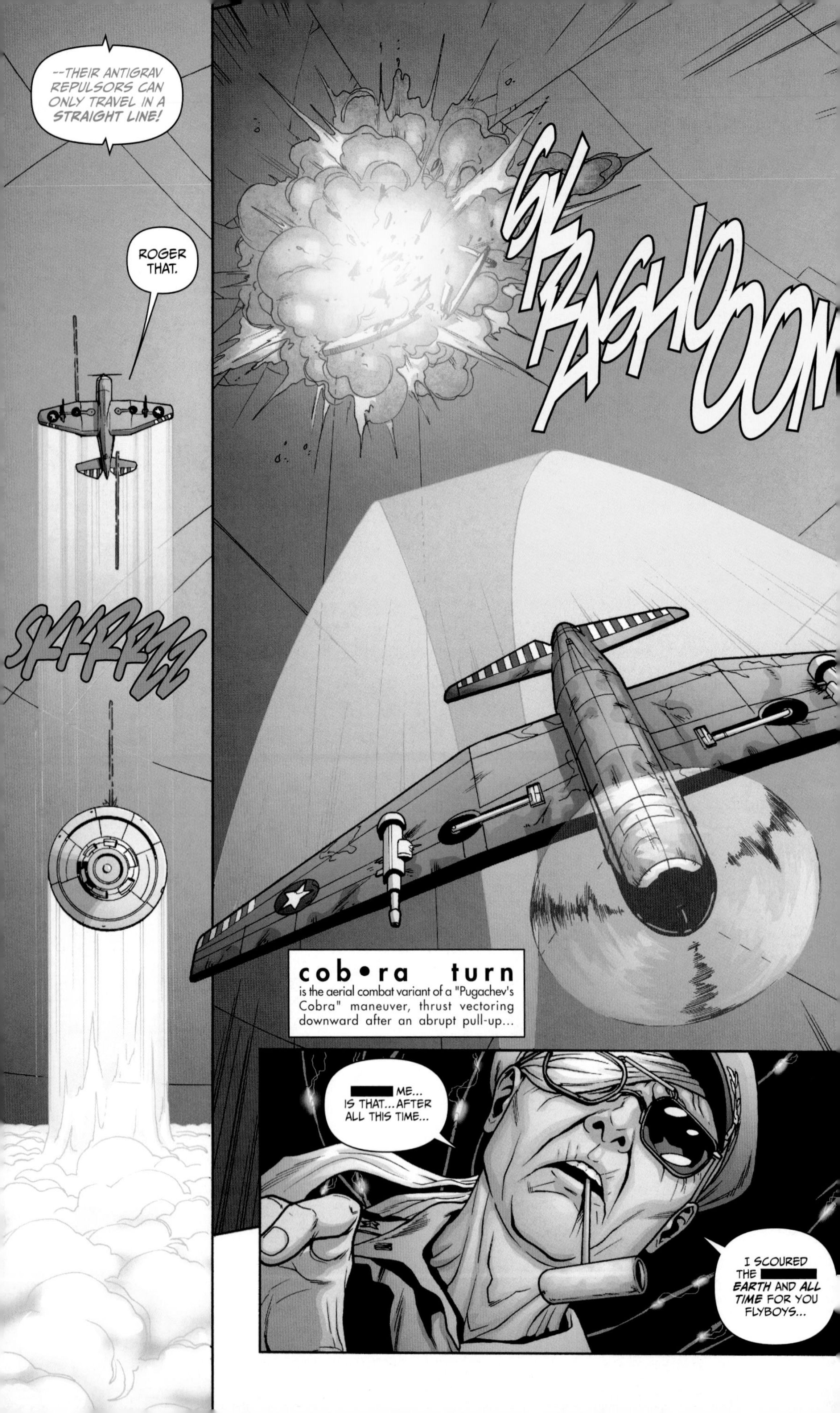
--THEIR ANTIGRAV REPULSORS CAN ONLY TRAVEL IN A STRAIGHT LINE!
ROGER THAT.
cob•ra turn
is the aerial combat variant of a "Pugachev's Cobra" maneuver, thrust vectoring downward after an abrupt pull-up...
[redacted] ME... IS THAT... AFTER ALL THIS TIME...
I SCOURED THE [redacted] EARTH AND ALL TIME FOR YOU FLYBOYS...

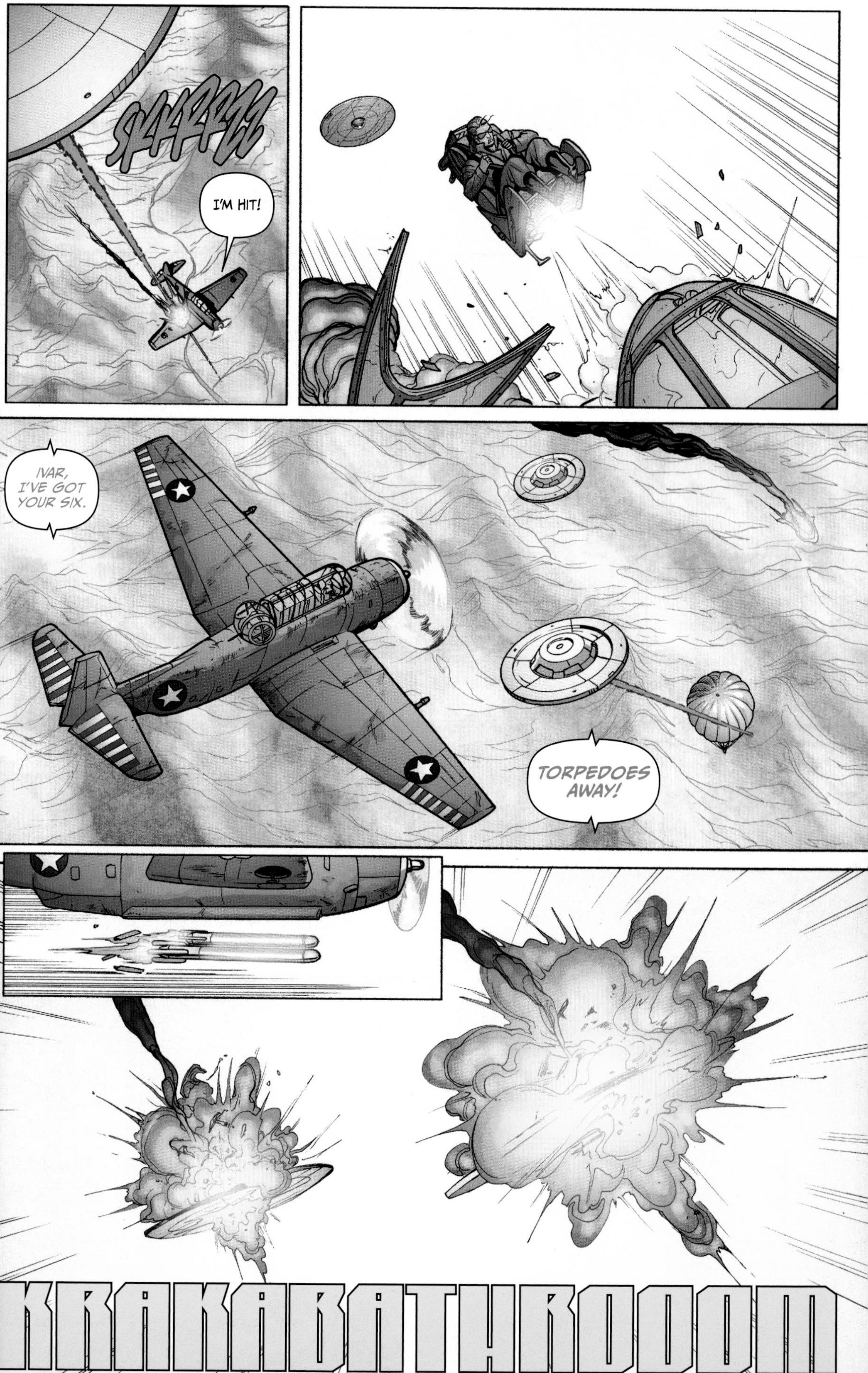
I'M HIT!
IVAR, I'VE GOT YOUR SIX.
TORPEDOES AWAY!
KRAKABATHROOOM

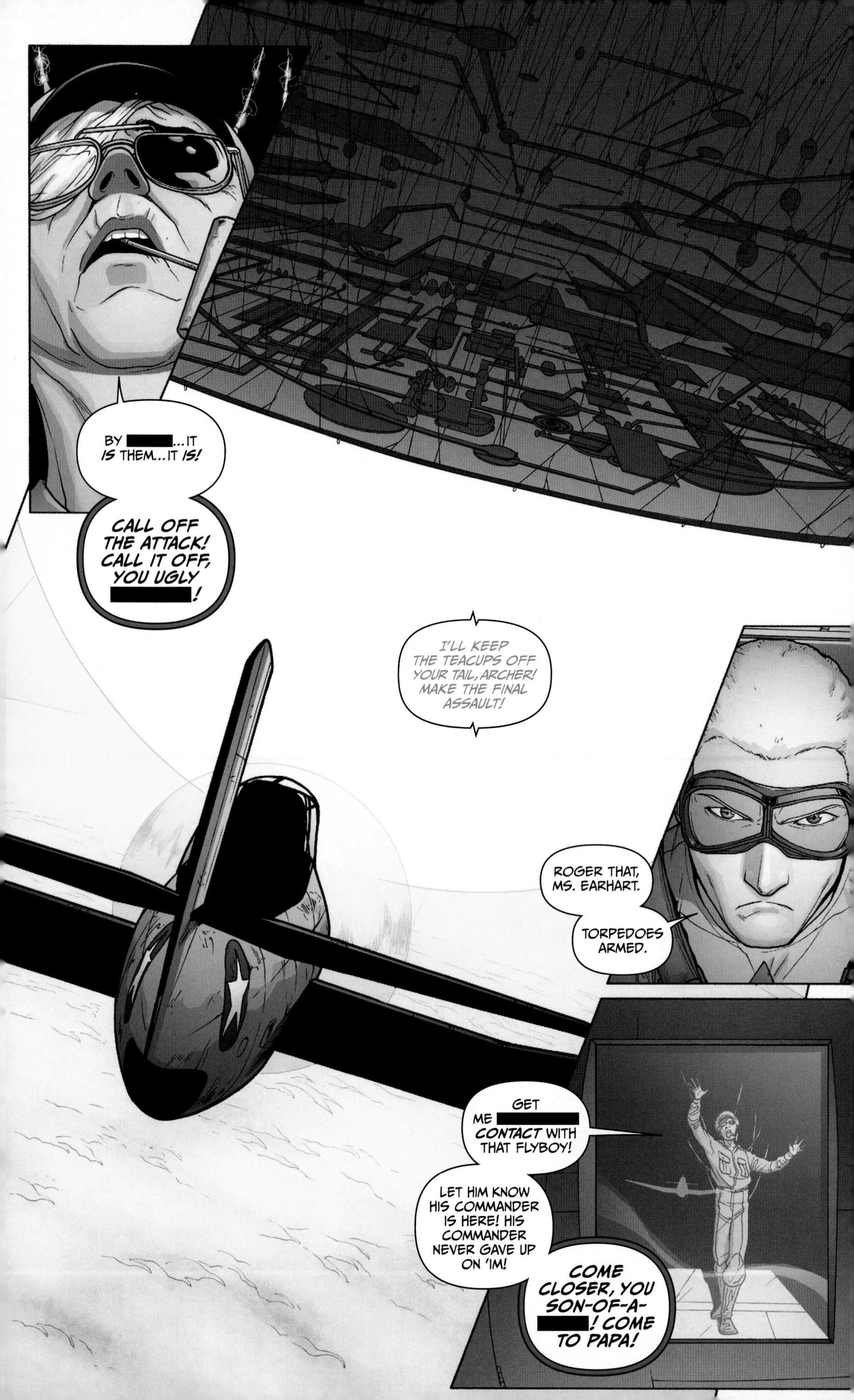
BY [redacted]...IT IS THEM...IT IS!
CALL OFF THE ATTACK! CALL IT OFF, YOU UGLY [redacted]!
I'LL KEEP THE TEACUPS OFF YOUR TAIL, ARCHER! MAKE THE FINAL ASSAULT!
ROGER THAT, MS. EARHART.
TORPEDOES ARMED.
GET ME [redacted] CONTACT WITH THAT FLYBOY!
LET HIM KNOW HIS COMMANDER IS HERE! HIS COMMANDER NEVER GAVE UP ON 'IM!
COME CLOSER, YOU SON-OF-A-[redacted]! COME TO PAPA!

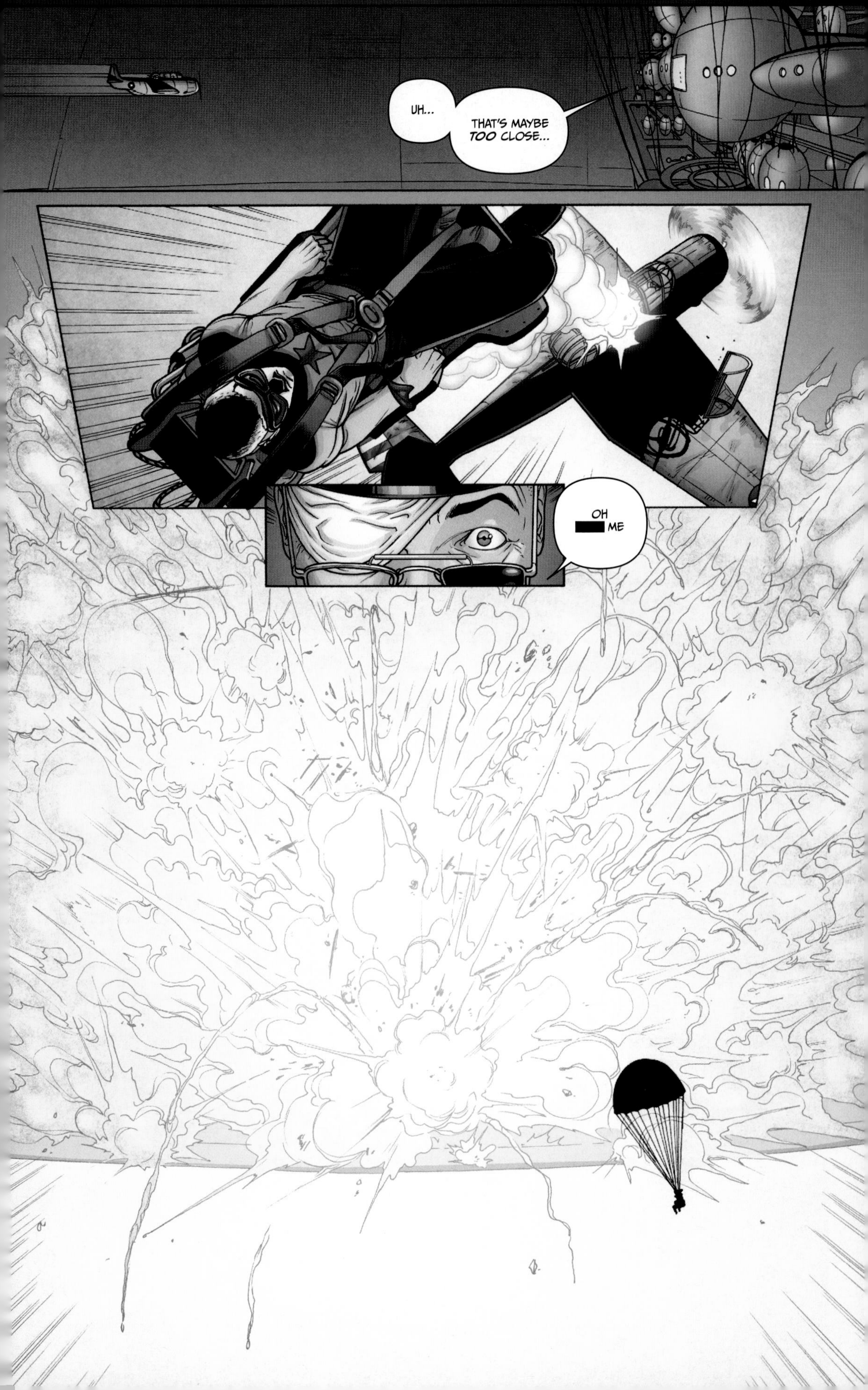
UH...
THAT'S MAYBE *TOO* CLOSE...
OH [redacted] ME

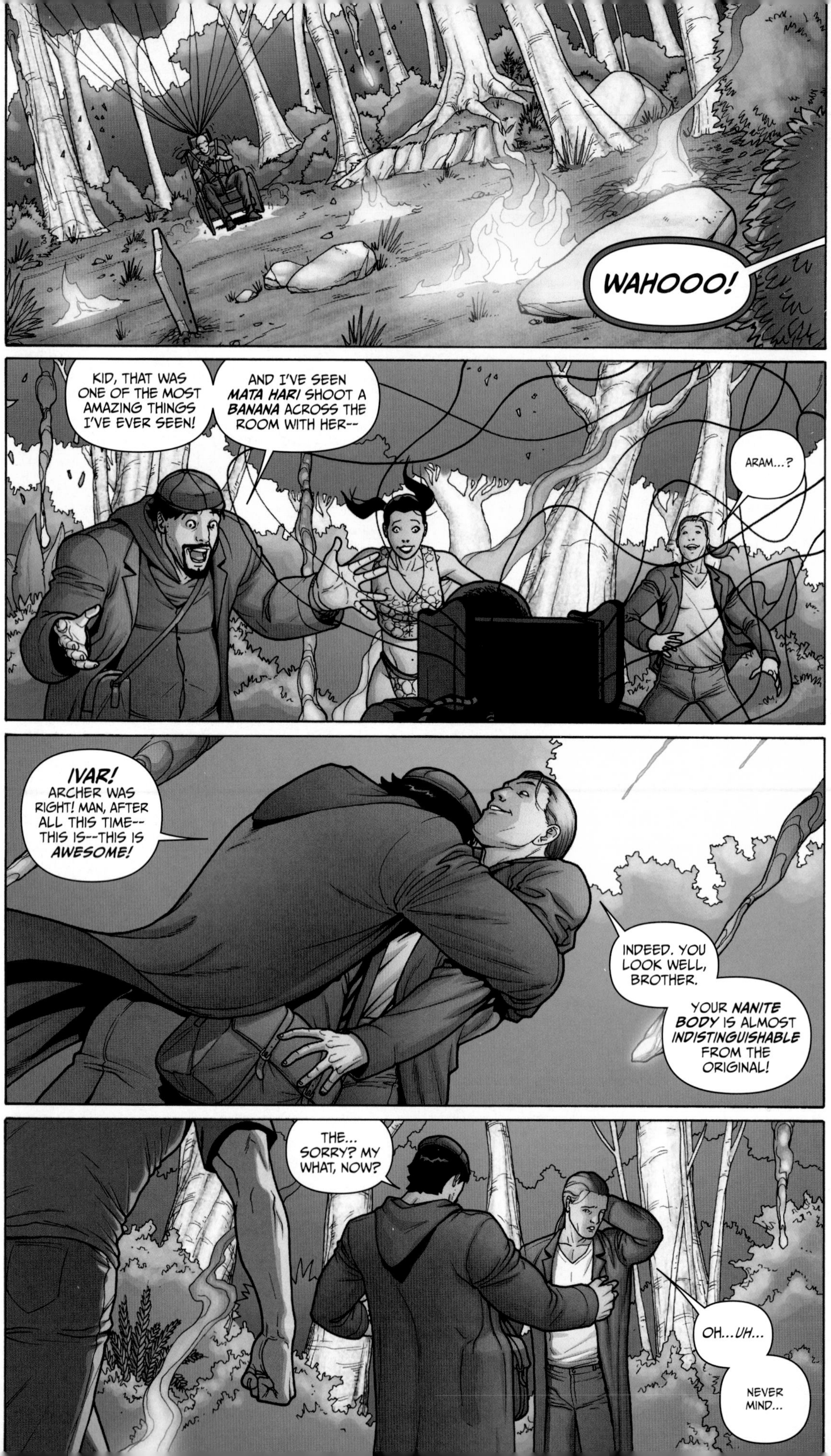
WAHOOO!
KID, THAT WAS ONE OF THE MOST AMAZING THINGS I'VE EVER SEEN!
AND I'VE SEEN *MATA HARI* SHOOT A *BANANA* ACROSS THE ROOM WITH HER--
ARAM...?
IVAR! ARCHER WAS RIGHT! MAN, AFTER ALL THIS TIME-- THIS IS--THIS IS *AWESOME!*
INDEED. YOU LOOK WELL, BROTHER.
YOUR *NANITE BODY* IS ALMOST *INDISTINGUISHABLE* FROM THE ORIGINAL!
THE... SORRY? MY WHAT, NOW?
OH...*UH*...
NEVER MIND...

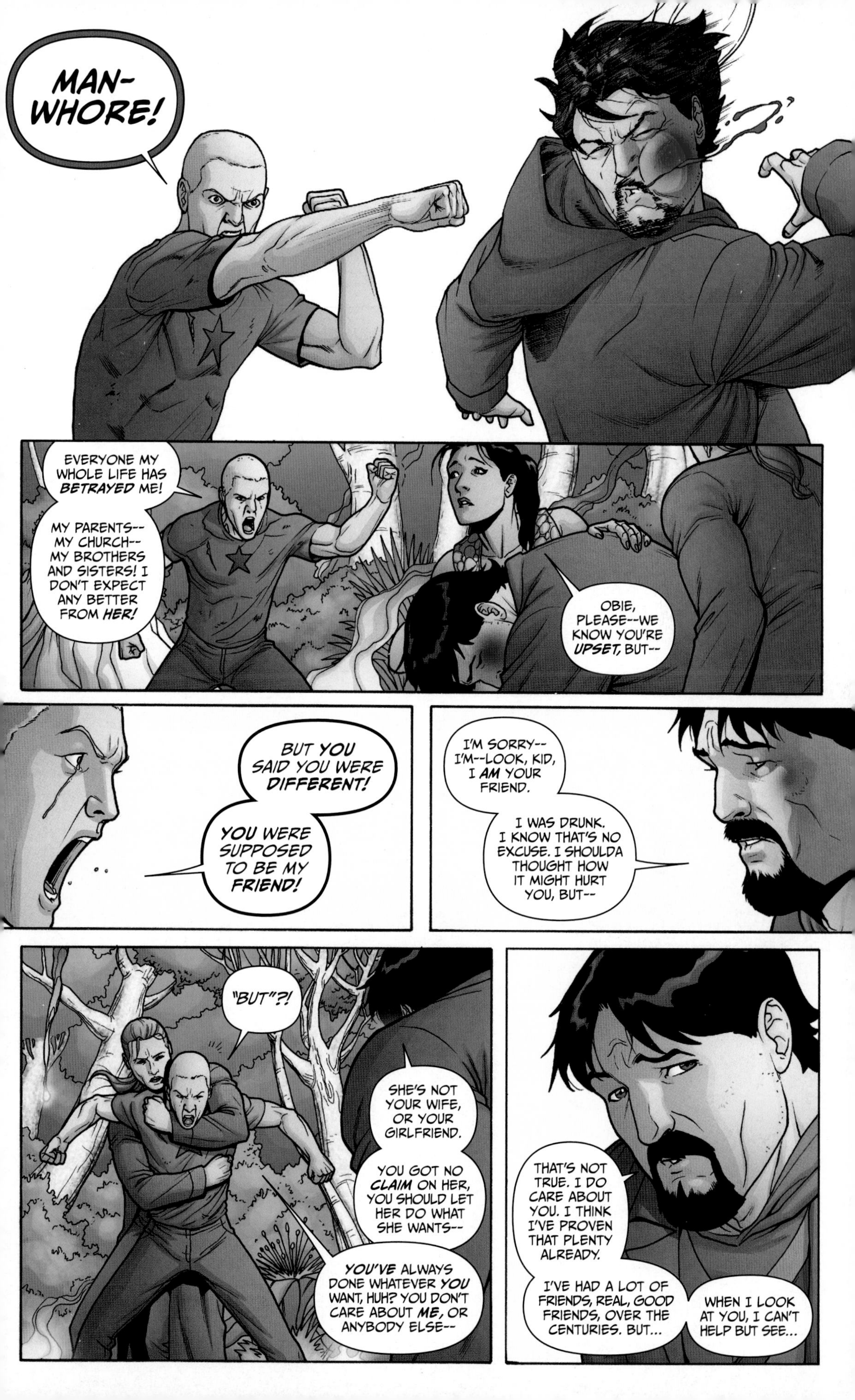
MAN-WHORE!
EVERYONE MY WHOLE LIFE HAS BETRAYED ME!
MY PARENTS-- MY CHURCH-- MY BROTHERS AND SISTERS! I DON'T EXPECT ANY BETTER FROM HER!
OBIE, PLEASE--WE KNOW YOU'RE UPSET, BUT--
BUT YOU SAID YOU WERE DIFFERENT!
YOU WERE SUPPOSED TO BE MY FRIEND!
I'M SORRY-- I'M--LOOK, KID, I AM YOUR FRIEND.
I WAS DRUNK. I KNOW THAT'S NO EXCUSE. I SHOULDA THOUGHT HOW IT MIGHT HURT YOU, BUT--
"BUT"?!
SHE'S NOT YOUR WIFE, OR YOUR GIRLFRIEND.
YOU GOT NO CLAIM ON HER, YOU SHOULD LET HER DO WHAT SHE WANTS--
YOU'VE ALWAYS DONE WHATEVER YOU WANT, HUH? YOU DON'T CARE ABOUT ME, OR ANYBODY ELSE--
THAT'S NOT TRUE. I DO CARE ABOUT YOU. I THINK I'VE PROVEN THAT PLENTY ALREADY.
I'VE HAD A LOT OF FRIENDS, REAL, GOOD FRIENDS, OVER THE CENTURIES. BUT...
WHEN I LOOK AT YOU, I CAN'T HELP BUT SEE...

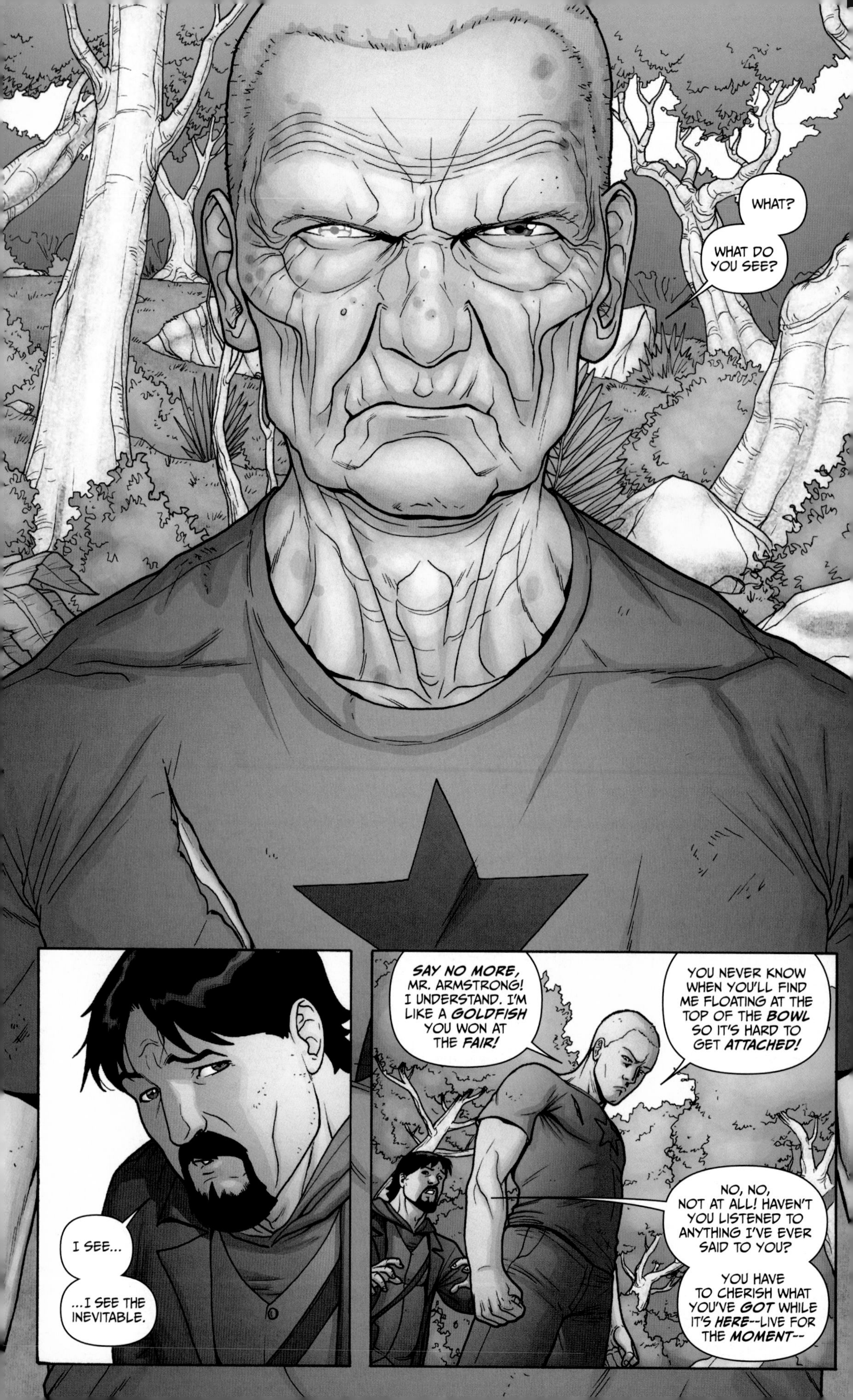
WHAT?
WHAT DO YOU SEE?
I SEE...
...I SEE THE INEVITABLE.
SAY NO MORE, MR. ARMSTRONG! I UNDERSTAND. I'M LIKE A GOLDFISH YOU WON AT THE FAIR!
YOU NEVER KNOW WHEN YOU'LL FIND ME FLOATING AT THE TOP OF THE BOWL SO IT'S HARD TO GET ATTACHED!
NO, NO, NOT AT ALL! HAVEN'T YOU LISTENED TO ANYTHING I'VE EVER SAID TO YOU?
YOU HAVE TO CHERISH WHAT YOU'VE GOT WHILE IT'S HERE--LIVE FOR THE MOMENT--

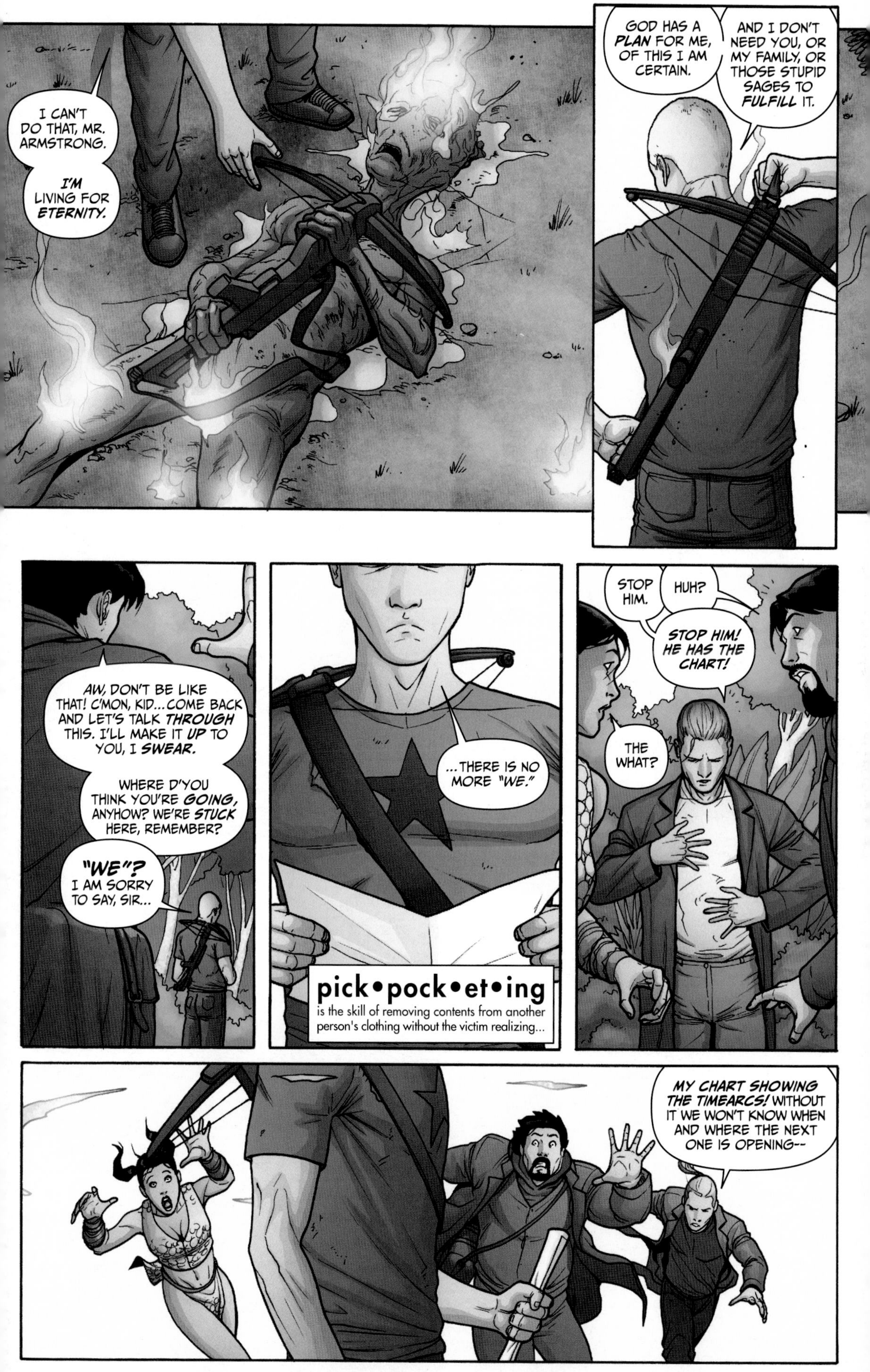
I CAN'T DO THAT, MR. ARMSTRONG.
I'M LIVING FOR ETERNITY.
GOD HAS A PLAN FOR ME, OF THIS I AM CERTAIN.
AND I DON'T NEED YOU, OR MY FAMILY, OR THOSE STUPID SAGES TO FULFILL IT.
AW, DON'T BE LIKE THAT! C'MON, KID...COME BACK AND LET'S TALK THROUGH THIS. I'LL MAKE IT UP TO YOU, I SWEAR.
WHERE D'YOU THINK YOU'RE GOING, ANYHOW? WE'RE STUCK HERE, REMEMBER?
"WE"? I AM SORRY TO SAY, SIR...
...THERE IS NO MORE "WE."
pick•pock•et•ing
is the skill of removing contents from another person's clothing without the victim realizing...
STOP HIM.
HUH?
STOP HIM! HE HAS THE CHART!
THE WHAT?
MY CHART SHOWING THE TIMEARCS! WITHOUT IT WE WON'T KNOW WHEN AND WHERE THE NEXT ONE IS OPENING--

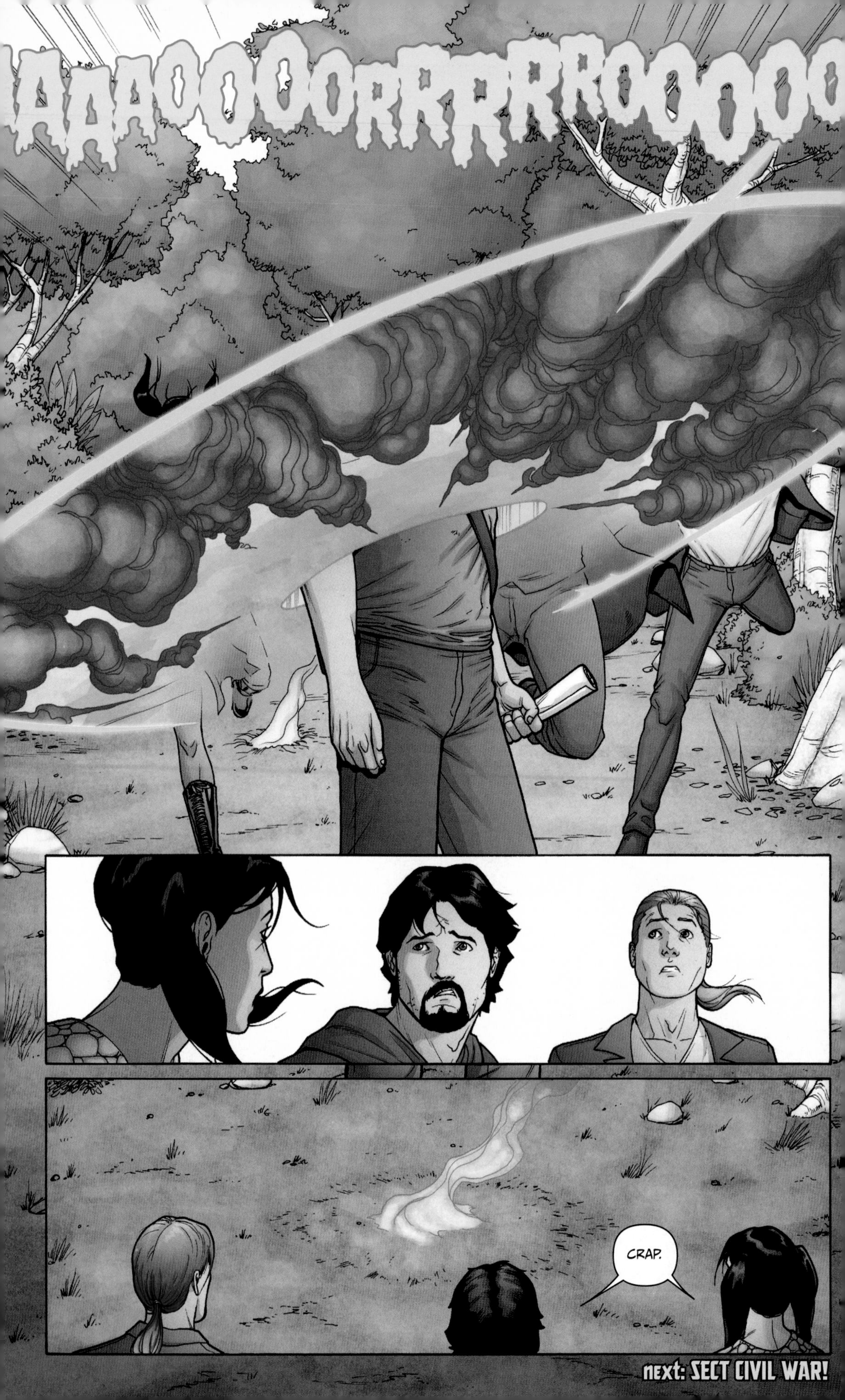
AAAOOORRRRROOOOO
CRAP.
next: SECT CIVIL WAR!

GALLERY

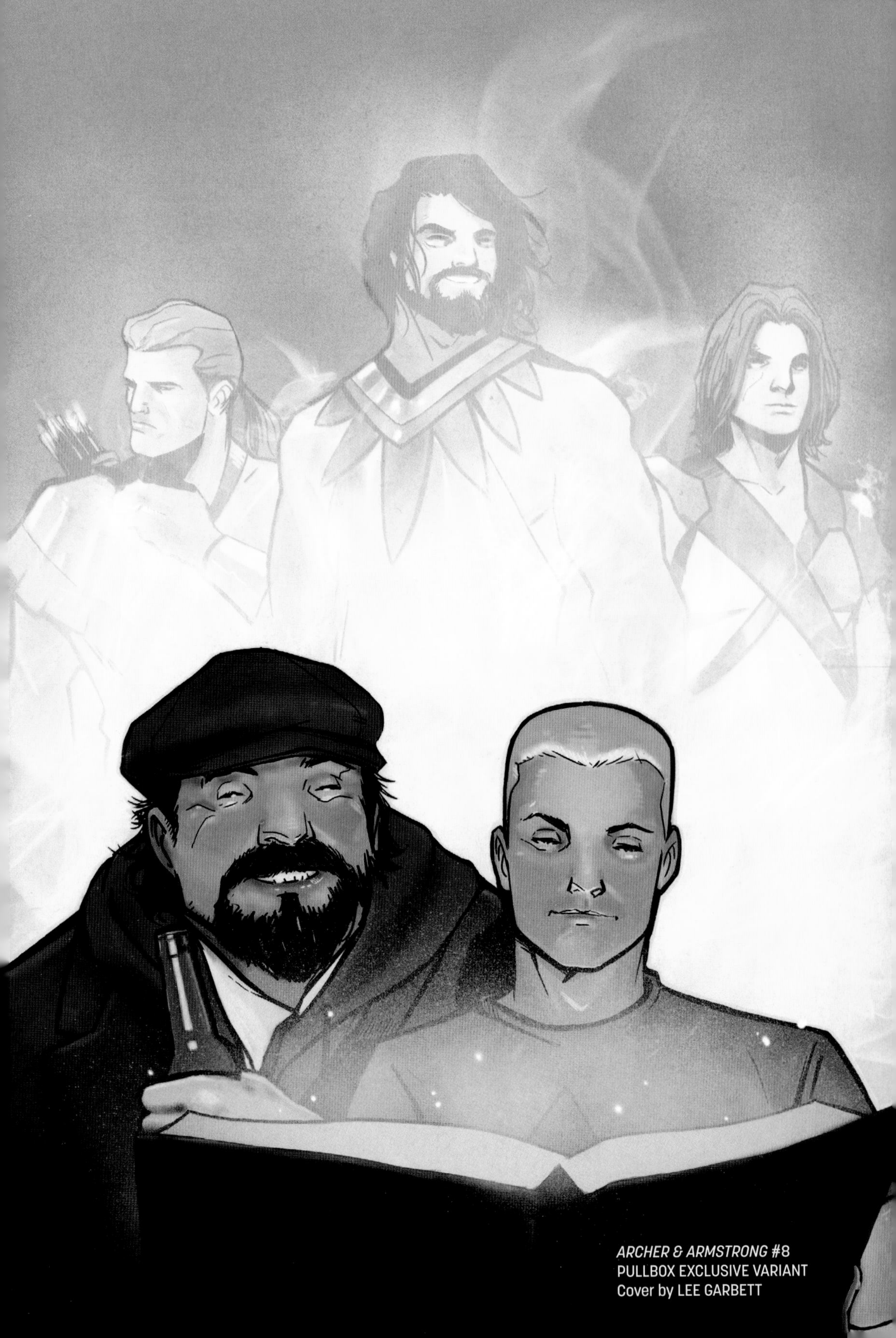

ARCHER & ARMSTRONG #8
PULLBOX EXCLUSIVE VARIANT
Cover by LEE GARBETT

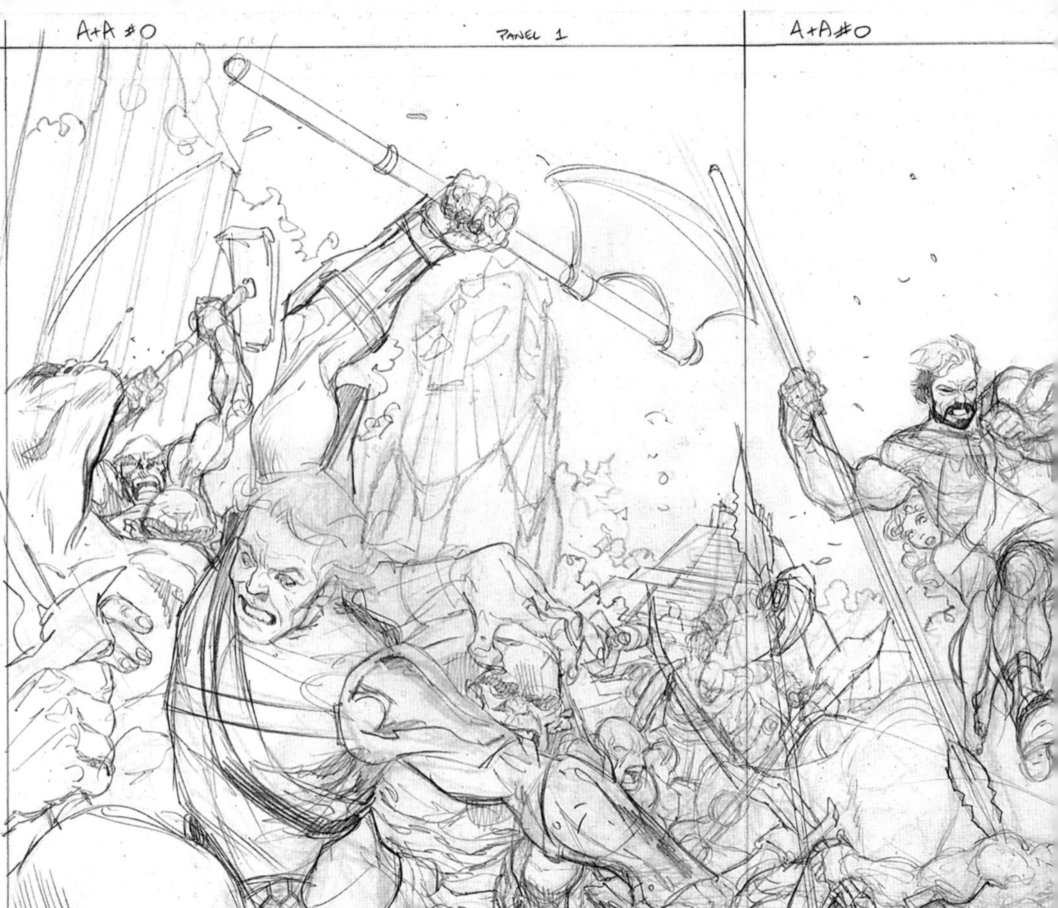
A+A #0
PANEL 1
A+A#0

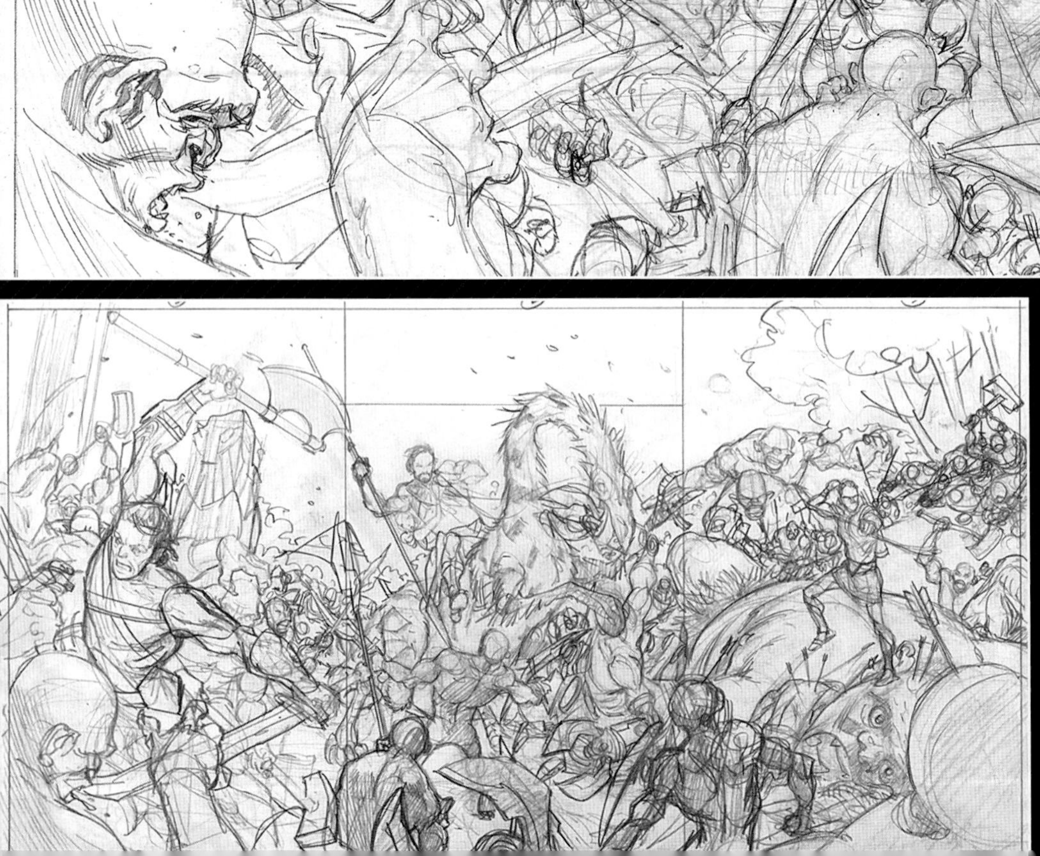

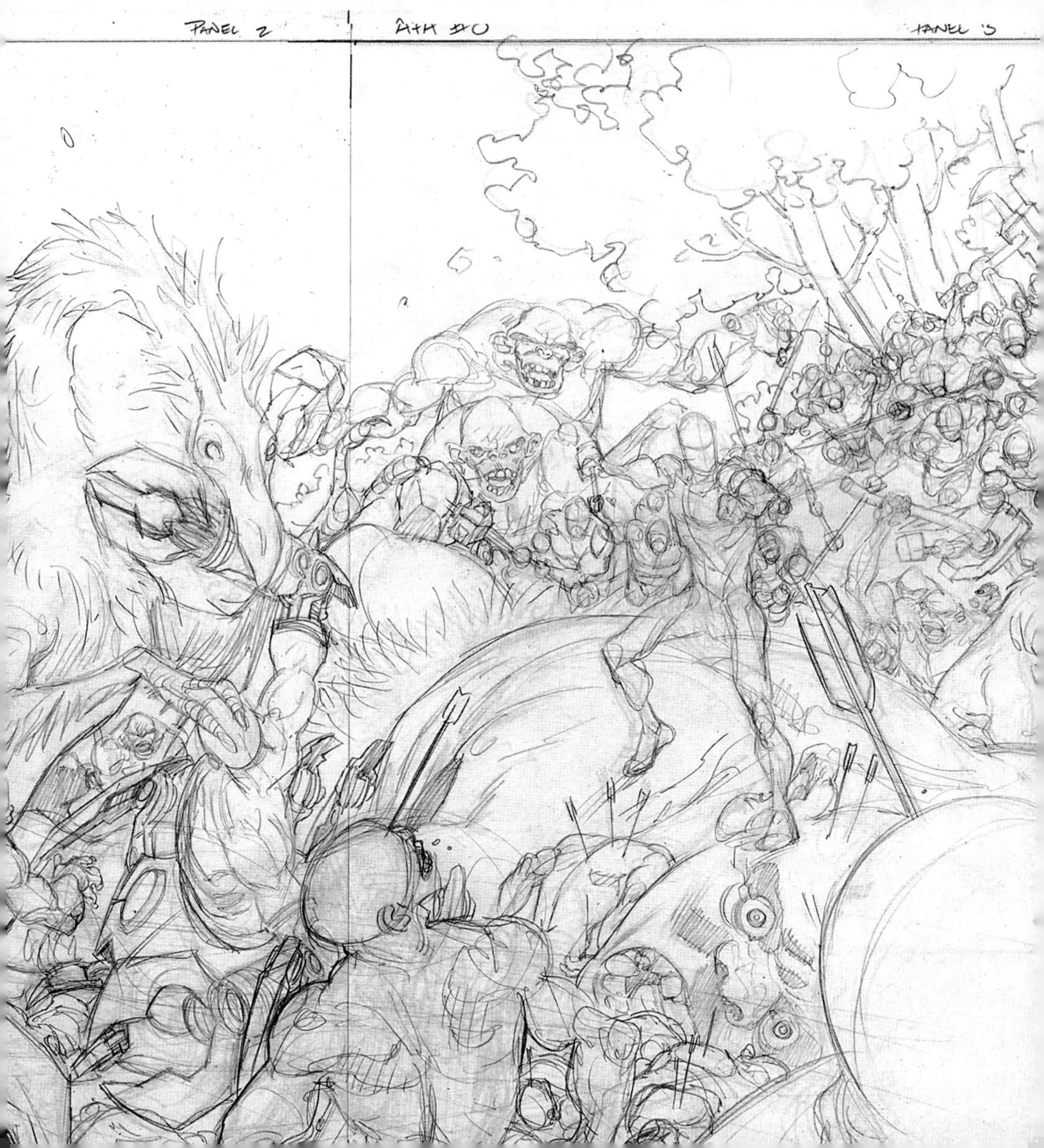
PANEL 2

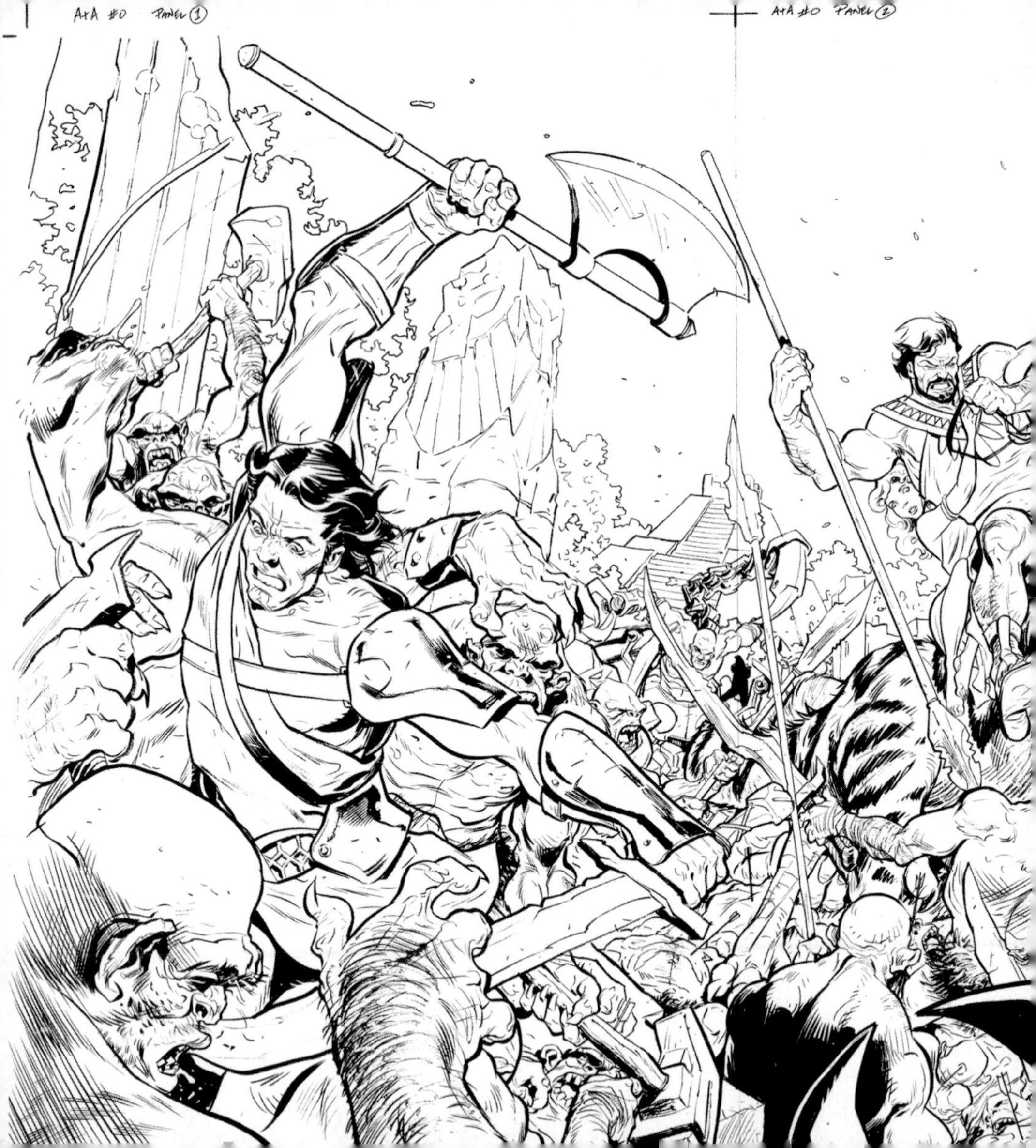
A+A #0 Panel 1
A+A #0 Panel 2

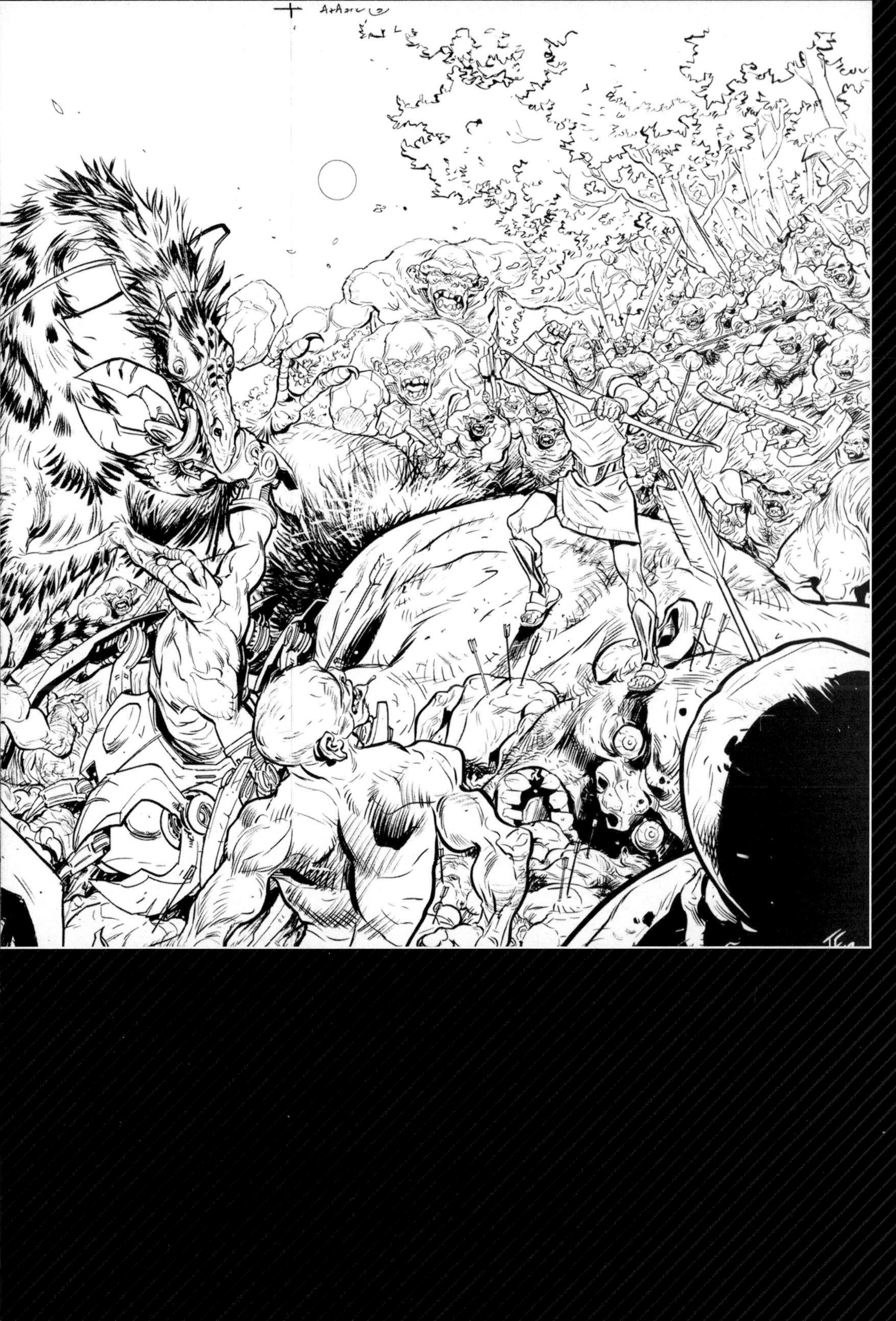

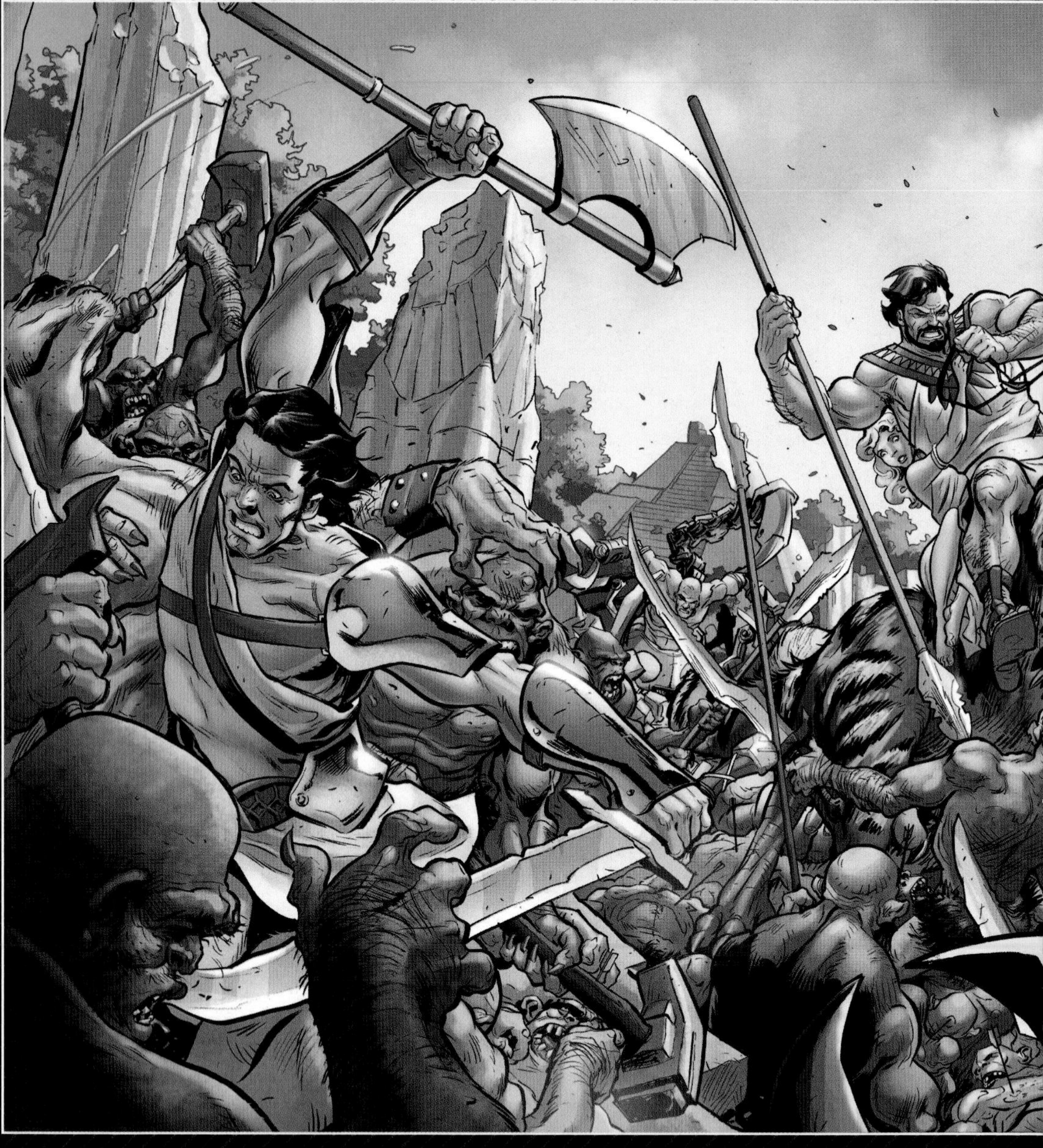

ARCHER & ARMSTRONG #0
WRAPAROUND GATEFOLD VARIANT
Cover by TOM FOWLER
Colors by BRIAN REBER

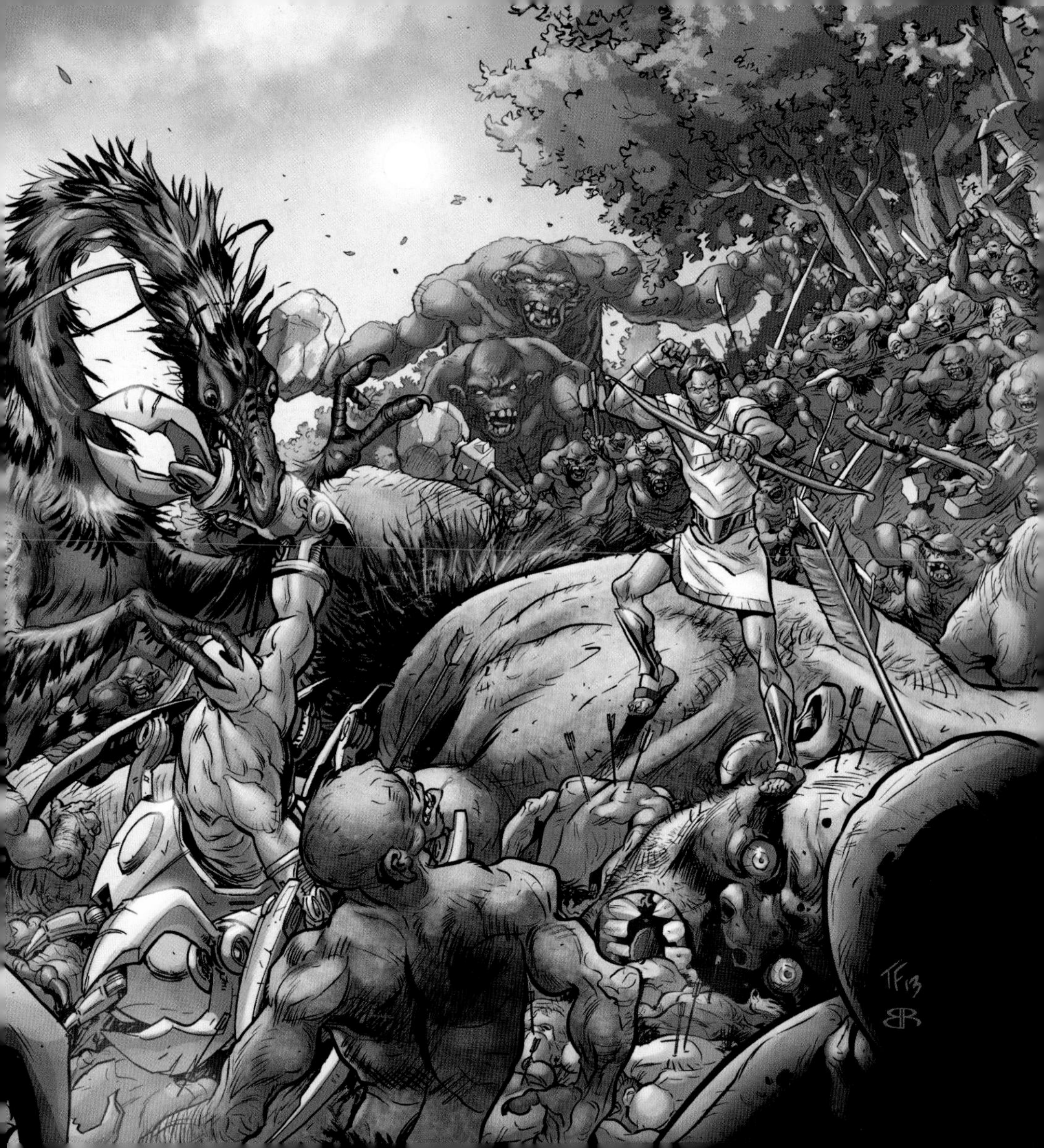

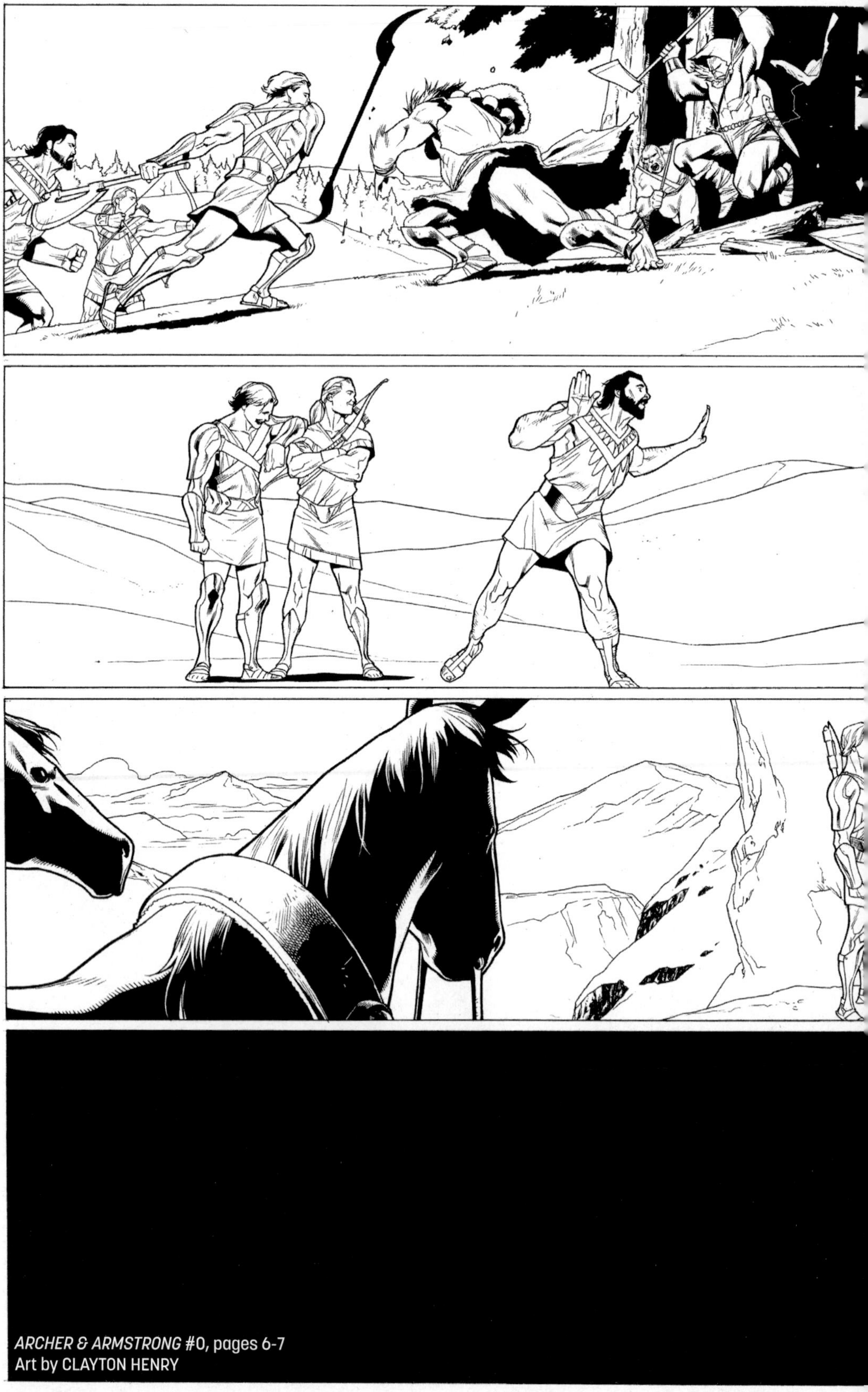

ARCHER & ARMSTRONG #0, pages 6-7
Art by CLAYTON HENRY

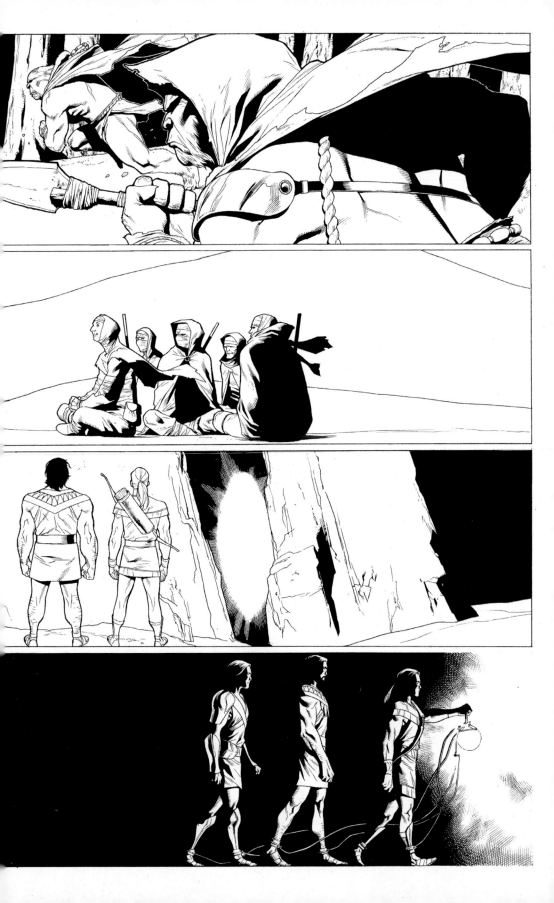

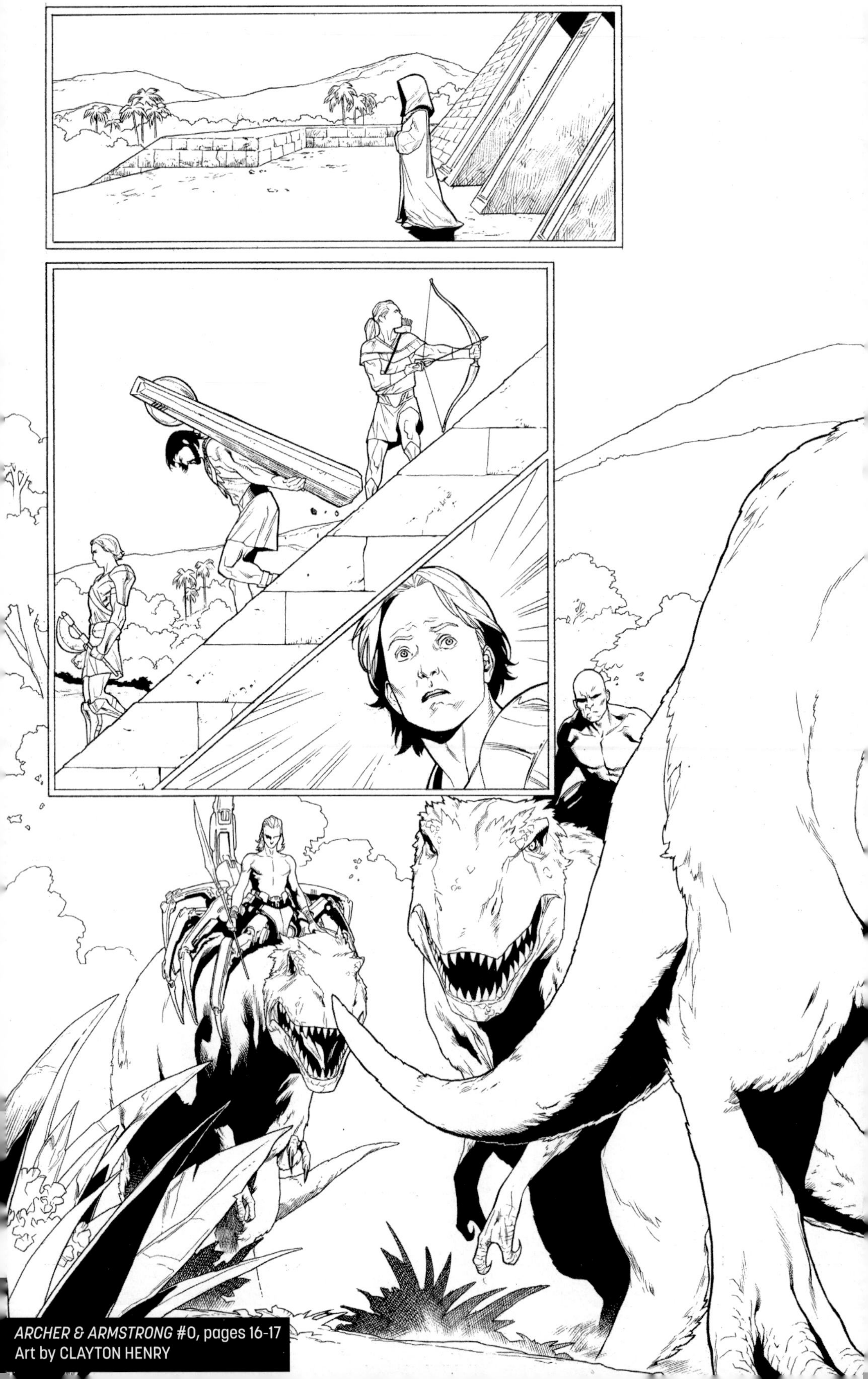

ARCHER & ARMSTRONG #0, pages 16-17
Art by CLAYTON HENRY

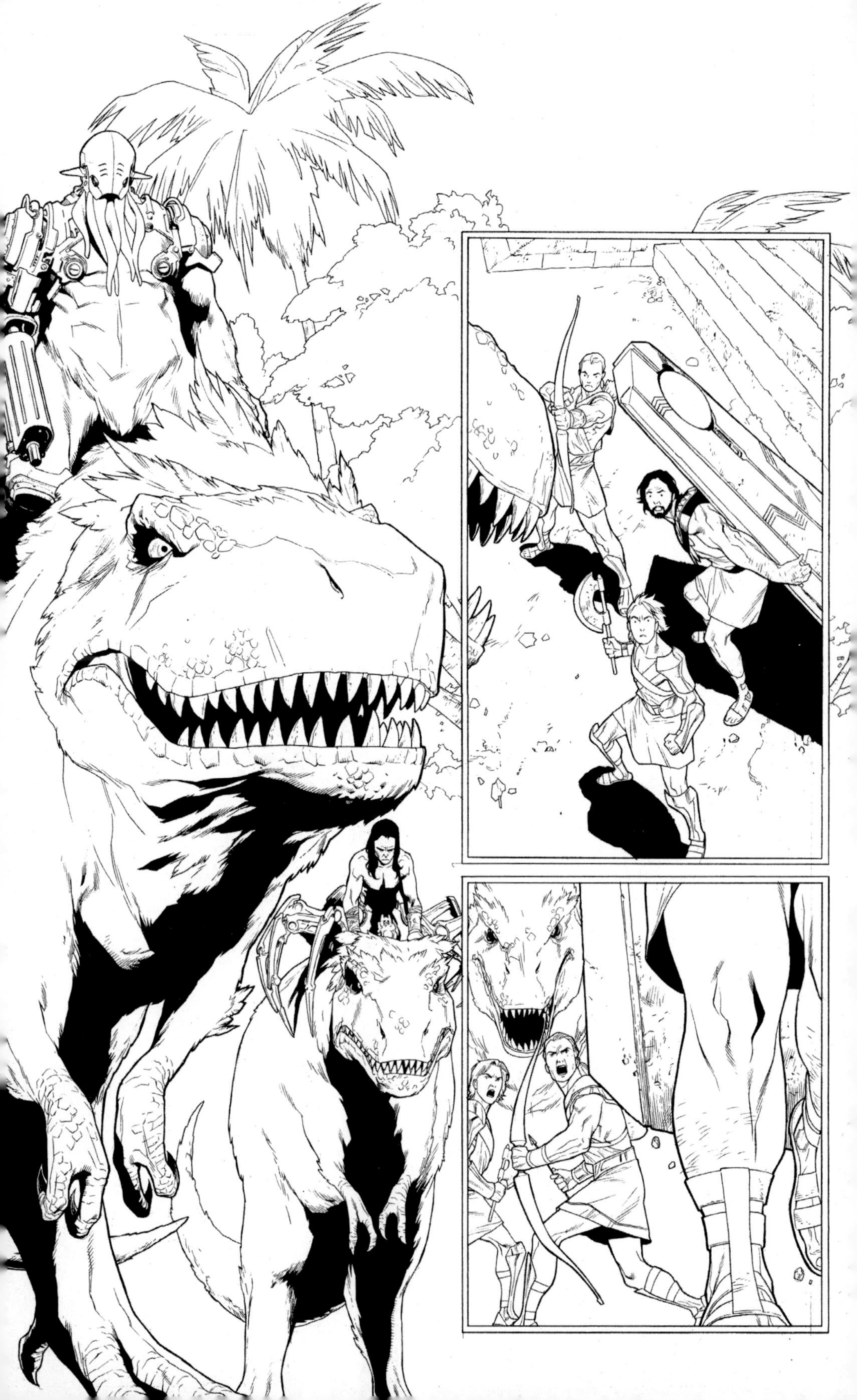

ARCHER & ARMSTRONG #10
PULLBOX EXCLUSIVE VARIANT
Cover by JUAN DOE

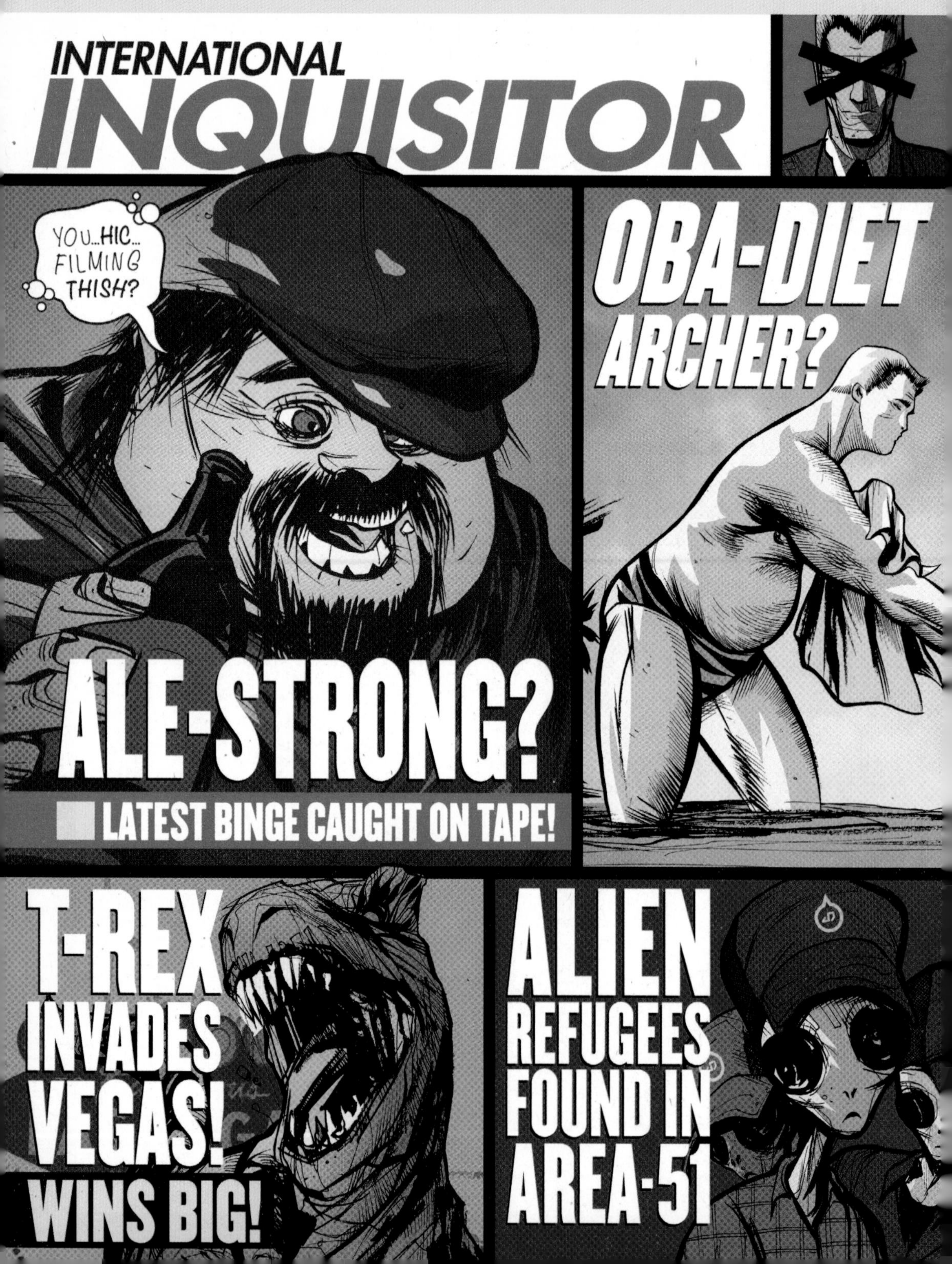
INTERNATIONAL
INQUISITOR
YOU...HIC... FILMING THISH?
OBA-DIET ARCHER?
ALE-STRONG?
LATEST BINGE CAUGHT ON TAPE!
T-REX INVADES VEGAS!
WINS BIG!
ALIEN REFUGEES FOUND IN AREA-51

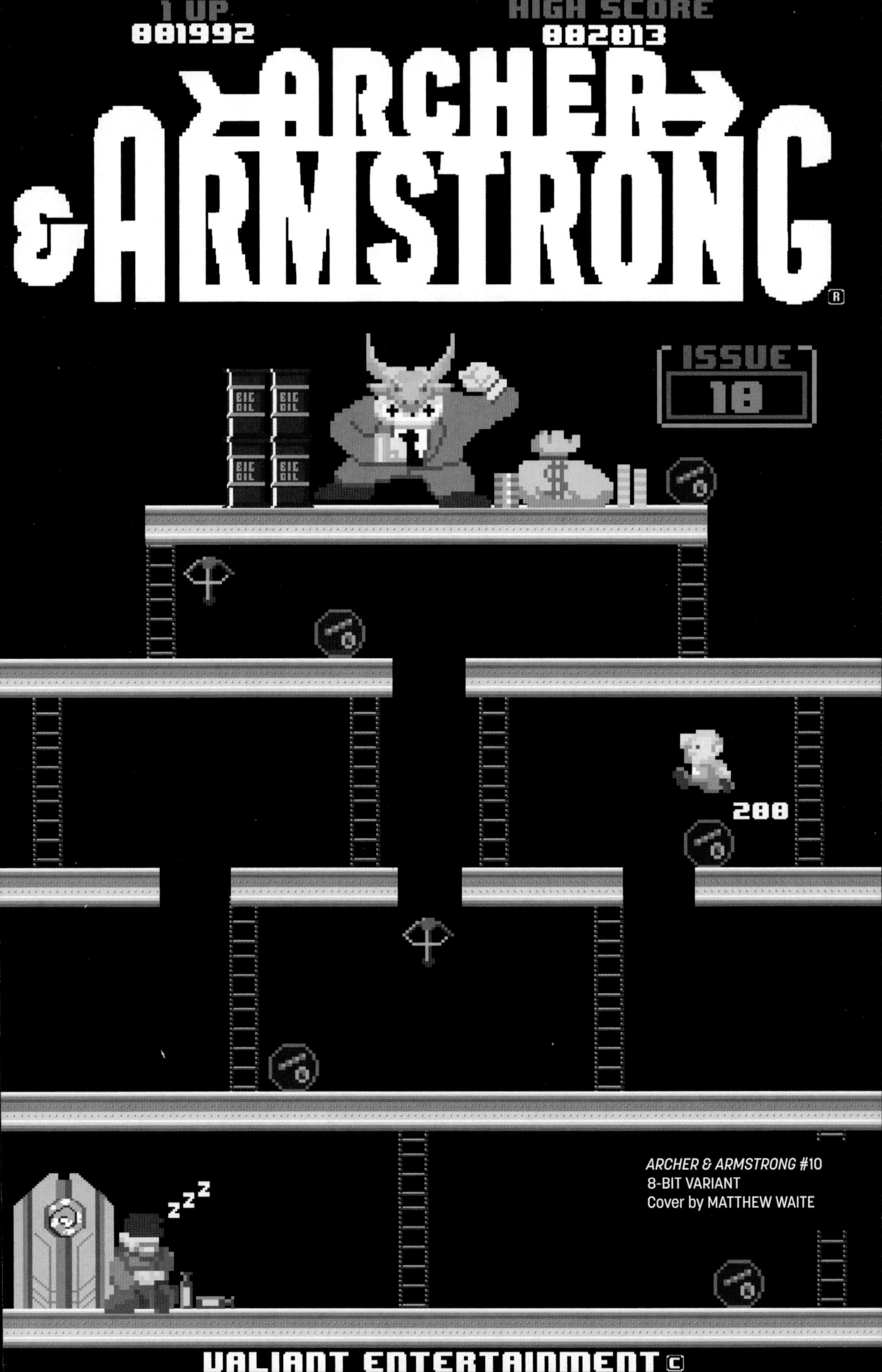
1 UP
001992
HIGH SCORE
002813
ARCHER & ARMSTRONG
ISSUE
10
BIG OIL
200
ARCHER & ARMSTRONG #10
8-BIT VARIANT
Cover by MATTHEW WAITE
VALIANT ENTERTAINMENT

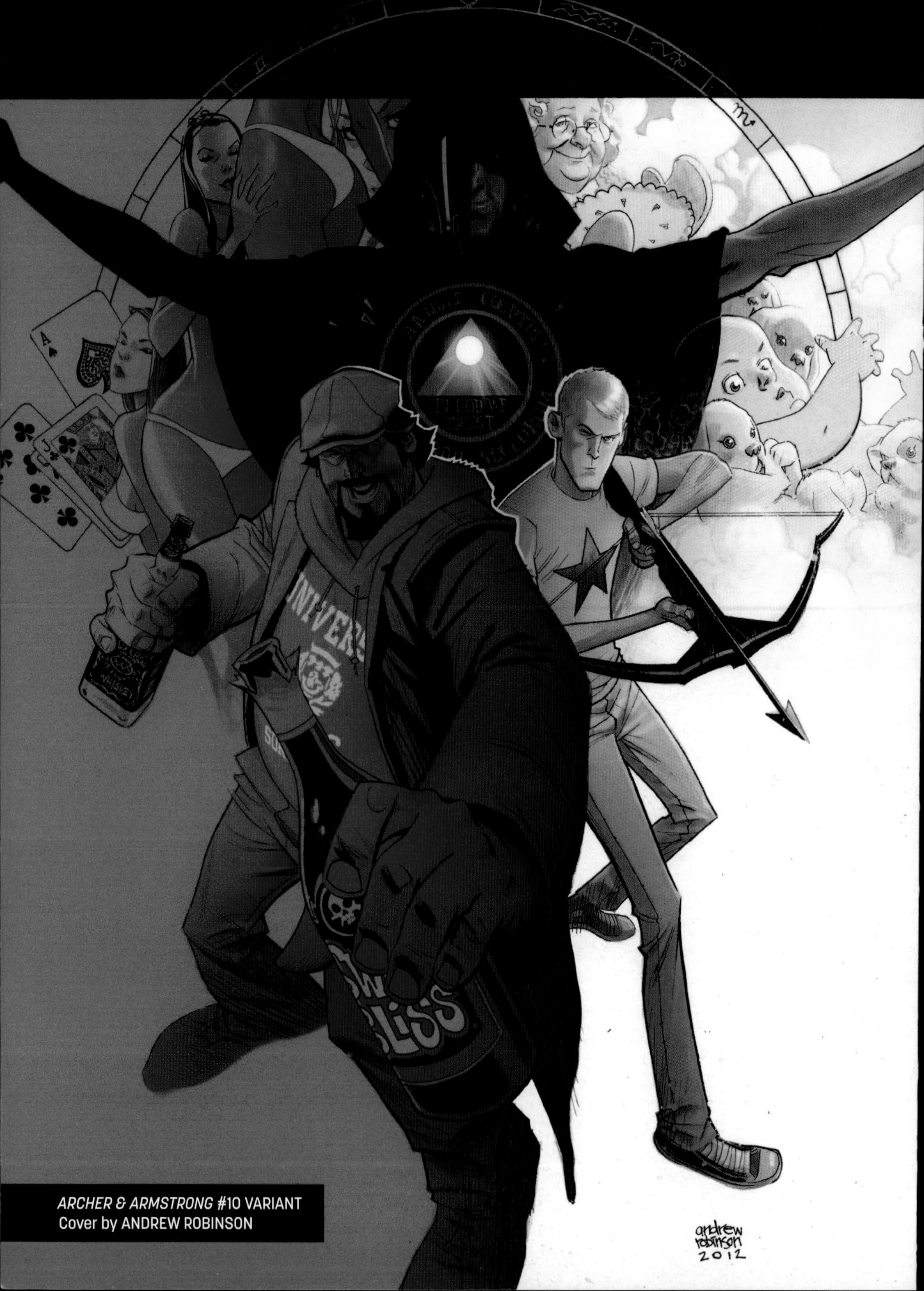
UNIVERS
WHISKEY
andrew robinson 2012

ARCHER & ARMSTRONG #10 VARIANT
Cover by ANDREW ROBINSON

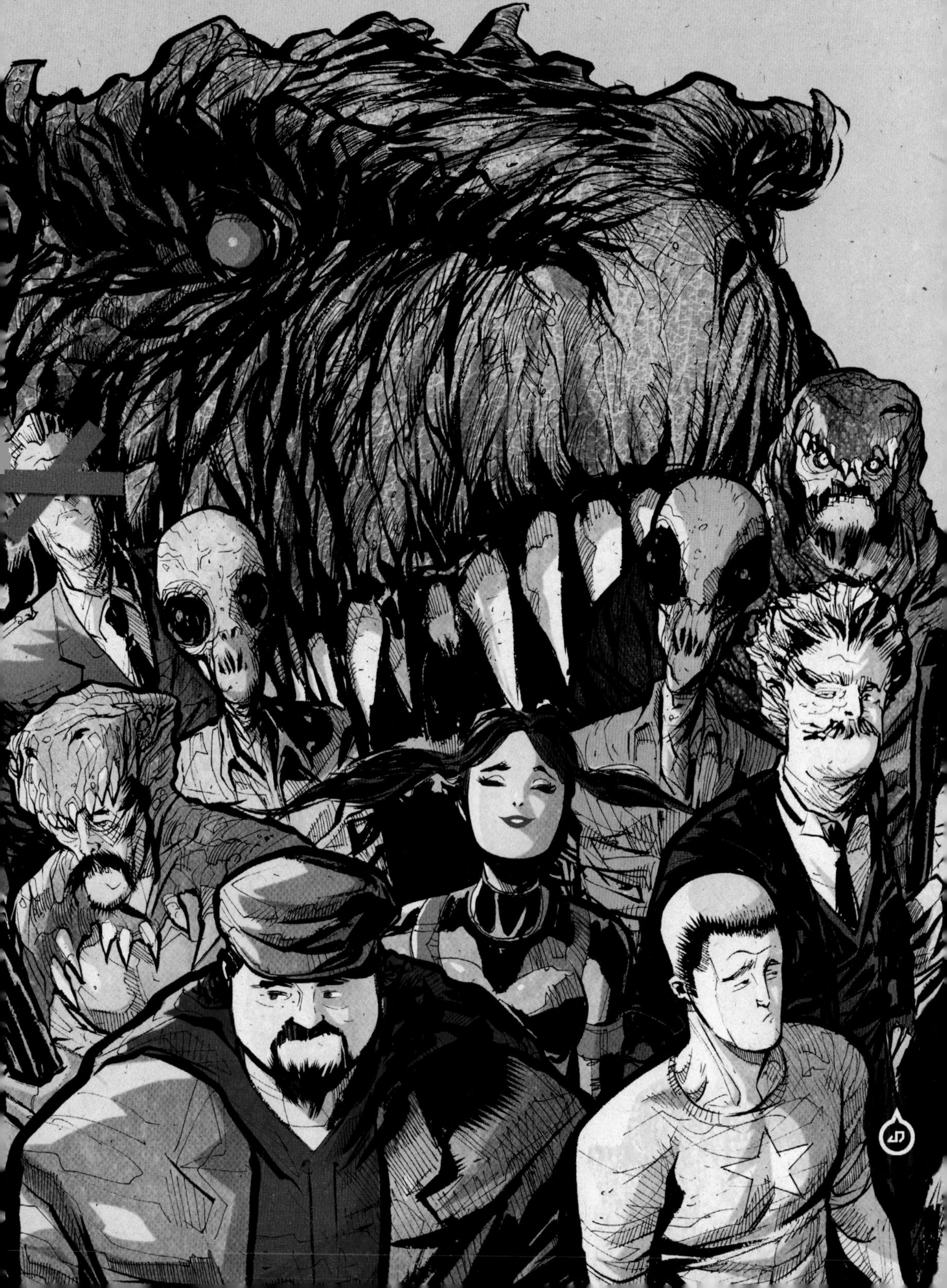

ARCHER & ARMSTRONG #11 VARIANT
Cover by JUAN DOE

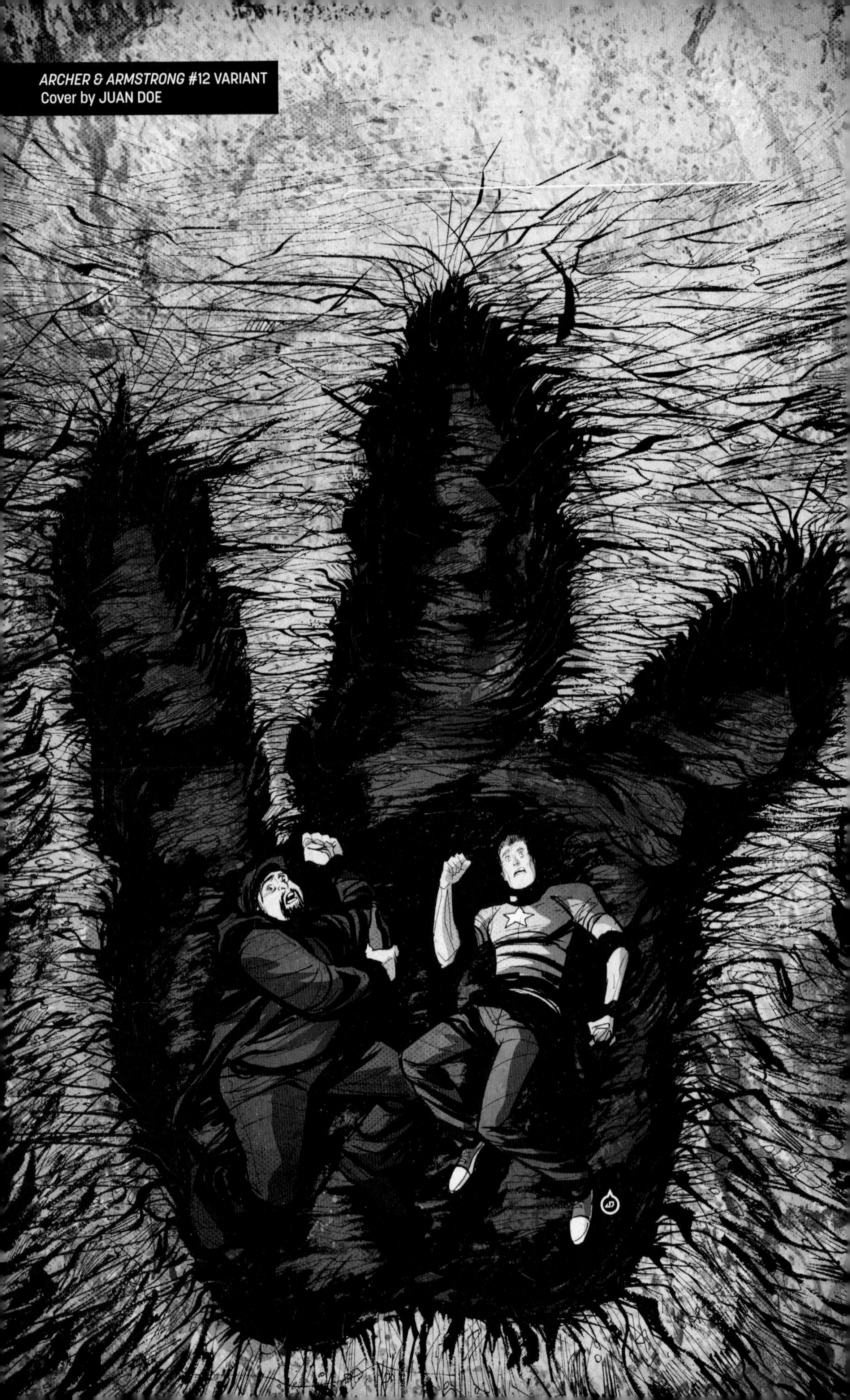

ARCHER & ARMSTRONG #12 VARIANT
Cover by JUAN DOE

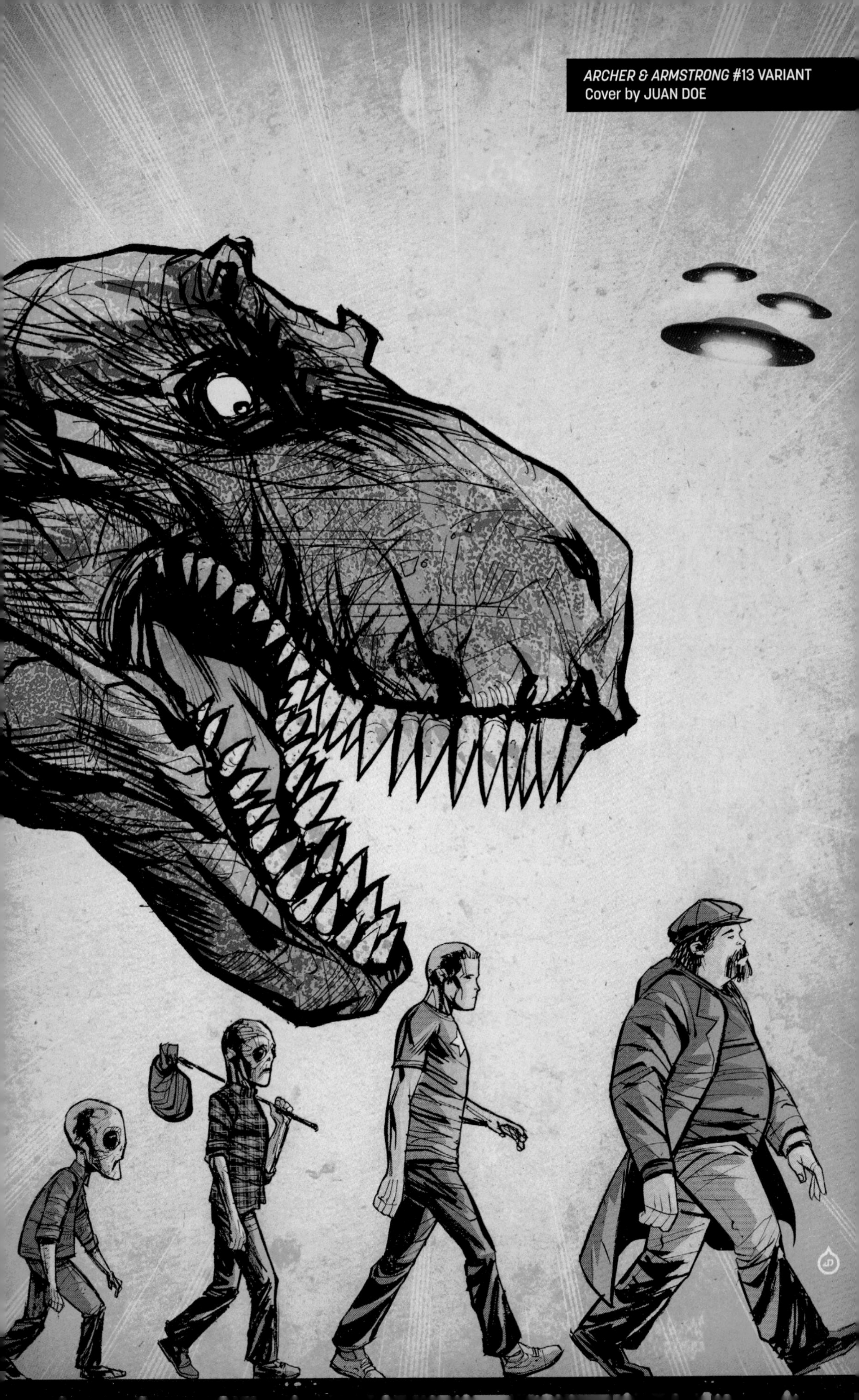

ARCHER & ARMSTRONG #13 VARIANT
Cover by JUAN DOE

VALIANT

VALIANT COLLECTIONS

TRADE PAPERBACKS

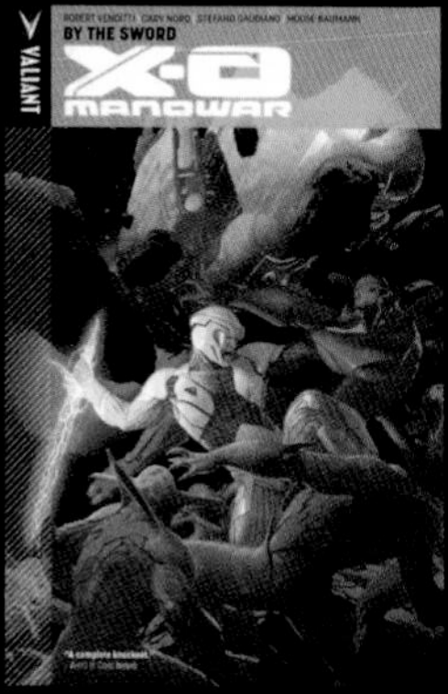
BY THE SWORD
X-O MANOWAR
VALIANT

X-O MANOWAR VOL. 1:
BY THE SWORD

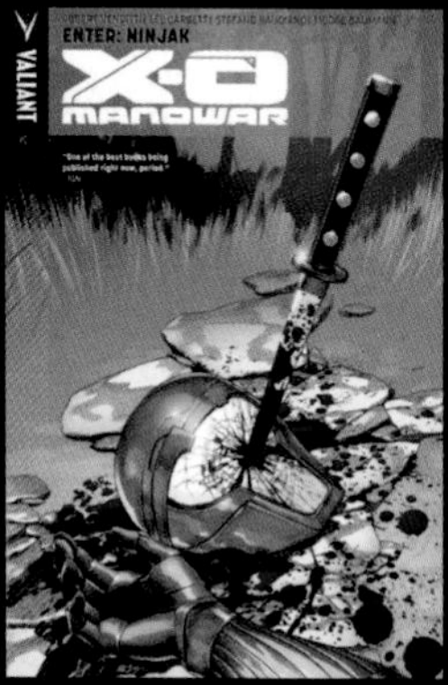
ENTER: NINJAK
X-O MANOWAR
VALIANT

X-O MANOWAR VOL. 2:
ENTER NINJAK

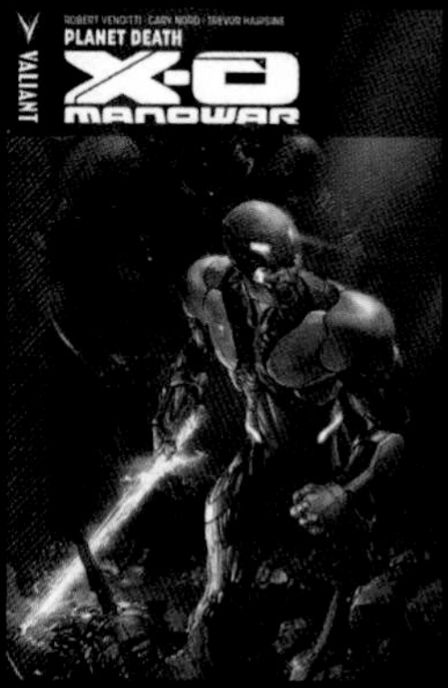
PLANET DEATH
X-O MANOWAR
VALIANT

X-O MANOWAR VOL. 3:
PLANET DEATH

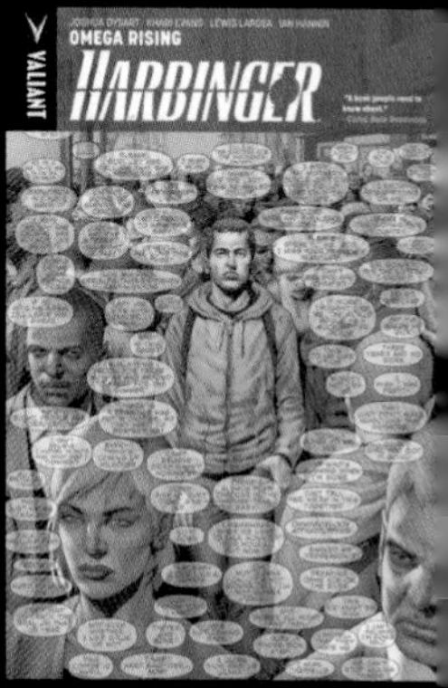
OMEGA RISING
HARBINGER
VALIANT

HARBINGER VOL. 1:
OMEGA RISING

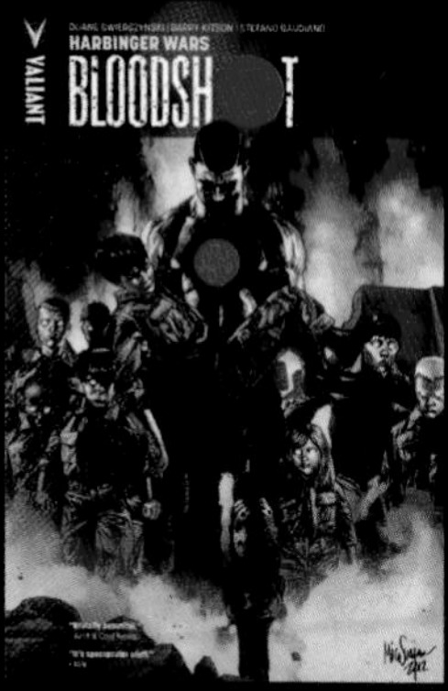
HARBINGER WARS
BLOODSHOT
VALIANT

BLOODSHOT VOL. 3:
HARBINGER WARS

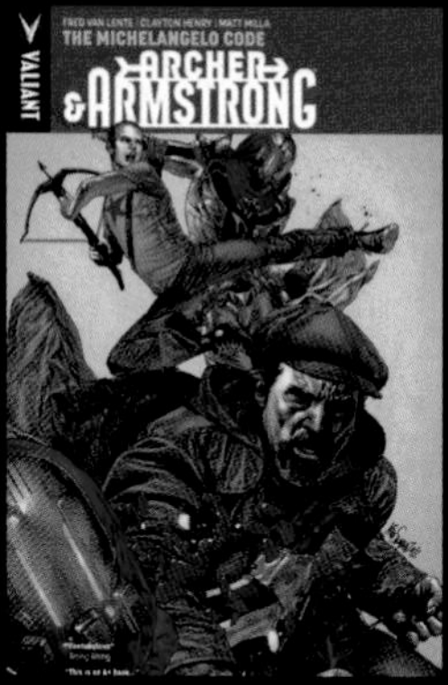
THE MICHELANGELO CODE
ARCHER & ARMSTRONG
VALIANT

ARCHER & ARMSTRONG VOL. 1:
THE MICHELANGELO CODE

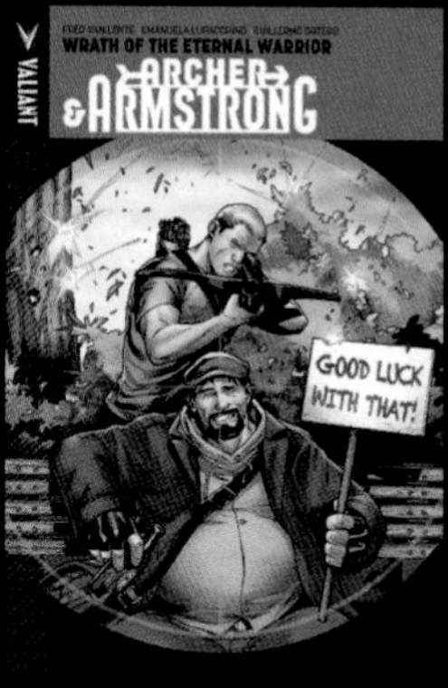
WRATH OF THE ETERNAL WARRIOR
ARCHER & ARMSTRONG
GOOD LUCK WITH THAT!
VALIANT

ARCHER & ARMSTRONG VOL. 2:
WRATH OF THE ETERNAL WARRIOR

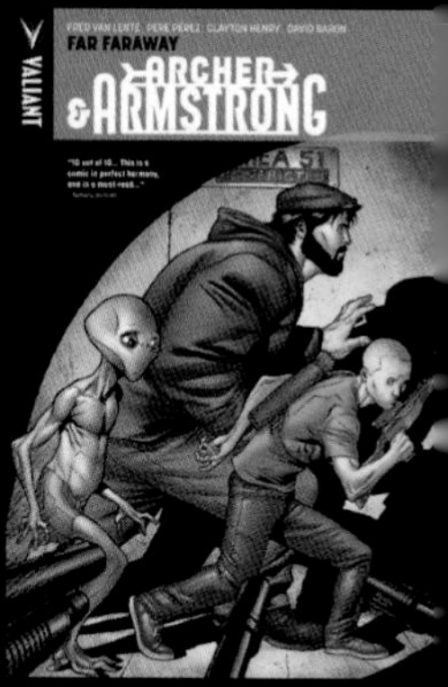
FAR FARAWAY
ARCHER & ARMSTRONG
VALIANT

ARCHER & ARMSTRONG VOL. 3:
FAR FARAWAY

DELUXE EDITIONS

X-O MANOWAR DELUXE EDITION BOOK 1

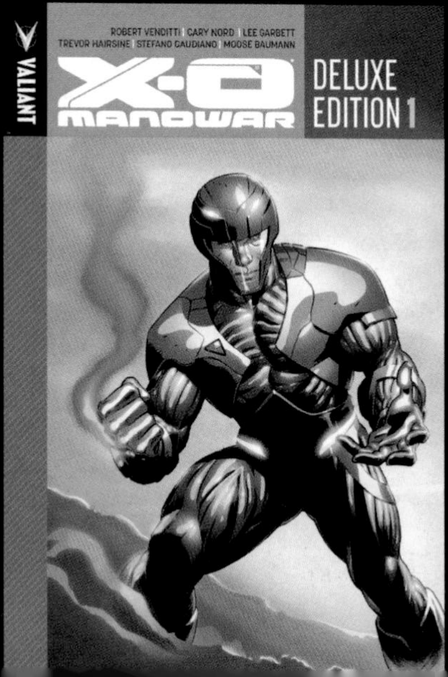
ROBERT VENDITTI | CARY NORD | LEE GARBETT
TREVOR HAIRSINE | STEFANO GAUDIANO | MOOSE BAUMANN
X-O MANOWAR
DELUXE EDITION 1
VALIANT

HARBINGER DELUXE EDITION BOOK 1

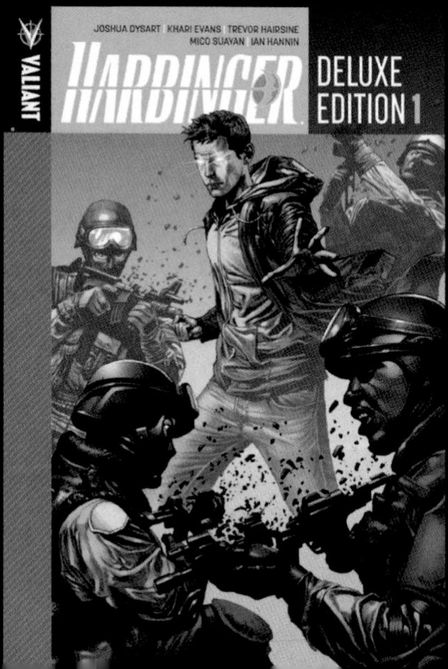
JOSHUA DYSART | KHARI EVANS | TREVOR HAIRSINE
MICO SUAYAN | IAN HANNIN
HARBINGER
DELUXE EDITION 1
VALIANT

THE STORY STARTS HERE.

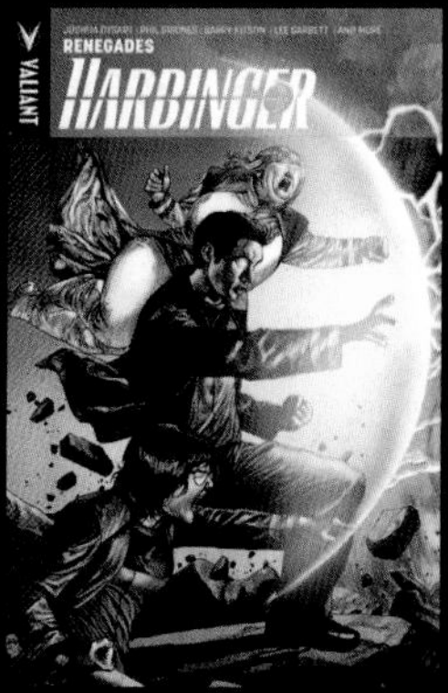
VALIANT
RENEGADES
HARBINGER

HARBINGER VOL. 2: RENEGADES

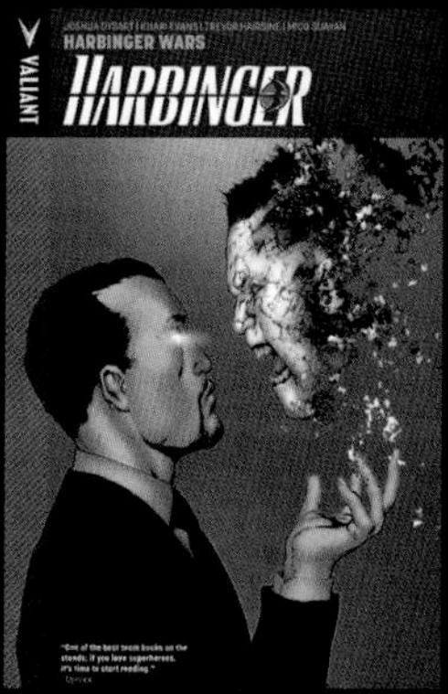
VALIANT
HARBINGER WARS
HARBINGER

HARBINGER VOL. 3: HARBINGER WARS

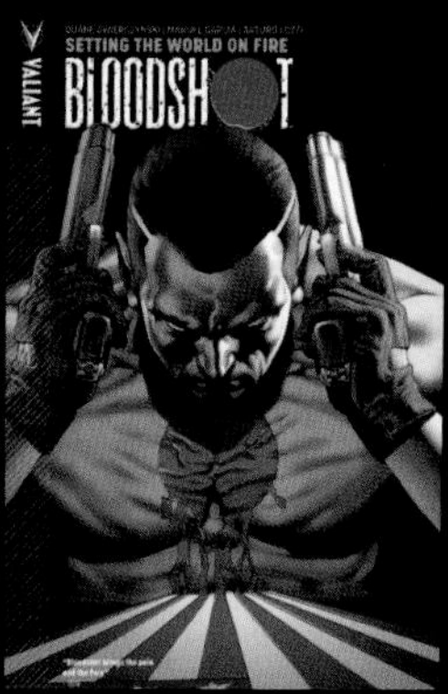
VALIANT
SETTING THE WORLD ON FIRE
BLOODSHOT

BLOODSHOT VOL. 1: SETTING THE WORLD ON FIRE

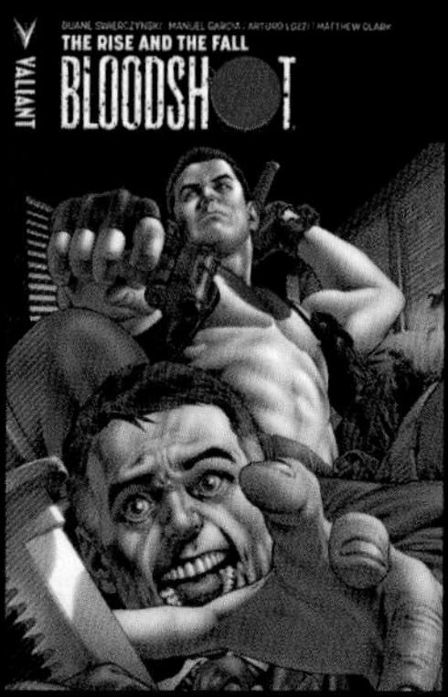
VALIANT
THE RISE AND THE FALL
BLOODSHOT

BLOODSHOT VOL. 2: THE RISE AND THE FALL

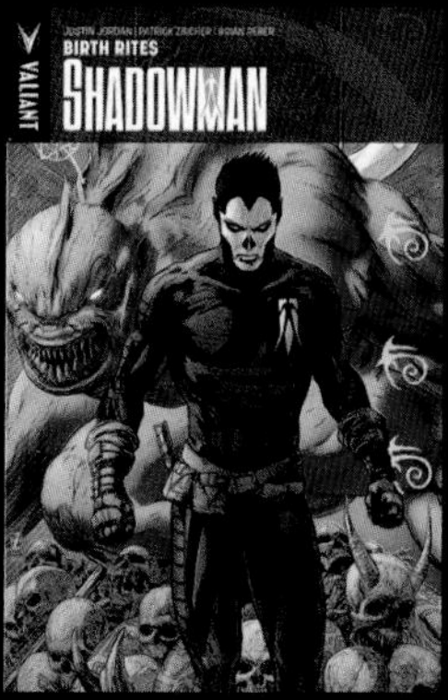
VALIANT
BIRTH RITES
SHADOWMAN

SHADOWMAN VOL. 1: BIRTH RITES

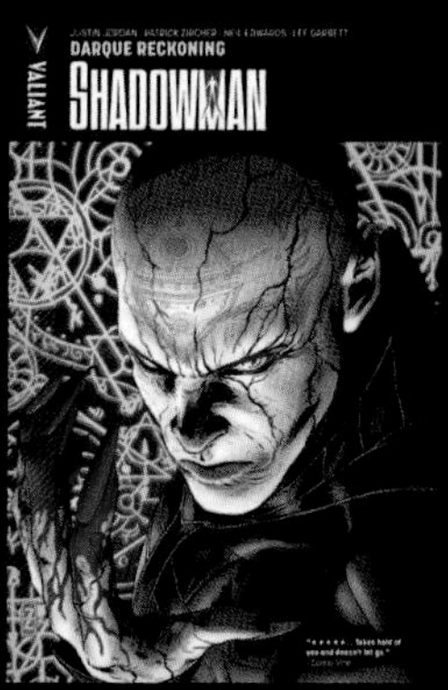
VALIANT
DARQUE RECKONING
SHADOWMAN

SHADOWMAN VOL. 2: DARQUE RECKONING

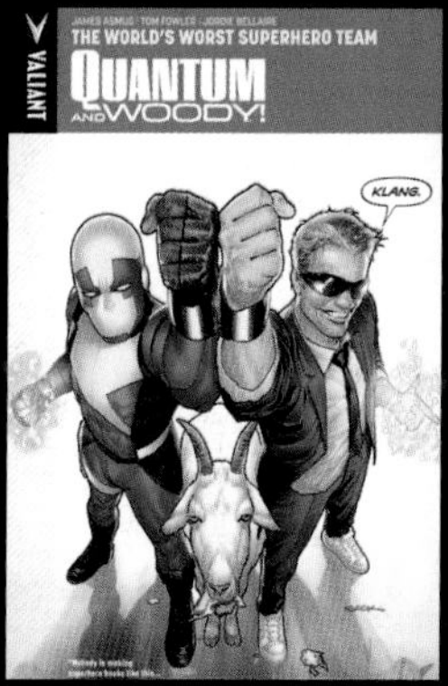
VALIANT
THE WORLD'S WORST SUPERHERO TEAM
QUANTUM AND WOODY!
KLANG.

QUANTUM AND WOODY VOL. 1: THE WORLD'S WORST SUPERHERO TEAM

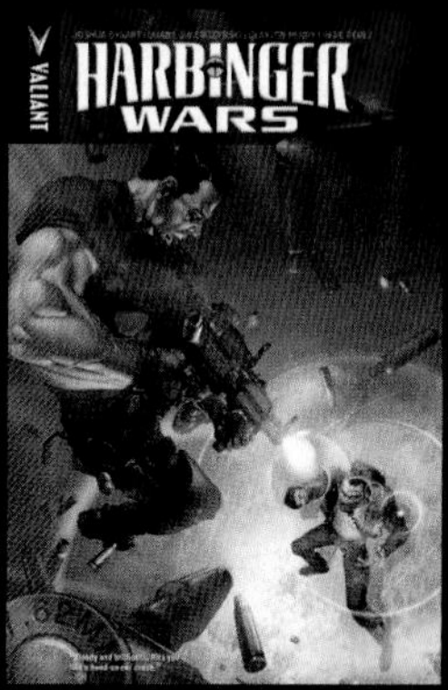
VALIANT
HARBINGER WARS

HARBINGER WARS

VALIANT MASTERS

VALIANT MASTERS: BLOODSHOT VOL. 1: BLOOD OF THE MACHINE

VALIANT MASTERS: NINJAK VOL. 1: BLACK WATER

VALIANT MASTERS: SHADOWMAN VOL. 1: SPIRITS WITHIN

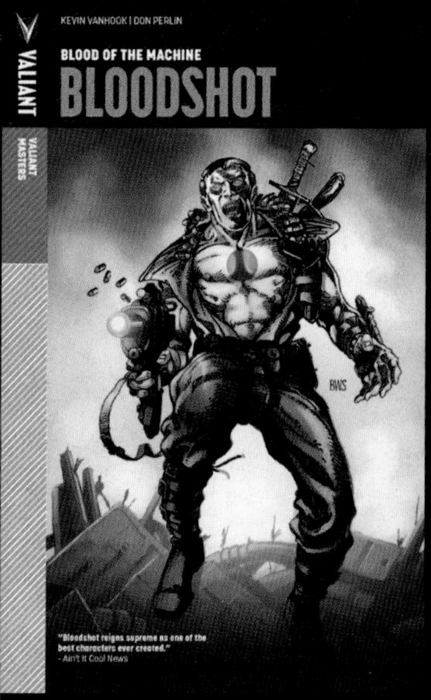
VALIANT
KEVIN VANHOOK | DON PERLIN
BLOOD OF THE MACHINE
BLOODSHOT
VALIANT MASTERS
"Bloodshot reigns supreme as one of the best characters ever created."
- Ain't It Cool News

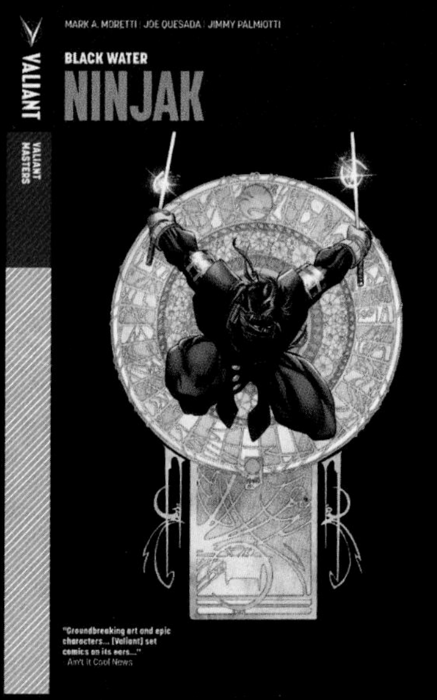
VALIANT
MARK A. MORETTI | JOE QUESADA | JIMMY PALMIOTTI
BLACK WATER
NINJAK
VALIANT MASTERS
"Groundbreaking art and epic characters... [Valiant] set comics on its ears..."
- Ain't It Cool News

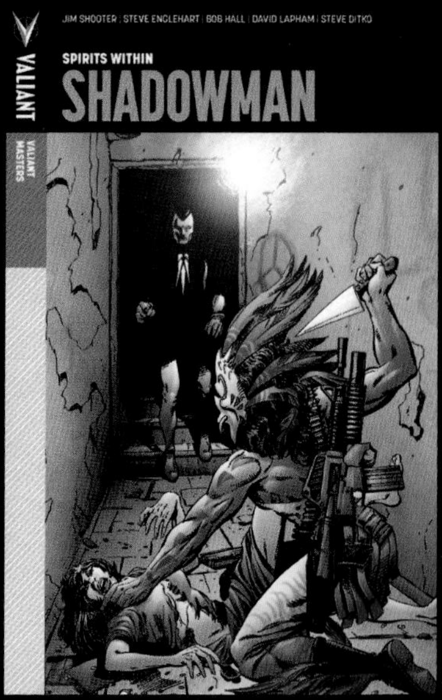
VALIANT
JIM SHOOTER | STEVE ENGLEHART | BOB HALL | DAVID LAPHAM | STEVE DITKO
SPIRITS WITHIN
SHADOWMAN
VALIANT MASTERS

VALIANT

ARCHER & ARMSTRONG

VOLUME FOUR: **SECT CIVIL WAR**

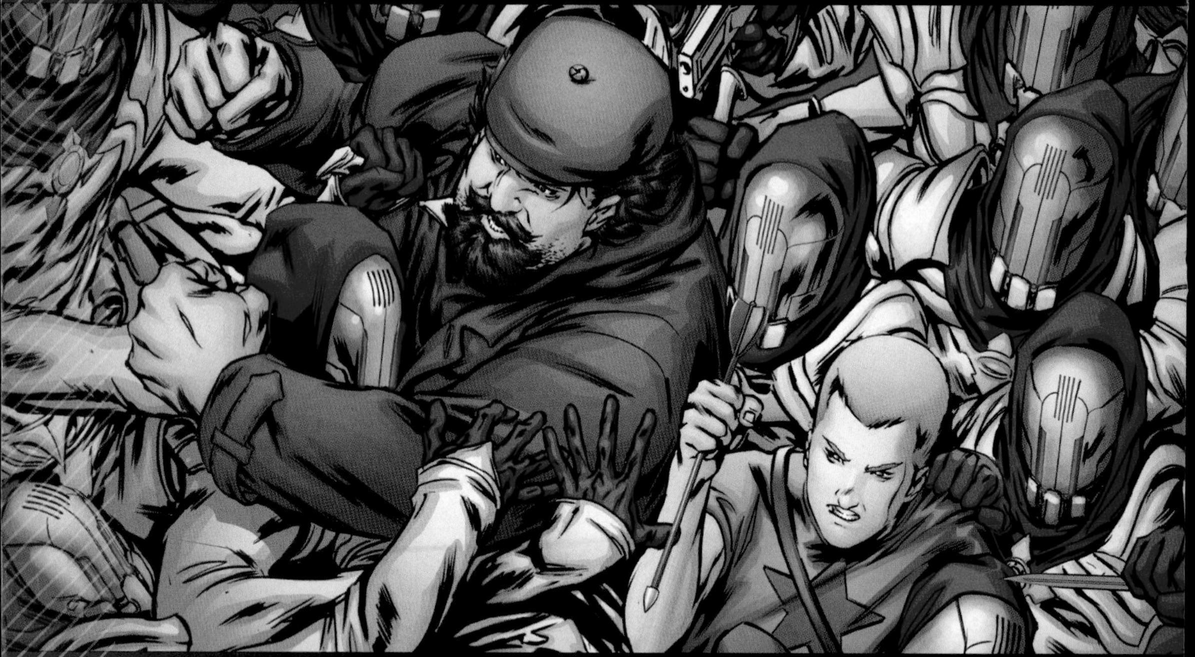

BROS BEFORE FOES!

For centuries, the cloak-and-dagger coalition of conspiracies collectively known as The Sect has worked together to bring silent oppression and undercover tyranny to a world that thought it was free. But, now after centuries of profit sharing and uneasy alliances, the factions of The Sect are about to erupt into open conflict...and the only men that can end the insanity are Archer & Armstrong! Too bad they're fighting for different sides! Why? How? And will either survive? The knockdown, drag-out A&A event of the year starts now - and no conspirator is safe!

Collecting ARCHER & ARMSTRONG #14-17 by New York Times best-selling writer Fred Van Lente (*Incredible Hercules*) and acclaimed artists Khari Evans (*Harbinger*) and ChrisCross (*Superman/Batman*), jump into the series that IGN calls "a must read" with an all-new adventure pitching Archer & Armstrong into their biggest battle yet!

TRADE PAPERBACK
ISBN: 978-1-939346-25-4

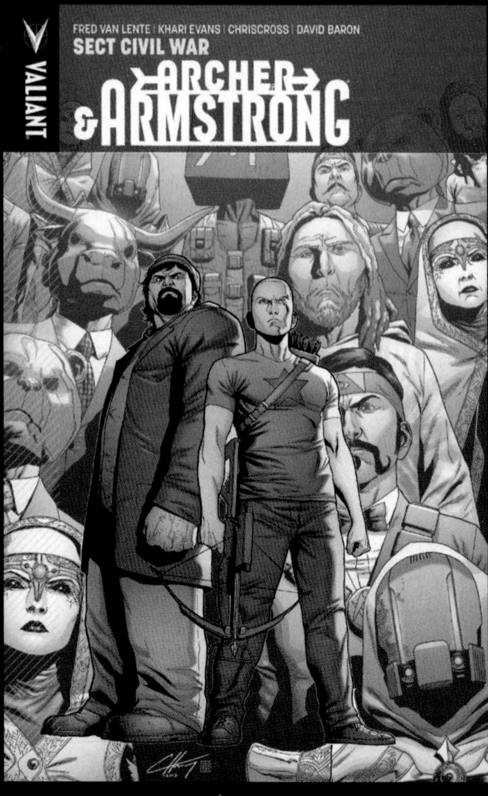
VALIANT
FRED VAN LENTE | KHARI EVANS | CHRISCROSS | DAVID BARON
SECT CIVIL WAR
ARCHER & ARMSTRONG